Doing History bridges the gap between the way history is studied in school or as represented in the media and the way it is studied at university level.

History as an academic discipline has dramatically changed in recent decades and has been enhanced by ideas from other disciplines, the influence of post-modernism and historians' incorporation of their own reflections into their work. *Doing History* presents the ideas and debates that shape how we 'do' history today, covering arguments about the nature of historical knowledge and the function of historical writing, whether we can ever really know what happened in the past, what sources historians depend on, and the relative value of popular and academic histories. This revised edition includes new chapters on public history and activist histories. It looks at global representations of the past across the centuries, and provides up-to-date suggestions for further reading, presenting the reader with a thorough and current introduction to studying history at an academic level as well as a pathway to progress this study further.

Clearly structured and accessibly written, it is an essential volume for all students embarking on the study of history.

Mark Donnelly is Associate Professor at St Mary's University, Twickenham, London, UK. He writes about history theory, public history and collective memory. He co-edited *Mad Dogs and Englishness: Popular Music and English Identities* (2017). He also co-wrote *Liberating Histories* (2019) with Claire Norton.

Claire Norton is Associate Professor at St Mary's University, Twickenham, London, UK. She is interested in how past-talk is used to articulate, legitimise and challenge identities, institutions and political discourses. She has written books on Ottoman manuscript textualities, Islamic-Christian interactions in the early modern world and history theory.

Doing History

Doing History

2nd edition

Mark Donnelly and Claire Norton

LONDON AND NEW YORK

This edition published 2021
by Routledge
2 Park Square, Milton Park, Abingdon, Oxon OX14 4RN

and by Routledge
52 Vanderbilt Avenue, New York, NY 10017

Routledge is an imprint of the Taylor & Francis Group, an informa business

First edition published by Routledge (2011)

British Library Cataloguing-in-Publication Data
A catalogue record for this book is available from the British Library

Library of Congress Cataloging-in-Publication Data
A catalog record has been requested for this book

ISBN: 978-1-138-30154-2 (hbk)
ISBN: 978-1-138-30155-9 (pbk)
ISBN: 978-1-003-10778-1 (ebk)

Typeset in Times New Roman
by Newgen Publishing UK

Printed in the United Kingdom
by Henry Ling Limited

For AFAZL with love

And for Clare, Katherine and Isobel

Contents

Acknowledgements

We are grateful to many people who have directly or indirectly helped us to write this book. The first edition developed out of a historiography module that we co-taught at St Mary's University, Twickenham, London. We would like to thank our colleagues and students for providing such a supportive environment in which to work. A number of people read draft copies of the original text and provided us with thoughtful and detailed comments. Specifically, we would like to thank Dan Stone for his thorough reading of the whole manuscript. At Routledge, we are very grateful to Eve Setch and Zoe Thomson for their support and patience in commissioning a second edition.

This revised book benefits from conversations that we've had with colleagues from many different countries. At the Institute of Historical Research 'Philosophy of History' seminar we owe a particular debt to Helena Hammond, Mark Mason, Kalle Pihlainen, Keith Jenkins, Peter Icke and Beverley Southgate. From the International Network for Theory of History, we are grateful to Berber Bevernage, Anton Froeyman, Gisele de Almeida, Broos Delanote, Kenan Van de Mieroop and Ramses Delafontaine. At our own research centre at St Mary's, we learned a great deal from our invited speakers. In addition to some of these speakers who have already been mentioned, we thank Marnie Hughes-Warrington, Martin Davies, Tyson Retz, Richard King, Helen Bendon and Emily Miller. We are very grateful to Georgia Bender for helping us with research and ideas for the new edition.

We also want to make a special mention of the late Alun Munslow, who consistently supported our various research projects since he wrote a report on the first edition of this book.

Lastly, we are grateful to our families for their ongoing support, encouragement and understanding.

Preface

How students are taught to 'do history' at university level differs from what they are taught before they begin their degree. This is understandable and, we would argue, desirable. Degree-level study *should* challenge students to think about subjects in new ways, even if sometimes the experience of working with unfamiliar concepts is initially disorienting. School history curricula largely assume that the historian's task is to write as accurately and fairly as possible about 'important' historical topics – the ones deemed worthy of attention by curriculum designers. In this context, the key questions about how historians write history are really about the acquisition and performance of particular skills and methods. At university, however, students are confronted (in most cases for the first time) with more philosophical issues relating to historical research and writing. What is history? Who is history for? What are the social and political functions of historical knowledge? Why do historians write about their subject in the way that they do? Is history the same thing as the past? Why are some historians writing about the past in radically unorthodox ways, producing texts that would not have been regarded as legitimate histories until fairly recently?

This book aims to introduce students to the kinds of questions described above, and to help them to take part in the discussions that such questions provoke. Most history degree courses include some theoretical or reflexive component, in which attention focuses on what historians are actually doing when they produce knowledge about the past. We are aware that some historians view such enquiry into their practices as self-indulgent, and a distraction from the more important business of researching the actual past. But in our view historians (and history students) *should* be able to discuss their research and writing in theoretical or philosophical terms (how do they know what they know, what is their role in the creation of historical knowledge and on what grounds might we accept or reject knowledge claims?) as well as being able to answer more conventional historical questions. Our justification for making this point is that all history writing is based (consciously or not) on philosophical assumptions about what historians do and what it means to write 'history'. In order to think critically about these assumptions, historians require some familiarity with key texts and writers in the 'philosophy of history' field. However, we are also aware that such texts are often austere, abstract and for many students problematic as an entry point into unfamiliar territory. *Doing History* is designed to serve as a better entry point, one that assumes that its readers do not already possess an extensive vocabulary of philosophical terms. We aim here to introduce students to the key historiographical debates that historians are currently concerned with, using a question- or problem-centred format. We want to familiarise students with the main concepts and terminology involved in these debates, and equip them to take part in discussions about the nature (and future) of history as a discipline on their own terms.

Doing History is not intended to be a philosophical monograph; it does not advance a thesis as such about the 'proper' way to write history, neither does it attempt to provide an overview of the discipline's various theoretical schools. Of course, we do not pretend that we are neutral or disinterested observers of an academic debate from which we stand apart. In the chapters that follow our intellectual sympathies are always fairly clear. But as Barbara Herrnstein Smith wrote, it is probably impossible to describe or represent the positions with which one disagrees as well as those one endorses.[1] Moreover, to claim that such supposed intellectual 'objectivity' and impartiality is possible would conflict with the wider arguments that we make throughout this book. We do believe, however, that we have critically and thoughtfully analysed the arguments of others, considered the evidence equally, and tried to represent the views of those with whom we agree and those with whom we disagree as fairly as possible.

One argument that we do endorse throughout this book is that philosophical issues about 'doing history' relate to all forms of historical practice. We do not see them as abstractions or as somehow isolated from the 'real' work of historians. We hope that readers will apply the terminology and concepts that they encounter here (and in their further reading) to their thinking about all other features of their work as historians. We have tried to show here how different perspectives about 'doing history' produce more than simply different interpretations of historical events, periods or processes. They determine whose stories from the past are told, whose voices from the past are heard, what counts as 'legitimate' history, who can become a professional historian, and which cultures and intellectual traditions are deemed worthy of our attention. In contrast to many other books that deal with similar historiographical issues, we have therefore tried to think about history writing in global terms rather than assume that scholarly history writing is a predominantly European and North American tradition. The single theme that runs through this book is the idea that how we 'do' history is always tied to particular times, places and cultures; it is never universal, invariant or somehow above the contingencies of a tradition.

Note

1 Barbara Herrnstein Smith, *Belief and Resistance: Dynamics of Contemporary Intellectual Controversy* (Cambridge, Mass: Harvard University Press, 1997) xix

PART I

WHAT IS HISTORY?

1 Introduction

Is history the same as the past?

The terms 'history' and 'the past' are often used interchangeably. History is commonly understood to mean past events. When we say that something or someone 'is history', we mean that their significance belongs only to the past. When something is said to be the best or the biggest in history, it is another way of saying that nothing of its type in the past can match its superiority. Media features on 'this week in history' consist of events that happened to occur between corresponding day/month ranges in the past. The apparent convertibility of the terms history/past is what lies behind the misleading idea that history is a naturally occurring substance. Both the past and history are assumed to be produced by the passage of time breaking away from the present. In this sense, describing something as historical is primarily a comment on its distance in time from now. This is important because, if we think of history in terms of its temporal distance from the present, it suggests that things become historical by themselves as the years pass.

Throughout this book, we will avoid giving the impression that there is anything natural about history. In our usage of the term, history refers to particular ways of thinking about the past, researching phenomena from the past and creating accounts. For us, history is produced by acts of writing, speech and other forms of communication. History is a matter of designation (by historians) and recognition (by audiences for histories). It is not something that generates its own forms naturally as the past is left behind by the accumulation of time. This might sound like a counter-intuitive and therefore uncomfortable line of thought for people to follow. After all, the idea that history is simply 'back there' waiting for us to come looking for it has become ingrained within our ways of thinking and talking. Phrases such 'going back in time' to look at a previous era, or 'bringing the past to life' contain this sense of history as a pre-formed, observable object. Moreover, as well as seeming to be counter-intuitive, thinking critically about the meaning of the term history is liable to be dismissed by some as an unnecessary and self-indulgent distraction from the 'real' work of researching past events. Why worry about 'what history is'? Why not just read histories or original sources? Our answer to such questions is contained within this book's title.

'Doing history' conveys how we prefer to use history as a term that names an activity or set of practices. History for us is something that people can choose to do, to create, to write, to produce, to perform and to imagine. If we use history as a noun to refer to a thing in this book, we usually mean history as the name of an academic discipline, with its various institutional infrastructures (school and college departments, journals, publishers, research institutes, archives and so on). Given that we regard history primarily as something that some people 'do', a series of questions follow. How do we currently do history, and has it always been done the same way? Where do the rules for doing history come from, and how are they kept in place? Why do we choose to produce histories at all? Whose interests are served or damaged by our current ways of doing history, and how might this change if we did history differently? These are the kinds of questions that we address in this book. In emphasising our preference for thinking about history as a set of practices, we should deal with one possible source of confusion straight away. Of course we accept that all kinds of actions, reactions, sequences of occurrences and transitions took place in the past. The French monarchy really was abolished in September 1792. Rosa Parks did refuse to move her seat on a bus in Alabama in December 1955. But these events, and countless others like them, are not 'historical' in and of themselves. For that to happen, they have to be brought within the modes of writing, speech and representation that are commonly recognised as 'history'.

The processes by which things from the past are designated as belonging to history are often overlooked. Historians disagree with each other about the accuracy and explanatory value of various accounts of the past – usually centring on issues of interpretation, categorisation and how sources have been used. But such disagreements are usually played out on the shared ground that the thing in dispute is unquestionably a historical object of enquiry. Indeed, when history was professionalised as an academic discipline in the nineteenth century it modelled itself on the natural sciences, incorporating their codes of objectivity and supposedly disinterested empirical investigation. This culminated in Carl Hempel's 'The Function of General Laws in History' (1942), which sought to relate individual explanations for historical events to the type of universal laws found in the sciences.[1] In the last decades of the twentieth century, however, the shared assumption that historical objects are 'real', that they exist independently from any modes of perception or thought, was brought into question. The key issue here was the role of language, not just in communicating the findings of research, but in constituting the objects of enquiry within a field of research in the first place. This focus on the shaping role of language was part of a broader 'linguistic turn' in philosophy, the humanities and social sciences from the 1960s onwards. Instead of assuming that language was capable of representing reality as accurately as possible, the linguistic turn set out from a more sceptical position. It held that language could produce effects of reality, but it could never articulate reality in itself. The production of reality effects in any given field (including history) resulted from the deployment of rhetorical techniques, agreed vocabularies, narrative strategies, reading practices and figures of speech. All of these combine to create a discourse – which means a particular way of talking or writing about something. Following the linguistic turn, thinkers such as Hayden White, Keith Jenkins, Elizabeth Ermarth, Alun Munslow and Beverley Southgate argued that history was just one type of discourse that was available for producing knowledge about the past. But what history could never be – and what it never had been – was a way of getting to the actuality of the past.

Many historians rejected the implications of the linguistic turn. Geoffrey Elton continued to regard history as an objective search to discover truth about the past.[2] Joyce Appleby, Lynn Hunt and Margaret Jacob argued for retaining the concept of a real and knowable past in *Telling the Truth about History* (1994), albeit a past that should be written about from a variety of cultural perspectives. A similar assumption appears in Richard J. Evans's *In Defence of History* (1997), in which the past is likened at various points to a sculptor's block of stone, a mountain observed by painters and a jigsaw puzzle. Each of these analogies conveys the sense that the past that historians study is singular and whole – after all, there is only one way of putting together a jigsaw puzzle that makes any sense. This notion of a singular past is crucial to historians' beliefs that they can produce authoritative and reliable accounts of it. (As we will explain later, we prefer to think in terms of plural pasts. But for convenience we will normally refer to 'the past' in this book).

For sceptics such as Jenkins and Ermarth, however, there is no way of comparing the past itself with an account of that past to check for reliability. The past is always absent, so it is never available as a referent. Of course, we can accept that all kinds of things took place 'before now', but we cannot go back to the time of the Norman Conquest, the Ottoman Empire or anything else as observers. Our knowledge of the past is derived from different kinds of texts (or sources). Historians work in the present, and from there they can only look at traces left behind from the past (like documents, objects, buildings, films and so on), talk to people about their memories of past events, or look at other people's versions of what they imagine the past might have been like (usually in the form of books, films or documentaries). In short, instead of thinking that history simply studies the past (which is always out of reach), it is more useful to think of history as being about the study of these *other* things (the traces, the memories, other people's versions of the past). History looks at surrogates of the past, not the past itself. In this line of thinking, statements about the 'accuracy' or 'truthfulness' of a historical account are held to relate to the ways in which the historian has used their research materials – the documents, the objects, other histories, the surrogates of the past. They do not relate to the past itself. This is why Keith Jenkins has argued that when it comes to dealing with historical knowledge, '"the past" is a useless notion'.[3] History as an activity, in other words, involves the writing of the past – albeit with a methodological reliance on the use of sources in a particular way – but it is not an exercise in reconstructing the past 'as it was'.

Why study history?

Historians (we include ourselves) often choose to answer this question instrumentally. We take it as an invitation to market our subject to whichever audience is in front of us. We compile audits of skills that can be acquired by studying history. We list the kinds of employment that history graduates typically move into. We tell prospective students how exciting and rewarding they will find our history courses. These are the safe and easy answers to the 'why study history?' question that we provide for students and academic managers. They have a certain value. History is a subject that helps students to think – the same can be said, of course, of many other subjects. Reading for a history degree requires students to expand their vocabularies, their categories of thought and their facility for linking texts and ideas together. History students learn to analyse complex sets of data, synthesise competing historical interpretations, read different kinds of primary and secondary texts critically, develop their reasoning skills and improve their capacity to undertake research. These are transferable and therefore marketable skills. This is why history graduates often move into careers in areas such as management, law, education, media, journalism and public administration.

But the 'why study history?' question also needs to be answered on a different level, one that relates to a philosophical view of history, or a theoretical understanding of what historical enquiry might be able to achieve. The question implies an existential challenge – what is the point of our doing what we do? Tony Judt wrote a powerful advocacy of studying history – specifically twentieth-century history – as a means of providing a context against which contemporary political challenges might appear more intelligible. He wrote:

> of all our contemporary illusions, the most dangerous is the one that underpins and accounts for all the others. And that is the idea that we live in a time without precedent: that what is happening to us is new and irreversible and that the past has nothing to teach us… except when it comes to ransacking it for serviceable precedents.[4]

According to Judt, history helps us to understand the 'perennial complexity' of our current dilemmas: social, political, moral, ethical and ideological. Only in cultures that seek to forget the recent past, he says – with the exception of those parts of the past that are selected for memorialisation – can ahistorical abstracts like the 'war on terror' or the threat of 'Islamo-Fascism' be taken seriously as justifications for policy decisions.[5] In a similar vein, Eric Hobsbawm argued in his memoirs that 'most historians, including all good ones, know that in investigating the past, even the remote past, they are also thinking and expressing opinions in terms of and about the present and its concerns. Understanding history is as important for citizens as for experts'.[6] We might add here that Hobsbawm's injunction can be turned on its head – thus, it is our understanding of the present that makes the study of the past intelligible.

In some respects it might seem surprising that eminent historians such as Judt and Hobsbawm feel the need to make the case for studying history. After all, the subject is a ubiquitous feature of the wider contemporary cultures of media, entertainment and national politics. We are constantly directed to think in historical terms. Placing things into what we call a historical context has never been more popular, or assumed to be so necessary and natural. We encounter what we take to be 'the past' everywhere, in a world in which everything is explained as being the end-point of a historical process. We revive old design styles, watch films like *My People, My Country,*[7] finance the preservation of old buildings, read parts of Anne Frank's diary, listen to critics argue about which decade had the 'best' pop music, watch television programmes where volunteers experience a highly contrived version of what life might have been like in an Iron Age settlement, a Victorian farm, a Tudor kitchen and any number of other simulations. We identify with earlier generations and wonder how we might have coped in their shoes. We look to history as a guide for acting now. We hope that it will unlock a way of making sense of ourselves in the world. Above all, we largely take it for granted that we are morally obliged to keep the past in mind. In today's culture it is always the (apparently important) anniversary of one thing or another. Each day the Wikipedia main page lists a set of anniversaries in its 'On this day' section. Historians of course seek to perpetuate this history-culture, always pointing to something from the past in order to make their point that nothing that we have now is completely new. 'Talk to any historian', complains Martin Davies, 'he or she always comes up with an antecedent to show that this *latest thing* is actually the same as the *same old thing*'.[8]

At some point in the development of our social imagination we internalised the idea that we can and should 'learn the lessons of history'. Certainly this is what historians have been telling people they should do since at least as far back as the time when Confucius was writing, some 2,500 years ago. Unless we learn from the past, the cliché says, we are condemned to repeat its most damaging excesses and wrong turnings. Historical knowledge in this line of reasoning is held to act as a kind of safeguard. In contemporary European cultures this way of thinking is most commonly applied in relation to the Third Reich and the Holocaust. We must study the Nazi era, the reasoning goes, or we risk becoming the next victims of mass murder, or perhaps the ones who do the killing. But before we accept this injunction, we should question the assumption that people who acquire historical knowledge are necessarily more likely to make good ethical choices. If, for example, we met a person whose bookshelves were full of Hitler biographies, perhaps we would feel reassured that here was someone who took seriously their duty to be on guard against the rise of neo-fascism. But equally, we might want to ask whether their motivations for having so many books about Hitler were darker and potentially more troubling. Reading history is not always and everywhere a morally improving activity. As Lawrence Langer has argued, for example, there is nothing to prevent political or military leaders who have their own genocidal ambitions from studying the Holocaust as a model of how to organise mass murder. In any case, we should recognise that sound ethical arguments against genocide could be made equally effectively with or without reference to historical precedents.

In fact, there is a long tradition of thought that regards the study of history as being at best a waste of time and at worst potentially harmful. An interesting entry point into this line of thinking is Hayden White's essay 'The Burden of History' (1966).[9] White argued here that history failed to match either the predictive value of science or the imaginative power of art. White traced some of the various ways in which historians (or historical consciousness) have featured in a negative light in works such as George Eliot's *Middlemarch* (1874), Henrik Ibsen's *Hedda Gabler* (1890), André Gide's *Immoralist* (1902) and Jean-Paul Sartre's *Nausea* (1938). Each of these writers shared common ground with the philosopher Friedrich Nietzsche, whose criticisms of history as it was often practised in the nineteenth century were set out in 'On the Uses and Disadvantages of History for Life' (1874). As White comments: 'Nietzsche hated history even more than he hated religion. History promoted a debilitating voyeurism in men, made them feel that they were latecomers to a world in which everything worth doing had already been done'.[10] In fact, Nietzsche rejected two particular ways of writing history that sought to memorialise or preserve the past – those he called 'monumental' and 'antiquarian' history. In place of this he advocated writing 'critical' history, at least until it succeeded as a way of overcoming the burdens of the past. The past had to be forgotten, he wrote, if it was not to become the gravedigger of the present.[11] In other words, the danger of some forms of thinking about history was that they served to justify how things were in the present by taking them to be the latest point in an unstoppable historical sequence. They shored up present arrangements (social, political, economic) by describing these arrangements as what the past always had in store for the future. Studying history, according to this critique, conditions us to think in old ways (always within the old co-ordinates) and prevents us from thinking in radically new ones. This is what Sande Cohen had in mind when he wrote that 'we are overhistoricised and undercritical' in relation to contemporary conditions (he wants us to pull apart the assumptions that are used to justify current arrangements, rather than think about how we might put them into a historical sequence and thus leave them undisturbed).[12] In 'The Burden of History', White echoed Nietzsche's dismissal of the virtues of studying the past for its own sake, describing such activity as 'wilful resistance to the attempt to close with the present world in all its strangeness and mystery'. Instead, he argued, history should be justified as 'a way of providing perspectives on the present that contribute to the solutions of problems peculiar to our own time'.[13] In effect, Hayden White was posing the 'why study history?' question in a different way – one that related to the functions of history.

In our view, although Judt/Hobsbawm on one side and Cohen/Davies on the other appear to disagree sharply, there are ways in which we can begin to reconcile their views. Judt and Hobsbawm advised us to study history in ways that show that those things we have come to regard as natural, pre-ordained, ahistorical and thus unchallengeable are in fact contingent, context-dependent and not permanent. Indeed, historians can and do argue that their subject's premise is that change is the only constant in human affairs. In that sense, history can be used as a tool for critical thinking. Equally, we can usefully read Cohen and Davies as a warning against taking at face value those forms of historical work that seek to normalise and naturalise current conditions (neo-liberal forms of capitalism, vast inequalities in resources and opportunities, the supremacy of the West and so on) by describing them as the only possible way in which things could have turned out. History might well have been what White called the 'conservative discipline *par excellence*',[14] but perhaps that tells us more about the kind of people who have traditionally written history – inside and outside the academy. There are no 'innate' properties to history as a subject, there are only decisions made by historians, as individuals and collectives, to write about the past in particular ways. In other words, there is no need for us to have a universal, invariant and general answer to the 'why study history?' question. Rather, we need more localised answers to more specific questions – why are we studying *this* history, in *these* particular ways, for *what* purposes and with *what* possible implications?

What are the functions of history?

John Tosh, in *Historians on History* (2009), suggests that historians have been collectively motivated by four main aspirations. Each of these aspirations implies a vision of history's principal function. The first was to 'discover what happened in the past and what it was like to live in the past'.[15] History is likened here to a detective enquiry, with the study of the past regarded as an end in itself, free from any claims to present-day political or social utility. History in this sense would primarily serve an aesthetic function, providing pleasure for like-minded individuals. This would include, for example, the use of history as nostalgia – historic walks, visiting old buildings and museums, collecting memorabilia. It would include the collection of information about a historical subject for purely personal reasons – known as antiquarianism.

Moreover, we should recognise here the processes of personal identification and transference that occur when we read and think about history. In other words, at some level history provides a form of escapism by enabling us to imagine that we are someone (or something) else – in much the same way that we project ourselves onto characters in novels or films.

The second aspiration was to write history that revealed the shape of human destiny. This built on assumptions about linear time and held that human history had an underlying plot. Before the eighteenth century this plot was commonly regarded to be a divine plan for the world. But since the Enlightenment it has come to be explained as a story of human progress, both material and moral. The idea of history following its own path toward a particular end – separate from the way that historians choose to impose their own patterns and sequences on past events – is known as teleological history. Accounts which claim to describe the unfolding of these paths – towards, say, the growth of liberal democracy, the rise of empires, the rise of western civilisation, the triumph of free-market capitalism – are called meta-narratives (meaning an all-encompassing account of how things came to be). The best examples of such meta-narratives are found in the nineteenth century. G.W.F. Hegel in *The Philosophy of History* (posthumously published in 1837) described history as something that operated according to discoverable laws. He saw history as the rational unfolding of the World-Mind or World-Spirit (via a long process of struggle and conflict) leading towards its destiny – the realisation of human freedom. Karl Marx in *Capital* (vol. 1, 1867) drew on Hegel's model but turned it on its head. In place of Hegel's belief that human history was the story of moving towards an ideal, Marx substituted the idea that human development was driven forward by material concerns, and more specifically by the clash of interests between rival groups involved in a given social model of production. Marx therefore re-described history's destiny as the overthrow of capitalism and the rise of a new, communist society. A more contemporary version of teleological history is Francis Fukuyama's thesis about the triumph of liberal democracy in *The End of History and the Last Man* (1992).

Another aspiration of historians has been to serve current political or ideological interests – most obviously in providing an agreed picture of a shared past for projects of nation building or the configuration of a national identity. All histories are ideological in the sense that they provide a view of the world and a perspective on what we should know about that world. This is why the kind of history that is taught within national education systems, or the kind of historical research that attracts national research funding, has political implications. Former UK Prime Minister Margaret Thatcher recalled how she fought the 'hardest battle' over history when her government designed a national curriculum for schools in the late 1980s. She wanted more weight given to British political history, and more emphasis on 'facts' rather than 'enquiry'. She wrote in her memoirs: 'No amount of imaginative sympathy for historical characters or situations can be a substitute for the initially tedious but ultimately rewarding business of memorizing what actually happened'[16]. By this she meant the key facts of iconic events of domestic and international state politics. Thatcher believed she was in a battle against left-wing ideologues whose views on history as a subject were formed in the counter-cultures of the 1960s and 1970s. These were the kind of historians who wrote 'history from below' – social and cultural history that gave a voice to people and groups from the past who were ignored in studies of high politics. This approach was initially dominated by concepts of class, but it came to produce what we now recognise as feminist history, black history, postcolonial history, and histories of sexual and other minorities. The ways in which these categories intersect and overlap can be seen in works such as David Roediger's *The Wages of Whiteness: Race and the Making of the American Working Class* (2007).

Finally, historians have aspired to draw insights and lessons from the historical record itself – to 'learn the lessons of the past'. As we have seen, this is sometimes presented in instrumental (and problematic) terms. Historians might invoke the idea of 'avoiding past mistakes' – for example, by describing the circumstances in which despotic regimes have come to power in the past. Similarly, they might draw analogies with the past as a way of understanding the present – what strategies did previous governments use to deal with economic depression? What kinds of challenges are involved in fighting colonial wars? How have minority groups in the past organised themselves effectively around a grievance? At a more general level, the idea of 'learning lessons from the past' assumes that historical knowledge aggregates. In other words, that it is cumulative – that all knowledge about the past represents a gain for humankind because it represents a form of intellectual progress.

History also has more concrete and pragmatic functions. The subject has its own professional infrastructure, much of it funded by public finance. It provides jobs for teachers at school and college/university level. In 2018, for example, there were more than 20,000 postsecondary history teachers in the USA – not including graduate teaching assistants.[17] In the UK in the same year there were around 3,500 historians employed by universities.[18] Within this sector of employment careers have to be advanced and reputations made, usually by writing and publishing 'original' research. Funding for this research has to be captured via competition between historians. Books need to be written because publishers require new material for their catalogues. Students want to be taught on 'up-to-date' courses, based around new research materials and recent scholarship. And there are opportunities in the media for historians who are able to communicate clearly about a subject of current concern.

What is historiography?

Historiography can be defined most simply as the study of the writing of history. Such studies can be conducted at the general level – that is, asking questions about the different ground-rules and practices of writing history since the age of Herodotus (*c*.480–*c*.420 BCE). But as a history student you will most often encounter the term historiography at the local level of historians' writings about a particular subject. So, for example, the historiography of the Spanish Civil War (1936–39) denotes the collection of published work on the subject produced by historians such as Rafael Abella, José Luis García Delgado, Mary Nash, Gabriel Jackson, Paul Preston, Helen Graham and Sheelagh Ellwood. Studying historiography should not be confused with using certain historians' books as transparent mediums to access 'the past'. Nor should it be seen as an invitation to 'name drop' historians or to strip out some quotes from their work. Instead, it should involve thinking about the particular ways in which the relevant specialist historians have conceptualised, researched and written about the subject at hand. How does their work differ from one another? At what points do these works converge? How do we explain historians' arrival at contending interpretations of the same subject, and how do we cope with their lack of agreement? Moreover, these history texts should be related to the specific times and cultures in which they were produced – in other words, we should apply the same critical procedures for reading historians' work that we apply to the raw data of historical sources (documents, testimony and artefacts).

Part of the challenge of studying degree-level history is to arrive at an understanding of the different ways in which the subject is currently researched and written. It pays anyone who writes history to reflect on the assumptions that stand behind how they do it. All history writing is based on a theoretical approach – an understanding of what historians do – and if you want to read historical accounts critically, rather than simply mine them for information, it helps if you can identify which approach is being used. This is not a question of detecting a historian's 'bias' in order to set it aside. Nor is it a question of separating historians into 'wrong' and 'right' camps. It is about developing the practices required to be a more rigorous and perceptive reader of historical texts and developing the vocabulary to be able to take part in the debate and continue the conversation.

When historians write their accounts they follow the rules that govern the writing of history – the ones that tell us how to 'do history'. These are the procedures, conventions and customs for working with the sources (the surrogates and traces of the past) and presenting a particular type of written text. The rules function as a kind of scholarly historians' etiquette. We might say as a shorthand here that history has its own 'genre rules' – just as there are genre rules for different categories of fiction, philosophy, law textbooks and so on. These rules or protocols are created and made habitual by a 'community of users' (including teachers, academics, editorial boards, and professional historical societies). The accepted ways of 'doing history' are rooted in the here-and-now of our cultures. They are what we have for now, they differ from the norms of a century ago, and most likely they will be different again at some point in the future. These rules are collectively known as the historical method. While some historians argue that the application of these protocols to the analysis of sources permits a degree of matching with an independently existing past, we would argue that studying the sources according to the rules produces a particular past that is conventionally called 'history' and that this past is not independent of the historian and their interpretation of the sources or explanatory frameworks used for understanding the world. Moreover, there are potentially equally valid ways of creating representations of the past. Whichever understanding of the function of the historical method (the rules governing the writing of history) that one prefers, the point remains that history students are faced with the task of learning to work in accordance with the current rules for doing the subject. In effect, this means that doing a history degree requires you to learn how 'to play the game' of academic history – learning how to think, talk and write like historians do now. Following the rules is a precondition of anyone having their work regarded as academic history. While some historians claim that these rules help us to get closer to the actuality of the past, we favour an approach that regards historical knowledge as always provisional, produced for specific purposes and constructed at specific times and places. We maintain that it is possible to work using the discourse of history in ways that have some social relevance in the present day. Studying for a history degree can be a worthwhile activity for any number of reasons that we hope to make clear in what follows.

Notes

1 Carl Hempel, 'The Function of General Laws in History', in *Journal of Philosophy*, 39/1 (1942) 35–48.
2 Geoffrey Elton, *The Practice of History* (Oxford: Blackwell, 2nd edn 1992) 73–4.
3 Keith Jenkins, *Re-figuring History: New Thoughts on an Old Discipline* (London: Routledge, 2003) 53.
4 Tony Judt, 'The World We Have Lost', in *Reappraisals: Reflections on the Forgotten Twentieth Century* (London: Vintage, 2009) 1–22, 19.
5 *Ibid.*, 16–19.
6 Eric Hobsbawm, *Interesting Times: A Twentieth-Century Life* (London: Abacus, 2002) 282.
7 This film was released in China as *Wo he wo de zu guo* in 2019 to mark the 70th anniversary of the People's Republic of China.
8 Martin L. Davies, *Historics: Why History Dominates Contemporary Society* (London: Routledge, 2006) 4.
9 Hayden White, 'The Burden of History' (1966), reprinted in *Tropics of Discourse: Essays in Cultural Criticism* (Baltimore, MD: Johns Hopkins University Press, 1978) 27–50.
10 White, 'Burden', 32.
11 Friedrich Nietzsche, 'On the Uses and Disadvantages of History for Life' (1874), reprinted in Daniel Breazeale (ed.) trans. R.J. Hollingdale, *Friedrich Nietzsche: Untimely Meditations* (Cambridge: CUP, 1997) 62.
12 Sande Cohen, *History Out of Joint* (Baltimore, MD: Johns Hopkins University Press, 2006) 125
13 White, 'Burden', 41.
14 *Ibid.*, 28.
15 John Tosh (ed.), *Historians on History* (Harlow: Pearson Education, 2nd edn 2009) 2.
16 Margaret Thatcher, *Downing Street Years* (London: Harper Collins, 1993) 595.
17 United States Department of Labor, Occupational Employment Statistics, 25–1,125 Statistics, History Teachers, Postsecondary www.bls.gov/oes/current/oes251125.htm#ind accessed 31 October 2019.
18 See Advance HE, Equality Challenge Unit, *Equality in Higher Education; Statistical Report 2018*, 38.r

Further reading

Georg G. Iggers, *Historiography in the Twentieth Century: From Scientific Objectivity to the Postmodern Challenge* (Middletown, CT: Wesleyan University Press, 2005). A lucid and economical survey of modern historiography, with a strong emphasis on national varieties of history writing. Iggers organises this book around three themes: the emergence of history as a professional discipline, the influence of the social sciences and the challenge of postmodernism.

Ulinka Rublack (ed.), *A Concise Companion to History* (Oxford: Oxford University Press, 2011). This is a wide-ranging and thought-provoking survey of contemporary historical practices. The book sets out to re-examine the relationship between history, reality and truth as it stood in the early twenty-first century, while taking care to avoid conflating the writing of 'history' and 'western history'. It begins with overview essays on world history, causation, historical knowledge and historians. These are followed by chapters of variable quality on 'themes and structures', which include power, population, gender, ethnicity, science, environmental history, emotions and the power of ideas.

John Tosh, *The Pursuit of History: Aims, Methods and New Directions in the Study of History* (Abingdon: Routledge, 2015). First published in 1984, the sixth edition of this book continues to serve as a useful guide for university history students. Tosh takes a more traditional position on metahistorical issues than we do throughout *Doing History*.

Dave Eaton, *World History Through Case Studies: Historical Skills in Practice* (New York: Bloomsbury Academic, 2019). As the title states, Eaton uses 20 case studies of global history to illustrate different ideas about 'how to think historically'. He breaks this down into five main areas: historical significance, historical empathy, evidence, continuity and change, and progress and decline. The content of the essays range from the prehistoric era to the globalisation of football today.

2

Pre-modern historians on history

Human society has probably always had a historical consciousness of some form; that is, people have been narrating their pasts and telling stories about the 'before now' for thousands of years. There can be found in all civilisations and communities a genre of narrative, be it oral or written, which we might today describe as something like history. These earlier authors of histories have contributed much to our knowledge of the times about which they wrote, and also to our comprehension of what history was understood to be by their societies. Many of the historiographical issues that they raised are still being discussed and debated today. Is the purpose of history to faithfully record the past, or to educate, to entertain, or to provide moral guidance for the benefit of individuals and society? What causes change over time in societies: the progress and development of civilisation, God, material conditions, economics, geographical or climatic factors, or class conflict? Is there a pattern to history? Is it linear or cyclical? What should the role of the historian be? Should she simply chronicle events that happened or attempt to analyse and explain why they happened? Should the personal beliefs and perspectives of the historian be allowed to influence their narrative or should the historian 'tell things *as they were done*'?[1] What is the appropriate subject matter of histories: wars, diplomacy, the activities of the political elite, explanations as to why empires rise and fall, the development of society, or the lives of the common people? Who were the intended audiences of histories? Lastly, what type of writing is history: is it like literature or more like a science? Inherent in this last distinction are wider issues concerning the epistemological status of history – in other words, what type of knowledge is history? Is it factual knowledge, like science, or is it more imaginative, like poetry or literature? In this chapter we will explore how these questions have been addressed in different societies and cultures over the past 2,500 years through an analysis of various histories and historians. Obviously, there is not the space for a detailed discussion of all the main historians and trends in historical writing from across the world (see the recommended reading for books that deal with this subject in more depth), so we will just look at some of the more important people and ideas that you may come across in your reading or studies: those historians whose ideas had a profound influence on different audiences and on later historians. Moreover, because we wish to challenge the preconception that historical consciousness was generally a modern European phenomenon, we will pay particular attention to the historical traditions and scholars from the Chinese, Islamic and Afro-Asian worlds.

History in the ancient world

The development of Hellenic culture in the east Mediterranean around 500 BCE is generally understood to mark a cultural shift from the mythical to a more rational or philosophical consciousness. This meant that communities began to seek explanations of events in terms of economic, sociological, political or demographic factors and not solely in terms of the actions of the gods. Simultaneously we see the emergence of what could be termed the first historians, people who attempted to find rational explanations for the course of human events particularly wars, diplomatic activities and the foundation of cities.[2]

In his *History of the Peloponnesian War*, written in the fifth century BCE, Thucydides aimed to provide an accurate and detailed political and military account of the war. However, he was not content with chronicling the major events of the war, he also wanted to analyse and explain the forces that underpinned the conflict. It is this desire to provide an explanation of events together with his critical attitude towards sources that has earned him the title of 'the father of history' among contemporary western historians. Thucydides was also one of the earliest scholars to make the distinction between poetry (or literature) and history – a distinction that is still debated by historians today. He accuses chroniclers of composing their narratives with the aim more of 'pleasing the ear than of telling the truth'.[3] In contrast, he argues that in writing his work he has striven to adhere to high standards of research and accuracy and thus 'from the evidence that has been given [...] the state of affairs in antiquity was pretty nearly such as I have described it'.[4] Thucydides claimed that he achieved such accuracy because he included facts 'only after investigating with the greatest possible accuracy each detail'.[5] Although he considered alternative explanations of events, he presented an account of what he believed to have actually happened. He used a similar range of sources to those of modern historians, including oral evidence, archeological or material remains, inscriptions and earlier histories or accounts of events, including, despite his reservations, accounts by Herodotus and Homer. However, one type of source that he used which modern historians would probably no longer consider to be valid was evidence supplied by the oracles.

History writing in China also has a long heritage. While there were historians before Confucius (551-479 BCE), he is one of the earliest and most famous of Chinese historians. Confucius is generally credited with having introduced moral edification as a historiographic principle in Chinese history writing: that is, he used history as a pedagogical tool to convey moral messages and to pass judgements on people and actions. By reducing literary excesses and repetitions, deleting records he deemed to be unimportant, and re-arranging the text, he re-worked and augmented the earlier annalistic history of the reigns of 12 dukes between 722 and 484 BCE entitled *Spring and Autumn Annals*, in order to convey moral judgements. Sima Qian, a later Chinese historian, says this about the *Annals*: 'It distinguishes what is suspicious and doubtful, clarifies right and wrong, and settles points which are uncertain. It calls good good and bad bad, honours the worthy, and condemns the unworthy'[6].

In the Chinese historiographic tradition history did not only provide a moral narrative that distinguished between vice and virtue, it could also be used as a guide to contemporary statecraft. Confucius argued that, because present problems are all re-enactments of past problems, the past could provide a suitable model from which to learn the principles of good statecraft. In this way Confucius understands history to have a cyclical pattern. However, the importance of history as a pedagogical tool did not diminish the commitment of Chinese historians to be faithful to the sources and to search for the truth: Confucius argued that although he could discuss the rituals of the Yia and Shang dynasties, he could not discuss those of the Qi and Song because there were insufficient documents.

Sima Qian (also sometimes transliterated as Ssu-ma Ch'ien), who was Grand Historian/Astrologer in the first century BCE, in many ways shared Confucius' belief in moral edification as a historiographical principle. However, in his history, the *Records of the Grand Historian*, he did not only emulate Confucius, he also created a new historical tradition with novel styles and forms of writing which had a very profound influence on Chinese historiography. His history differs from that of Thucydides as it has a much greater geographical, chronological and thematic scope. While the subject of Thucydides's history was the Peloponnesian war, Sima Qian organised his vast encyclopaedic work into five broad categories: basic annals, chronological tables, hereditary houses, biographies, and treatises on human institutions such as astronomy, economics, hydraulic engineering, religion, calendars and music. While the first three sections provide a rather traditional history of the dynastic houses, reigns of individual emperors and hereditary office-holding families, the section on biographies describes the lives of a variety of individuals including poets, philosophers, tycoons, bandits, officials, diviners, foreigners and minor royalty. Sima Qian used this biographical form to highlight the actions of people in the past because he believed it was the job of the historian to pass judgement on the lives of individuals in order to highlight moral lessons. This use of biography as a tool for teaching morality was a historiographical innovation, which subsequently characterised Chinese history writing for nearly two millennia and can also be seen in western European history writing, particularly from the seventeenth to the nineteenth centuries. For example, Samuel Smiles in his late nineteenth-century work *Self-Help; with illustrations of Conduct and Perseverance* gives biographies of a series of engineers, businessmen, craftsmen and inventors in order to present 'lessons of industry, perseverance, and self-culture' to his audience.[7]

Another precedent that Sima Qian introduced, which remained a feature of Chinese writing until the twentieth century, was the practice of providing a commentary at different points throughout the text. He introduced his commentaries with the phrase 'The Grand Historian remarked' and used these sections to comment on historical events, critique historical figures and highlight the meaning of different stories.[8] This acknowledgement of the role of the historian in judging the lives of individuals and commentating on various aspects of the past is very different to the view among many twentieth-century historians that historians should remain objective and distant from the events they record and should only explain past events and not comment on them. However, Sima Qian combined his didactic approach to the writing of history with a careful regard for establishing what he saw as the truth. He believed that an equally important task of the historian was to correct the historical record in cases where people were erroneously judged as worthy of moral emulation or demonised as traitors: as he says 'because Su Ch'in died a traitor's death, the world has united in scoffing at him […] For this reason I have set forth this account of his deeds, arranging them in proper chronological order, so that he may not forever suffer from an evil reputation'.[9]

His attitude towards sources is similar to that of Thucydides and modern historians. He uses more than 75 written documents, memorials and inscriptions, and for events that occurred during his lifetime, he uses his own personal observations and oral information from other key figures. When faced with new information not included in earlier classical books, he compared it with that found in other documents in order to verify it, and where he judged that there was not sufficient information to provide a reliable and accurate account of events he accordingly did not provide one. Moreover, by not attributing the success or failure of events to the will of heaven, but to more earthly causal factors, he made explicit the power of human agency in shaping human history, which is a feature of more modern historical writing as well.

In ancient China history was not only used for pedagogical purposes, it also had a political role. It was read by rulers and administrators as a guide to statecraft and to provide practical insights into current political problems. It was also used, more polemically, to legitimise the rule of new dynasties, which would commission the writing of a history in order to confirm that their succession was legitimate and that there had been a rightful continuation of power and authority. This official endorsement that history writing received in ancient China was bureaucratised further under the Tang, with the establishment of the History Bureau. However, history did not inevitably become mere political propaganda, as such histories were still written within a framework that emphasised the importance of historical truth, fidelity to the sources and the importance of producing an account of what 'really happened'. Moreover, various safeguards were introduced to ensure that historians could remain faithful to the sources and free from undue official pressure. However, this is not to say that at times historians did not write partisan or sycophantic histories.

While the Byzantine historian Anna Comnena (discussed below) is often described as the first female historian, this reflects a rather Eurocentric view, as the famous Chinese scholar and historian Ban Zhao (as spelt Pan Chao) predates Anna Comnena by about 1,000 years.[10] Ban Zhao was the highly educated and accomplished daughter of Ban Biao, a famous historian who worked on a sequel to Sima Qian's *Records of the Grand Historian* entitled the *Han Shu* – a history of the Han dynasty. Following his death, and that of her brother who had taken over the task of finishing the history, Ban Zhao was commissioned by the Emperor Ho to complete the work, suggesting she was already a very well-respected scholar. We know that she at least completed the 'Eight Tables' and the 'Treatise on Astronomy' that her brother had started, but it is entirely possible that she also revised and re-edited the entire *Han Shu*.[11] As a result of her labour she became the de facto historian to the Imperial Court of China, although she did not hold this title.[12] Her work was used as a model for later histories of subsequent dynasties. She was also an adviser to, and confidant of, the Empress, who effectively ruled China, and the author of numerous other literary texts, including poetry and a moralistic manual entitled *Lessons for Women*.[13]

There was also a flourishing tradition of history writing in China throughout the ancient, pre-modern and modern periods by private individuals. Such works were not only encyclopaedic or histories of dynasties, but included treatises, synoptic works and miscellanies. These works still generally adhered to the conventions and methodologies of Chinese historical writing though. For example, Liu Shiji (661–721 CE) argued for the critical evaluation of sources, the impartial reconstruction of historical narratives through truthful recording and the avoidance of distortion, concealment and embellishment. He still adhered to the idea that the principal function of history was to apportion blame and praise, but argued that the historian could only act as moral adjudicator with a truthful and accurate account of the past.[14]

Writing around the same time as Liu Shiji, Bede's *The Ecclesiastical History of the English People* provides an account of events mainly in the seventh and early eighth century and is crucial for our knowledge of early English history. Similar to Sima Qian, Bede primarily understands history to have a moral and didactic component. Historical events, or the lives of historical individuals, should act as examples or guides to moral action: 'If history records good things of good men, the thoughtful hearer is encouraged to imitate what is good; or if it records evil of wicked men, the devout, religious listener or reader is encouraged to avoid all that is sinful'[15].

A key function of history for Bede, who was a member of a monastic order, was to spread Christianity and to strengthen the faith of existing Christians. He is therefore essentially writing within a Christian framework and his explanations of events are in religious terms. For example, he explains periods of prosperity in Britain as arising from Britons respecting God's laws, and conversely, negative events and disasters are the result of their misdeeds. This religious framework also means that his history includes many accounts of miraculous happenings.

Bede uses a variety of written and oral sources and also names these sources in his text. One of his most important sources was Abbot Albinus, who himself had collected numerous written and oral accounts of traditions in the Kent region and who passed them to Northelm, who gave them to Bede. Northelm also supplied Bede with evidence about Britain from letters and documents kept in the archives of the Roman church in Rome. Bede clearly distinguishes between direct and indirect accounts of events and notes when the details of an event have been obtained from hearsay or rumour.

Pre-modern Islamic history

Many pre-modern histories such as Bede's are written within a religious framework, be it Christian, Islamic or the heavenly order that Confucius and other Chinese scholars referred to. History writing in an early Islamic context was relatively varied, ranging from *hadith,* which was a genre that recorded the deeds and words of the prophet, to chronicle histories, biographies and universal histories. A good example of an Islamic universal history is that written by Ibn al-Athir in the twelfth/thirteenth centuries CE. Ibn al-Athir's 12-volume world history *al-Kamil fi'l-ta'rikh* [*The Perfect* or *Complete Work of History*] has been described as the highpoint of Islamic annalistic historiography.[16] This comprehensive work begins with an account of creation and a narration of Persian, Roman, Jewish and Arab histories from the pre-Islamic era, before providing a history of the early Islamic caliphate and subsequent Islamic dynasties.[17] It is arranged chronologically in an annalistic fashion, and as such is a paradigmatic example of pre-modern Islamic history writing. However, Ibn al-Athir was also quite innovative in terms of style and approach. For example, despite the annalistic format whereby all events occurring in a particular year are narrated together, Ibn al-Athir at times related a single event or series of related events that stretched over a period of a few years in a single section, thus creating a narrative based on subject matter rather than chronology. This occured far more frequently when he was writing the history of events occurring between 614 and 620 in the Islamic calendar (1217–1223 CE), including his account of the Fifth Crusade, Mesopotamian affairs after the fall of the Zengids and the Mongol attack.[18] Moreover, when sources gave contradictory accounts of events that Ibn al-Athir could not effectively harmonise into one narrative, he included different versions of the same event, promising to settle the dispute if further evidence came to light.[19]

Ibn al-Athir summarised and synthesised a variety of different histories and sources in his narration of pre-Islamic and early Islamic history, most notably the universal history of the ninth/tenth century historian al-Tabari. For events nearer his own time, he supplemented his sources with oral information derived from family members and contacts employed in the Zengid dynasty and the administration of Saladin, as well as official documents such as muster rolls and the official correspondence of government ministers.[20] Ibn al-Athir's history is truly universal in content, at least from an Islamic perspective. It covers events and provides information on polities and societies throughout the Islamic world, including details about the Abbasid caliphate in Baghdad, encounters with European crusaders in Syria and Palestine, factional power struggles among the Seljuk sultans, the political machinations of the Ghurid dynasty in South Asia, as well as the activities of Turkish nomads in the far east of Central Asia and the Amoravid and Almohad dynasties in Anadalusia. Ibn al-Athir not only concentrated on political, dynastic or military history. He also provided valuable information on the economic conditions of his own time, including the prices of various goods, the disruption of trade routes by the Mongols and trade disputes occurring between other states in the Persian Gulf.[21]

The introduction to his work, like that of many pre-modern histories, contains both a defence of history as a worthy subject of study and an explanation of what he understood history to be. For Ibn al-Athir, an interest in the past was a natural human activity found in all societies. In particular, he argued history has a didactic component, in that it provides moral lessons and guidance for audiences. It can also act as a kind of ultimate tribunal bestowing a good reputation on the worthy and a bad one on the wicked. Like Bede's history, his account of the past is also set within a religious framework, with the will of God lying behind all events, thereby reducing the importance of the role of people. He thus frequently commented on the transitory nature of human life and the vicissitudes of fortune. However, on occasion he wrote as if he did hold individuals responsible for their own actions. Similarly, despite the exemplary rather than explanatory nature of his work, he did sometimes attempt to explain the cause of events and speculated on possible alternative outcomes or hypothetical histories. Historiographically, therefore, there are considerable similarities between the approach of Ibn al-Athir and those of classical and medieval Christian European scholars and Chinese historians.[22]

Byzantine history

Writing in the twelfth century, slightly earlier than Ibn al-Athir, Anna Comnena, the daughter of the Byzantine Emperor Alexius, also wrote a multivolume history that dealt in part with the crusades. Her work, *The Alexiad,* was not a universal history, and had more in common with Ibn al-Athir's panegyric history celebrating the deeds of the Zengid dynasty entitled *The Resplendent History of the Atabeg Dynasty*, in that it was a eulogistic history of her family, the Comneni, and more specifically a military and political history of the Byzantine Empire during the reign of her father, Alexius. Her history is lively, informative and passionate. In the preface to the *The Alexiad* she sets out her understanding of the function of history: 'The stream of Time, irresistible, ever-moving, carries off and bears away all things that come to birth and plunges them into utter darkness [...] The science of History is a great bulwark against this stream of Time [...] it holds in a tight grasp whatever it can seize on the surface, and will not allow it to slip away into the depths of oblivion'[23]. More specifically, she makes explicit the political nature of history writing with her comment that, 'having realized the effects wrought by Time, [I] desire now by means of my writings to give an account of my father's deeds, which do not deserve to be consigned to Forgetfulness'.[24] Anna Comnena is aware of the potential criticisms that writing about her father might occasion and states that she will be completely unbiased and not allow filial piety and her love for her family to interfere with her objective description of events and people.[25] Indeed she takes great care to distinguish her work as history and not panegyric. This leads to one of the most interesting features of her work, the presence of extensive authorial interventions or self-interjections into the text. Although there was a tradition of such interventions in Byzantine historiography, both Anna Comnena and the historian Michael Psellos use the technique more extensively than other Byzantine historians.[26] Such interventions foreground the self-consciousness of the writer and draw attention to their role as author of the text. Some of her interventions seem relatively innocuous, as when discussing a Norman trick Anna Comnena notes: '[W]hen I think of all this it makes me smile and laughter rises to my lips, as I wield my pen by the lamp'[27]. Other interventions, however, more explicitly reflect her concern that her credentials as a historian will be affected by her personal closeness to her subject and that she will be accused of bias and partiality. They are therefore methodological and are intended to demarcate her work as history rather than panegyric. For example, when defending her mother against criticisms for having accompanied her father, Alexius, on campaign, she notes that 'I could have said a great deal more about this empress were it not that being a daughter might produce the suspicion of falsehood and the (accusation) that we are favouring the mother'.[28] Similarly, when defending her father's use of strategy rather than military conflict, she comments, 'For I have many times said in my defense that it is not favour towards my father which produces these words but the nature of circumstances. For does anything on the side of truth itself hinder one from being both a father lover and at the same time a lover of truth?'[29]

In addition to providing details of court life, military engagements and the deeds of her family, *The Alexiad* also provides an account of the First Crusade from the perspective of the Byzantine elite. Unsurprisingly, she depicts those crusaders who remained loyal to Alexius as pious and chivalrous, but portrays those who eventually attacked her father as faithless, covetous men. Her textual portraits of various historical protagonists provide one of the most interesting features of her history. Through these often very detailed descriptions she informs the reader of the moral and physical traits of members of the Byzantine aristocracy, their friends and their enemies. However, there is a tendency for her portraits to project the aristocracy as embodying ideal types rather than be realistic depictions, although she does personalise each description to a degree.[30]

Not all pre-modern Islamic histories were annalistic, biographical or linear. The work of Ibn Khaldun is an excellent example of cyclical history. Ibn Khaldun was a fourteenth-century North African scholar and bureaucrat. He was well educated and occupied a number of high government, legal and academic posts for a variety of different rulers, including that of prime minister for the Hafsid ruler, and chief judge and professor of law in Egypt.

Ibn Khaldun's most famous work is *The Muqaddimah* (*The Prolegomena*). Although now considered to be a work in its own right, it was originally meant to be the introduction and chapter one of Ibn Khaldun's longer and universal history of the Arabs, non-Arabs and Berbers, the *Kitab al-'ibar* [*The Book of Lessons*]. *The Muqaddimah* consists of an introduction which discusses historiography and the types of errors that historians commonly make, and six sub-chapters which deal with: human civilisation and the influence that the physical environment has on society; Bedouin civilisation; royal authority; urban civilisation; crafts and ways of making a living; and science.

For Ibn Khaldun history is more than 'information about political events, dynasties and, occurrences of the remote past'; it is 'an attempt to get at the truth, [a] subtle explanation of the causes and origins of existing things and deep knowledge of the how and why of events'.[31] In order to provide such an explanation and 'to establish the truth and soundness of information about factual happenings, a requirement to consider is the conformity [...] with general conditions. Therefore it is necessary to investigate whether it is possible that the reported facts could have happened'.[32] He continues that 'if he [the historian] trusts historical information in its plain transmitted form and has no clear knowledge of the principles resulting from custom, the fundamental facts of politics, the nature of civilization, or the conditions governing human social organization, and if, furthermore, he does not evaluate remote or ancient material through comparison with near or contemporary material, he often cannot avoid [...] deviating from the path of truth'.[33] A historian must therefore 'know the principles of politics, the nature of things, and the differences among nations, places and periods with regard to ways of life, character qualities, customs, sects, schools, and everything else [...] He must compare similarities or differences between present and past conditions. He must know the causes of the similarities in certain cases and of the differences in others'.[34] Ibn Khaldun illustrated his argument with a variety of case studies. For example, he challenged claims that there was a city built wholly of copper in the Sijimasah desert by arguing that none of the travellers and guides who regularly traverse the desert have ever seen it, and also that metal does not usually exist in quantities sufficient to build an entire city from it.[35]

For Ibn Khaldun, therefore, historical ideas should reflect reality; that is, they should conform to, or cohere with, the rules that govern social organisation. Consequently, it is fundamental for historians to have knowledge of these rules and of how society in all its aspects works, including a theory of social co-operation, urbanisation, social organisation and political power. His exhortation to historians to be aware of the underlying rules governing society, politics, authority and social organisation is possibly the most innovative aspect of *The Muqaddimah* and can be considered one of the earliest attempts to discern and explain the structural patterns that govern changes in human political and social organisations. For Ibn Khaldun, history is far more than a reconstruction of the past: it 'is information about human social organization' and should explain why and how societies came into being and how and why they change over time.[36] Essentially, Ibn Khaldun can be seen as a pioneer of what later became known in the West in the nineteenth century as sociology. Moreover, his exploration of the influence of the environment on human nature and society in the first sub-chapter of *The Muqaddimah* pre-empts Fernand Braudel's emphasis on the role of the environment in his twentieth-century epic history of the Mediterranean.[37]

Also of significance is the manner in which Ibn Khaldun combines his unique understanding of the term *asabiyye* (social solidarity or group feeling) with the Aristotelian circle-of-justice model of a functioning state and the life-cycle metaphor in order to explain the various stages that states go through. For Ibn Khaldun, *asabiyye* was a key element of human society and can also be considered as the basic motor of societal change: it explains the difference between different social organisations and also why some are bigger, more successful or more durable than others. A social group with strong group cohesiveness (*asabiyye*) will achieve predominance over other groups and its leader may therefore be able to establish a dynasty. However, to establish a dynasty requires the support of a large number of people and thus requires the development of cities and towns, which in turn permits the development of the arts, crafts and sciences. As the cities develop, the men whose social solidarity sustains the ruling elite become more alienated and their power is weakened, which ultimately leads to them being superseded by an outside military force whose group solidarity is much stronger. States therefore follow a life-cycle pattern: they emerge, develop, mature and then decline. Ibn Khaldun thus conceived of history as having a cyclical pattern with civilisations rising then collapsing and others subsequently taking their place. Cyclical ideas of history can also be found in Buddhist and Hindu histories, in some classical western histories (especially Edward Gibbon's *The History of the Decline and Fall of the Roman Empire*) and also in some modern economic histories. Andre Gunder Frank, for example, developed the Soviet economist Kondratiev's idea of there being waves of fast and slow economic growth, and suggested the existence of long and short economic cycles which have affected economic development in the world system.[38]

Early modern Ottoman historians

Mustafa Naima was a late seventeenth/early eighteenth century Ottoman historian whose history of the Ottoman Empire from 1591 to1660 became one of the most famous and defining histories for the period. Naima had a bureaucratic career in the Ottoman government, serving as chief army archivist, chief to the head accountancy bureau and secretary to various elite Ottomans. He was also, between 1697 and 1704 *vak'anüvis* (event-writer). The term *vak'anüvis* can have two meanings: a recording secretary who kept the minutes of government; or an official state historian. Naima was both. His duty was to keep a written record of the events of the Ottoman state in a daybook, but he was also commissioned to write a history of the Ottoman Empire.

Naima's history is, on the surface, typical of Islamic annalistic chronicles. It is organised according to year, so events that last for a number of years are broken up into different sections. Military events and affairs of state dominate, but he also included biographies of deceased members of the Ottoman elite. This emphasis on the history of the Ottoman state and government reflects his understanding of the function of history. Just as for the Chinese historians discussed above, for Naima, the purpose of history is didactic: it should educate the reader. The section of his preface entitled 'On History' makes this point quite forcefully, as he notes that history increases the keenness of scholars' intellects; makes the attentiveness of wise men broader; serves as a standard of judgement; gives the elite secrets which would otherwise have been concealed; gives men insight into the causes of decay and decline in civilisations and thus allows men to foresee what will be the result of actions and the consequences of particular circumstances.[39] History should therefore provide a record of past and present events in order to provide examples of good government practice as a guide to current administrators. Throughout his history, Naima gives advice on leadership, on factions and influencing sultans and on reforms. In this regard, Naima is continuing a long tradition of Islamic scholars who received court or state patronage and who wrote histories that provided useful political and moral lessons.

As to how Naima wrote his history, he was trying to provide a synthesis of all available histories for this period in order to construct the most reliable account. He mainly relied upon Katib Çelebi's *Fezleke* (*Memorandum*) and incorporated large sections from this and other histories into his own work. However, Naima was not uncritically copying these texts and it cannot be understood as plagiarism. By choosing what to incorporate and also by making small changes to the text, Naima and other Ottoman historians who composed histories in a similar manner were, effectively, commentating and passing judgement on the views of earlier historians: they were, in effect, engaging in what could be termed academic dialogue.

Moreover, Naima took great pains to challenge and verify his sources. Where different accounts of particular events existed, he usually reproduced all the versions and then either offered his view as to which he believed was the more probable version or left it to the reader to decide by saying 'God alone knows'. Sometimes he notes that he tried to reconcile events by speaking to members of the elite who may have had more direct knowledge of the event in question. On one occasion he follows two different versions of an event with a poem, which is very informative as to his understanding of the function of history and how, or whether, one should try to reconcile conflicting accounts:

> Certainly some call the lover cypress and some *elif*
> The aim of them all is one, but the telling differs.[40]

Both the cypress tree and the Arabic letter *elif* are upright and straight and are thus commonly used as metaphors to describe the physical and moral attributes of a beloved. The poem suggests that for Naima at times there may be two different narratives of a historical event, but they, like the cypress and the letter *elif*, can serve the same function: they can both allow the reader to draw the same moral lesson. This suggests that Naima did not believe that the function of history was always to try to accurately represent the past or tell *the* truth about what *really* happened, but that sometimes the moral or didactic aspect took precedence. This is not to say that Naima adopted an uncritical attitude towards sources. He was aware of the partisan nature of some of his sources, and he tried to take a more neutral stance when incorporating sections from them. In particular, he notes that he omitted some of the polemic from the pro-clerical account of the bureaucrat Manarzade, who was one of his main sources.

In many ways, western European historians of the same period were approaching the study of history in a similar manner. Philosopher and historian David Hume and Edward Gibbon both wrote histories that were largely based upon accounts by others, rather than primary sources.[41] However, they were committed to trying to establish a true account of the past, and through critical scrutiny of these accounts attempted to remove any evidence of legends, myths or politically partisan bias from the works. Moreover, both historians strove to write exemplary narratives that provided apposite moral lessons and concentrated on issues of political life, governance and questions of rulership.

In his Preface, Naima, like Ibn Khaldun, provides some guidelines for historians. These include a duty to be reliable and not make spurious or foolish claims (to tell the truth and substantiate it); to disregard the rumours and gossip of the common people and to concentrate on documented statements of reliable men who know how to record what actually happened; to not simply tell a story but also to incorporate useful information into the narrative and allow the reader to draw the moral for themselves; to speak frankly and fairly (to not be partisan or biased); to avoid obscure expressions; to quote in full any interesting correspondence, anecdotes and prose that can be obtained; and to discuss astrology only when appropriate. With the exception of this last point, these guidelines are reminiscent of those used by modern historians.

As we saw above, it was not only Islamic historians who were writing in a broadly bureaucratic context and who saw one of the primary functions of historical texts as providing important lessons for governing the state, a similar approach to history was evident in China. In the early modern period under the Ming dynasty, the protocols or rules of writing history were becoming more standardised and began to resemble very much the historical method of today's academic historians. A comprehensive compilation and vetting of sources, standardised rules for recounting events, adherence to the truth, impartial evaluation and narrative concision were all commonplace in many official and private histories.

Progressive, linear history and modernity

Historiographical traditions in the nineteenth and twentieth centuries have both continued and developed some of the characteristics seen in earlier historical practices, and also introduced new features. Although not all histories possess all of these traits, the key aspects of modern history writing include: a commitment to objectivity; a desire to provide causal explanations, not simply chronologies of past events; an interest in epistemology (theories of historical knowledge); a belief that history is a scientific discipline; and an understanding of history as a coherent, progressive and thus linear process which ultimately leads to social advancement and greater freedom. The two most significant characteristics are possibly the last two. The notion that history is scientific and progressive is very much a response to the discourse of modernity. Modernity is generally taken to be characterised by a commitment to empiricism as the best means of verifying knowledge about the world; beliefs in human intentionality, secularism, and progress; the idea that scientific and technological development is the best solution to problems; and the desire to improve society.

The natural sciences, with their emphasis on the scientific method, the key role of empirical observation and the idea that laws governed the natural world, had a profound influence on historians in the nineteenth century, causing them to speculate about whether human society, past and present, could similarly be accurately described by empirical observation and was subject to discoverable laws. Such a response to history writing was expressed in the positivist writings of Auguste Comte, who argued that the history of human society demonstrated a progressive three-stage path leading from primitive society, where the world was understood primarily in religious terms, through the metaphysical stage, when alternative views of the world were sought, and ultimately to the positive stage in the nineteenth century, when an empirical methodology was employed to make sense of the world. Comte argued that historians could, through a rational and scientific analysis of empirical data (sources), identify the structural laws which govern or guide human development and social change. The discovery of such laws would then allow one to speculate on the future development of human society. Positivist historians therefore adhere to a progressive theory of history. Moreover, they see it as a science, and, they argue, just as with the natural sciences, there are natural laws governing society. The apparent existence of these laws enables historians to formulate hypotheses about the development of societies, which can then be empirically tested and amended if necessary. As we will see, positivism had a significant influence on many of the historiographical developments that occurred at the end of the nineteenth and during the twentieth century.

The notion of history as linear and progressive has been interpreted very differently by historians. In addition to the positivist movement described above, it can have an economic aspect, as in Marx's explanation of history, a nationalistic aspect, as in Whig history, and a racist aspect, as in the case of colonial and some Eurocentric histories. Although its most famous proponent was the early nineteenth-century historian Macaulay, Whig history writing emerged in Britain in the eighteenth century and takes its name from the Whig political party. Many have accused Whig history of being party political propaganda rather than history, and it is certainly true that politics and history were very much intertwined for Whig historians. For example, when the Whigs were returned to political power in 1830, Macaulay played a key role in the administration. However, as we have seen above, many historians have had close links with the government or state bureaucracy over the past 2,500 years, and continued to do so throughout the twentieth century. The British wartime Prime Minister Winston Churchill, for example, won the Nobel prize for literature for his historical writings. Whig historians interpreted the early modern period as a narrative of progress culminating in the development of distinctive British political institutions and society. They saw history as explaining and justifying not only the key events of British history, but also the existing social system, institutions and government. For the Whigs, British history was a narrative of how Britain became democratic, free and successful.

Many other historians also emphasised the continual development, and superiority, of European civilisation. Hegel, Ranke and Marx argued that Asian society was primitive and unchanging – without a history or historical consciousness – and it could only be brought into the modern world and the progressive course of history through western European intervention. Such histories therefore provided a perfect explanation of, and justification for, European colonial exploits in the nineteenth and twentieth centuries.

This idea of Afro-Asia being under-developed particularly when compared to the West was further developed in the twentieth century by Eurocentric historians who argued that either on the basis of race (Weber), environment (Diamond and Jones), Christianity (Mann) or western rational culture (Jones and Landes) that the West, over the past 600 years, developed economically, intellectually and culturally faster than the rest of the world and that this led to the inevitable pre-eminence or dominance of the western countries and their culture.[42] Such a view has since been challenged in a variety of ways by non-Eurocentric scholars including Blaut, Goody, Frank and Hobson among others.[43]

Notes

1 Thomas Blundevill, *The True Order and Methode of Wryting and Reading Hystories* (London: William Seres, 1574) unpaginated, quoted in Beverley Southgate, *History: What and Why? Ancient, Modern and Postmodern Perspectives.* (London: Routledge, 2nd edn 2001) 21.

2 M.C. Lemon, *Philosophy of History: A Guide for Students* (London: Routledge, 2003) particularly chapters 2 and 3.

3 Thucydides, *History of the Peleponnesian War*, four vols, trans. C.F. Smith, Loeb Classical Library (London: Heinemann, 1969) 1.21.1 quoted in Marnie Hughes-Warrington, *Fifty Key Thinkers on History* (London: Routledge, 2000) 320.

4 *Ibid.*, 1.21.1.

5 *Ibid.*, 1.22.2.

6 S. Qian, 'Shih chi 130: the Postface of the Grand Historian', in B. Watson, *Ssu-ma Ch'ien, Grand Historian of China* (New York: Columbia University Press, 1958) 51, quoted in Hughes-Warrington, *Fifty Key Thinkers* 292.

7 Samuel Smiles, *Self-Help; with Illustrations of Conduct and Perseverance* (London: John Murray, 1890) vi.

8 On-cho Ng and Q. Edward Wang, *Mirroring the Past: The Writing and Use of History in Imperial China* (Honolulu: University of Hawai'i Press, 2005) 63.

9 Quoted in G.R. Hardy, 'Objectivity and Interpretation in the "Shih chi"' (Ph.D. thesis, Yale University, 1988) 156 and subsequently in Hughes-Warrington, *Fifty Key Thinkers* 293.

10 Laiou, however, describes her possibly more accurately as 'the only secular women historian of the European Middle Ages', 'Introduction', 1.

11 Nancy Lee Swann, *Pan Chao: Foremost Woman Scholar of China First Century A.D.* (New York: Russell and Russell, 1968, originally published in 1932) 69 and 152.

12 *Ibid.*, xi.

13 *Ibid.*, 43 and see also chapter xii especially 153.

14 Ng and Wang, *Mirroring the Past* xv-xvi.

15 Bede, *The Ecclesiastical History of the English People* trans. J. McClure and R. Collins (Oxford: Oxford University Press, 1994) preface, also quoted in Hughes-Warrington, *Fifty Key Thinkers* 1.

16 For an English translation of sections of the work, see *The Chronicle of Ibn al-Athir for the Crusading Period from al-Kamil fi'l-ta'rikh.* Parts One and Two translated and with an introduction by D.S. Richards (Aldershot: Ashgate, 2006–7)

17 F. Rosenthal, 'Ibn al-Athir', in *Encyclopaedia of Islam* P.J. Bearman et al. (eds), (Leiden: Brill, 2004) CD-ROM ed. Windows Version.

18 D.S. Richards, 'Ibn al-Athir and the Later Parts of the *Kamil*: a Study of Aims and Methods', in D.O. Morgan (ed.), *Medieval Historical Writing in the Christian and Islamic Worlds* (London: School of Oriental and African Studies, 1982) 82–3.

19 *Ibid.*, 88–9.

20 *Ibid.*, 89–90.

21 *Ibid.*, 86.

22 *Ibid.*, 93–5.

23 *The Alexiad of Anna Comnena* trans. E.R.A. Sewter (Harmondsworth: Penguin, 1969, reprinted 1985) 17, quoted in Angeliki Laiou, 'Introduction: Why Anna Komnene?', in Thalia Gouma-Peterson (ed.) *Anna Komnene and Her Times* (New York: Garland Publishing Inc., 2000) 5.

24 Laiou, 'Introduction', 3–4.

25 *Ibid.*, 6.

26 Ruth Macrides, 'The Historian in the History', in Costas N. Constantinides, et al. (eds) ΦΙΛΕΛΛΗΝ *Studies in Honour of Robert Browning* (Venice: Istituto Ellenico di Studi Bizantini e Postbizantini di Venezia per tutti i paesi del mondo, 1996) 210.

27 Quoted in Macrides, 'The Historian', 218.

28 *Ibid.*, 219.

29 *Ibid.*

30 Laiou, 'Introduction', 8–13.

31 Ibn Khaldun, *The Muqaddimah: An Introduction to History* trans. and introduced by Franz Rosenthal with a new introduction by Bruce B. Lawrence (Princeton: Princeton University Press, 2005) 5.

32 *Ibid.*, 38.
33 *Ibid.*, 11.
34 *Ibid.*, 24.
35 *Ibid.*, 37.
36 *Ibid.*, 35.
37 Fernand Braudel, *The Mediterranean and the Mediterranean World in the Age of Philip II* (University of California Press, reprint edition 1996).
38 Andre Gunder Frank, *ReOrient: Global Economy in the Asian Age* (University of California Press, 1998).
39 Lewis V. Thomas, *A Study of Naima* ed. Norman Itzkowitz (New York: New York University Press, 1972) 110–11.
40 Mustafa Naima, *Tarih-i Naima* also known as *Ravat al-husayn fi khulāsat-i akhbar al-khāfikayn* (Istanbul: Matbaa-i âmire, 1281–3 [1864–6]) 277.
41 David Hume, *The History of England*, an e-version based on the 1778 edition is available at the Online Library of Liberty http://oll.libertyfund.org/ToC/0011.php accessed 1 December 2010; Edward Gibbon, *The Decline and Fall of the Roman Empire* (London: Strahan and Cadell, 1776–89).
42 Max Weber, *The Protestant Ethic and the Spirit of Capitalism* (New York: Scribners 1958); Jared Diamond, *Guns, Germs and Steel: The Fates of Human Societies* (New York: Norton, 1997); Eric Jones, *The European Miracle: Environments, Economies and Geopolitics in the History of Europe and Asia* (Cambridge: Cambridge University Press, 1981); Michael Mann, *The Sources of Social Power: vol. 1 A History of Power from the Beginning to A.D.1760* (Cambridge: Cambridge University Press, 1986); David Landes, *The Wealth and Poverty of Nations: Why Some are so Rich and Some are so Poor* (New York: Norton, 1998). See J.M. Blaut, *Eight Eurocentric Historians* (London: The Guildford Press, 2000) for a detailed discussion of the above historians.
43 J.M. Blaut, *The Colonizer's Model of the World: Geographical Diffusionism and Eurocentric History* (London: The Guildford Press, 1993); Blaut, *Eight Eurocentric*; Jack Goody, *The East in the West* (Cambridge: Cambridge University Press, 1996); Frank, *ReOrient*; John M. Hobson, *The Eastern Origins of Western Civilisation* (Cambridge: Cambridge University Press, 2004).

Further reading

Marnie Hughes-Warrington, *Fifty Key Thinkers on History* (London: Routledge, 2000). Offers an excellent summary of 50 historians writing during the 2,500 years from across the world.

Georg G. Iggers and Q. Edward Wang, with contributions from Supriya Mukherjee, *A Global History of Modern Historiography* (Harlow: Pearson Longman, 2008). This is a detailed examination of Islamic, Chinese and South Asian historical trends and developments from the eighteenth century onwards with most emphasis on the twentieth century.

Ibn Khaldun, *The Muqaddimah: An Introduction to History* trans. and introduced by Franz Rosenthal with a new introduction by Bruce B. Lawrence (Princeton: Princeton University Press, 2005).

Rhoads Murphy, *Ottoman Historians and Historiography* (Istanbul: Eren Yayincilik, 2010).

On-cho Ng and Q. Edward Wang, *Mirroring the Past: The Writing and Use of History in Imperial China* (Honolulu: University of Hawai'i Press, 2005). Explores Chinese historiography over 3,000 years.

Huaiqi Wu, *An Historical Sketch of Chinese Historiography* (Germany: Springer-Verlag, 2018).

Fozia Bora, *Writing History in the Medieval Islamic World* (London: I.B. Tauris, 2019).

Daniel Woolf, *A Concise History of History* (Cambridge: Cambridge University Press, 2019).

3 Academic history

In nineteenth-century Germany two different traditions of writing about the past came together: antiquarianism, which emphasised the empirical recovery of the past through the collection and investigation of material remains; and that of the philosophical historians, who speculated about historical development in general terms. Historians increasingly started to think about the meaning of history, while simultaneously searching for reliable documents or artefacts that could be used as evidence for their arguments. One of the most famous German historians to be involved in this transformation of history writing was Leopold von Ranke. Ranke was a nineteenth-century German professor of history who is generally, rightly or wrongly, credited with developing the modern historical method and being one of the fathers of historical science and modern academic history. He argued that all available evidence should be studied; encouraged source criticism as a methodological norm, particularly of documents held in state archives; stressed the purpose of history as being simply to show 'how things essentially happened' [*wie es eigentlich gewesen*]; and discouraged historians from demonstrating any personal views or opinions in their writing. The Rankean tradition had a profound effect upon historical studies in the twentieth century, and many historians claim to have their historical roots in the Rankean approach. One of the key features of modern historical writing is an interest in the epistemology of history; that is, how we acquire and verify historical knowledge. The conflation of Ranke's practical research methodology with a set of philosophical theories, namely Anglo-American empiricism, realist (or representationalist) theories of knowledge and correspondence theories of truth and meaning, led to some historians interpreting Ranke's maxim *wie es eigentlich gewesen* to mean that history should show 'what actually happened' rather than 'how things essentially happened'. This resulted in truth being understood, in the context of historical writing, in exclusively factual or empirical terms: something that contrasts with Naima's understanding of truth as having a moral dimension.

Munslow and Jenkins have argued that, for the sake of convenience, modern historians can be (very) broadly classified into three different categories or genres on the basis of their epistemologies of historical knowledge: reconstructionists (who adopt a very Rankean approach); constructionists; and deconstructionists (or postmodernists).[1] While historians do not always easily fit into one of these categories, they are a useful tool for beginning to think about how twentieth-century historians conceptualise the discipline of history writing and what constitutes 'proper' history, its function, and the type of questions it should try to answer.

Nationalism, Ranke and history in the university

Although Ranke has been credited with developing or articulating the critical methodology crucial to academic history, and in particular with placing an emphasis on a hermeneutical approach to primary sources (that is, the critical interpretation of texts), it is important not to overemphasise the innovation of such practices. In Germany in the eighteenth century the practices of textual criticism used in theology were gradually adopted by historians, who began to stress the importance of identifying and using genuine primary sources as a basis of history writing, rather than simply relying upon the accounts of earlier historians. Source criticism thus became the key component of academic history at German universities and historians began to claim that it was this source criticism that enabled them to produce verifiable historical knowledge. It is perhaps preferable to see Ranke as the spokesman for, rather than innovator of, this particular methodology and attitude towards documentary primary sources. Moreover, it is important to remember that the professionalisation of history as embodied by Ranke and his colleagues was contingent on the wider socio-political context of the time. The nineteenth century was a time of nationalism and the establishment of nation states, and governments were quick to realise the role that histories, particularly those that focused on the political, diplomatic and military struggles between what were now seen as different nations, could play in providing a cohesive identity for newly established and older nation-states. Therefore, states began to establish increasingly professionalised archives. Around this time, to further facilitate the production of suitable histories, the state also began printing collections of government documents, all of which helped to make the Rankean emphasis on political history and documents of state more normative and dominant.[2]

The emphasis that Ranke placed on source criticism and the increasing professionalisation of historical studies was not exclusively a European development. Ranke's view of history is quite similar to that of the seventeenth- and eighteenth-century Chinese school of evidential learning, whose adherents initially began to use philology, etymology, epigraphy and phonology in order to try to determine the original meaning of the Confucian classics, and subsequently applied similar techniques to their analysis of historical sources. They subjected earlier histories to considerable scrutiny, and compared their accounts of events with all available sources to determine accuracy. They were also similarly concerned with establishing the truth of what had happened and their motto was an old Han-era adage: 'To seek truth in actual facts'.[3] Many of these historians were also teachers working in academies, rather than bureaucrats, so they too constituted a collaborative scholarly community of learning similar to that found in German universities.

Ranke's view of the history profession was challenged, however, by some of his contemporaries. Droysen, for example, believed that Ranke had overemphasised the importance of source criticism and sidelined that of interpretation. For Droysen, sources alone could not yield historical knowledge: they could be turned into historical information or knowledge only when interpreted by a historian. As he said:

> [T]hose who consider it to be the highest task of the historian that he does not add anything of his own thinking, but simply lets the facts speak for themselves, do not see that the facts themselves do not speak except through the words of someone who has seized and understood them.[4]

This debate about the role that interpretation should play in the writing of history subsequently became a key feature of twentieth-century historiographical arguments. Similarly, although some of Ranke's contemporaries argued that history should reflect the rational progress of humanity, Ranke disagreed that history either had a shape or that it was linear and progressive. He also disagreed with the assertion that human society (past and present) was governed by laws which could be discovered through a careful study of the evidence. For Ranke, the key job of the historian was to describe rather than explain human actions. However, he did believe that historians, through their study of the past, could make manifest God's presence in the world, and that, by understanding the interconnection of facts and events, the divine course of human history would be made manifest.[5]

Reconstructionist history

Historians writing in the Rankean and empiricist tradition can be described as reconstructionist. They emphasise the importance of critical source analysis (ideally of state documents) as *the* basis of historical knowledge. However, they also interpret Ranke's injunction to only 'show what actually happened' as meaning that the historian should refrain from allowing their perspectives, opinions and biases to influence the history that they write. This emphasis on the historian reconstructing the past in a neutral manner has encouraged reconstructionists to eschew vociferously the validity of employing explanatory theories or laws in their analysis of the evidence. This suspicion of both theory and the use of laws or structures to explain human society has led to a tendency for reconstructionists to focus on retelling events, rather than attempting to explain social processes or the structures that govern society. They therefore tend to ask 'what happened' questions. Because of the critical role that primary sources play in upholding epistemologies, reconstructionist historians tend to favour those sources which they perceive are less biased or subjective – in particular state documents, or to use Marwick's term 'documents of record', such as edicts, the minutes of state meetings or discussions in parliament, court records and local parish records.[6] This bias towards particular sources results in a propensity towards writing political or diplomatic history.

Influenced by Ranke, reconstructionists argue that the past should be studied for its own sake and therefore professional academic historians should only be motivated by the first of Tosh's functions of history discussed in Chapter 1: the desire to discover what happened in the past. In particular, history should not be used didactically: it should not teach moral lessons, nor provide advice on good governance or statecraft as was the case in much Chinese history writing. It should be used neither to reveal human destiny, nor to foresee where human society is heading. Perhaps most importantly, it should not serve political or ideological ends: that is, it should not be used to legitimise particular claims to power, nor to establish a communal identity. This is not as easy as it sounds because, while historians may not consciously intend their histories to serve such functions, they generally unconsciously do so.

Arthur Marwick and Geoffrey Elton are perhaps the most vociferous exponents of reconstructionist or Rankean traditionalist historiography. However, as a consequence of the adoption of the Rankean methodology as *the* model for professional, academic history across the world, and the instinctive commonsense appeal of empiricism, realist (also known as representationalist) epistemologies and the correspondence theory of truth, their views are shared by many other historians. For Elton, a Tudor political historian, history is very much a practical discipline and he is especially averse to the contamination, as he sees it, of history by ideas and methods from other disciplines and the introduction of theory and theoretical models. He therefore has little time for those who adhere to a particular model of history, be it linear, cyclical or teleological, nor for those who argue for the existence of laws or structures that govern the development of human society. According to Elton, professional historians can access the truth simply through a critical study of all available, relevant primary sources; by asking questions of the evidence that are free from bias; by keeping an open mind; and by presenting their ideas in a clear and intelligible form. There are therefore some similarities between Elton's guide to being a good historian and that of the Ottoman historian Naima, suggesting that the precepts of Rankean professionalism are not as modern nor as European as some have suggested.

History from below – social science-influenced, constructionist history

Although the Rankean model of historical studies was adopted internationally in the late nineteenth century as *the* model for professional academic history, it was very quickly critiqued not only in western countries but in Latin America and Japan. These critiques focused on two main points. Firstly, that Rankean history, with its strict focus on diplomatic and political history, ignored the political and social consequences of the emergence of a mass, industrialised public. Secondly, that its exclusive focus on the critical analysis of sources was too narrow and it therefore tended to neglect the social context of historical development and did not try to explain, particularly with reference to laws or theories, societal change.

In response to this first criticism a large number of histories began to be written that focused less on great men and more on ordinary individuals. This type of history is commonly known as 'history from below' or 'people's history' and has been used to cover a number of different approaches to writing history and explanations of historical change. What all the different approaches have in common, though, is a concentration on the lives of ordinary people, people previously often excluded from history: women, peasants, the industrial or urban working classes, ethnic minorities and the poor. As these people rarely left written records of their lives and beliefs, such an approach often necessitates either the reinterpretation or re-reading of traditional sources such as court records or other state documents, or the use of alternative sources such as ballads, cartoons or folktales. Just as this new approach to narrating the past changed the types of sources that historians used, it also altered the type of history written, with historians increasingly writing social and economic rather than political and diplomatic history. Three of the most well-known approaches to 'history from below' are those influenced by Marxism, what is often described as the Annales school and postcolonial or subaltern history.

All three approaches can be understood as embodying a constructionist approach to history writing. Constructionism is another conceptual category that covers a great diversity of historians who exhibit a broad range of different attitudes towards the theory, practice and writing of history. However, they all generally share a belief in the value, or necessity, of using theoretical concepts to interpret historical evidence and explain human society. Constructionists believe that the task of the historian is not simply to chronicle the main or important events of the past, but to discern or provide a coherent narrative to link these events together into a larger story or meta-narrative. Moreover, they also want to be able to explain social, political and economic change over time. As we saw above, the idea that there were discoverable structural laws that governed human behaviour and the development of human society was first suggested by Ibn Khaldun in the fourteenth century, although it was developed in more depth by Auguste Comte in the nineteenth century. This idea became very popular among the new socio-economic historians of the twentieth century, who variously stressed the benefits of using economic, demographic, environmental, sociological, anthropological or statistical models for explaining human society. Constructionists therefore conceive of human societies as organisations whose development is determined by discoverable law-governed processes. They argue that all histories implicitly or explicitly use explanatory theories or presuppositions about how human society or human behaviour works to interpret evidence of the past. They claim that, in contrast to reconstructionists, they are explicit about the theories they employ and, moreover, these models, because they are often expressed in propositional terms, are amenable to testing and verification. In this manner constructionists argue that the use of theories does not render their historical narratives subjective, because they are always amenable to further testing. Marxist-influenced approaches, the Annales school and early postcolonial or subaltern histories are all examples of constructionist approaches to writing history. Other examples include historians who ascribe explanatory value in a historical context to the environment, ecology or climate in some form. For example, Jared Diamond's thesis explicating the rise of the West argues that it was a consequence of the unique geography of Europe. Similarly, Jack A. Goldstone explains uprisings, revolutions and rebellions in seventeenth-century China, England and the Ottoman Empire as a result of ecological crises.[7]

Although constructionists do focus on individual events, their interest in theories that elucidate human behaviour and societal change means that they tend to try to locate individual events within a broader explanatory framework that will make clear the structures of society and explain change. Their histories therefore tend to be more problem centred and they ask 'how' questions; for example, how and why politics, the economy and culture have changed over time. Moreover, these two concerns also affect the types of sources they use. Rather than favouring state documents of record, they use sources that can provide data that is amenable to statistical analysis (such as parish records, census material, criminal records and wills), sources that can be read against the grain to provide information on ordinary people, such as court records, as well as more unusual sources including the physical landscape and cartoons.

Marxism and socio-economic approaches to history

The writings of the nineteenth-century philosopher, political theorist, revolutionary thinker and historian Karl Marx have had a profound influence on twentieth-century society and history writing. Marx's investigation into history was prompted by a desire to uncover the laws that governed human development and explained societal change. As we saw in Chapter 1, Marx's theory of historical change drew on Hegel's model of the dialectic – in which recurrent conflicts produce change and improved resolutions of the arrangements that produced the original conflict, thus producing a linear pattern of improvement. However, unlike Ibn Khaldun, who suggested that 'group feeling' explained societal change, Marx employed the idea of class conflict. As he said at the beginning of the *Communist Manifesto*:

> [T]he history of all hitherto existing societies is the history of class struggles. Freeman and slave, patrician and plebeian, lord and serf, guild-master and journeyman, in a word, oppressor and oppressed, stood in constant opposition to one another, carried on an uninterrupted, now hidden, now open fight, a fight that each time ended, either in a revolutionary re-constitution of society at large, or in the common ruin of the contending classes.[8]

Marx's theory of historical change can be described as follows. Humans are social animals who naturally form societies in order to meet their material requirements. The productive forces (which include labour, and the means of production such as technologies, raw materials, skills and equipment) determine or constrain the possible economic structures that a society can develop. These in turn significantly influence the form of the superstructure (the political and legal institutions) and the various ideologies and discourses (religious, philosophical, moral and artistic beliefs) prevalent in that society. Different kinds of society therefore develop as a result of the particular combination of productive forces in existence at any specific time. To understand the institutions, laws, politics, culture and morality of a society it is necessary to understand the nature of its productive forces and its mode of production. The mode of production can be described as the stage of economic development of a society manifested in a particular combination of the productive forces and the relations of production (that is, the power relations governing society's assets as expressed in law, the relations between people and their work and between the various social classes). As Marx argued:

> The mode of production of material life conditions the general character of the social, political and spiritual processes of life. It is not the consciousness of men that determines their existence, but, on the contrary, their social existence determines their consciousness.[9]

Marx identified a number of main modes of production: primitive communal; the Asiatic mode of production; ancient; feudalism; capitalism; and communism. This understanding of society and historical change is termed historical materialism.

For Marx, the motor of historical change is the contradiction between the modes of production and the relations of production that erupts in the form of class conflict. Society will be stable while there is equilibrium between the social relations, the political system and ideological superstructure, and the modes of production. However, over time the productive forces begin to be held back from further development because they outstrip the social relations appropriate to them: in other words, the economic structure can no longer facilitate the development of the forces of production. This creates a tension, which manifests itself as conflict between different classes, between distinct groups defined by their different relations to the means of production and their place in the productive system. If this conflict is resolved by a revolution, then the previous economic structure will be replaced by one more suited to the development of the existing forces of production; property and social relations will also be transformed; and a new mode of production will be in force. Therfore for Marx, political struggles do not cause change in society, but are instead themselves the effects of changes which are caused by economic forces. Marx argued that human societies gradually change and develop and move their way through the various modes of production and, although currently the capitalist mode is dominant, ultimately at some point in the future there will be a revolution and communism will become the dominant mode. Therefore, for Marx, history does have a pattern but, although society moves through epochal changes, it is not cyclical; instead, history is essentially linear and progressive.

The key aspects of Marx's theory that historians later adopted were his emphasis not only on the role that economic factors had in determining or influencing the form of a society's institutions and ideologies, but also the role they played in historical change. Equally influential was his idea of class conflict as a motor of historical change, particularly as it gave agency back to groups of people who had traditionally been seen in historical accounts as passive participants. For example, French Marxist-orientated historians applied their understanding of Marx initially to the French Revolution, which they interpreted as a bourgeois revolution that ended the feudal mode of production and ushered in the capitalist mode.

The writings of Marx also had a profound influence on some British historians, particularly those of the British Marxist School, which included, among others, E.P. Thompson, Christopher Hill, Rodney Hilton and Eric Hobsbawm. Thompson was a Marxist intellectual who transformed the writing of labour history. His most famous work, and the greatest work of this school of historians, is the social history *The Making of the English Working Class* (1963), in which he challenged not only the Fabian orthodoxy which saw the majority of working people as passive victims, but also the approaches of economic historians who saw working people simply as an undifferentiated labour force, and the 'pilgrim's progress' model which teleologically figures key working men as pioneers of later social developments such as the welfare state or a socialist commonwealth.[10] Instead, Thompson argued for the agency of the working people: 'I am seeking to rescue the poor stockinger, the Luddite cropper, the "obsolete" hand-loom weaver [...] from the enormous condescension of posterity'[11]. His approach was Marxist in that he argued that the changing means of production engendered by the Industrial Revolution affected the formation of class. However, Thompson, like many historians, did not slavishly adhere to Marx's theories in their entirety, but argued that they could be re-interpreted to take account of different circumstances. Thus, although he argued for an analysis of historical change and development based upon class struggle, he did not simply employ the concept of class as either an abstract term or as something arising deterministically from a change in the means of production (i.e. technological change). Instead, he saw class in cultural terms, as something that happens in human relations when some people, as a result of common experiences, articulate their interests in opposition to those of other people whose interests differ. For Thompson, therefore, just like Marx, there is a degree of antagonism between classes. However, class is not conceived of as a thing, but instead as a relationship.[12]

Hobsbawm similarly believed that the best model for explaining change over the past 1,000 years was Marxist materialism. Like Marx, he argued that the main factor that led to societal change was conflict between groups who had different relationships with the means of production. Hobsbawm believed that, much of the time, conflict was inevitable. For example, he argued that factory workers in the early nineteenth century worked in such appalling conditions that rebellion was unavoidable. These conditions led to a series of ultimately unsuccessful revolutions across Europe and the consequent rise of the liberal bourgeoisie and the triumph of capitalism. Hobsbawm, rather than concur with the standard interpretation of Luddite 'machine breaking' by workers as an animalistic or instinctive reaction to the pressures of misery, argued instead that it could be interpreted as the workers reacting proactively to the threat to their livelihood brought about by the total transformation of productive relations that the introduction of such machinery brought about.[13] Although Hobsbawm was originally a labour historian, his later work covers peasant and agrarian studies (the rural labouring classes), world history, peasant revolutionary movements and historiography.

Marxism also had a significant influence on post-independence Indian history writing and there was a gradual shift away from the Rankean topics of political, military and diplomatic history in favour of social and economic subjects.

However, the Rankean commitment to a critical analysis of primary sources and objectivity remained. One of the most influential Marxist Indian historians was D.D. Kosambi who in his work *Introduction to the Study of Indian History* focused on social formations, class conflict and material life.[14] In a similar manner to Thompson, Kosambi and other Indian historians re-interpreted Marx's historical theory, borrowing the elements that had value and ignoring those that did not seem appropriate to their situation. By re-interpreting the Mughal period of Indian history as a form of Indian feudalism, Kosambi demonstrated that Marx's concept of the Asiatic mode of production was not relevant to the situation in early modern south Asia and also challenged the notion that south Asian communities had essentially lacked a historical consciousness before the arrival of the British. His groundbreaking work was the stimulus for further histories of the Mughal agrarian system.[15]

Marxist historiography also flourished in post-Second World War Japan. For many Japanese historians, Marx's historical model of the transition of societies from ancient slavery through feudalism and on to capitalism and communism provided a valuable framework for analysing the transition in medieval Japanese society from slavery to feudalism and also explained and gave significance to peasant rebellions and mass movements.[16] However, the main pre-occupation of Japanese Marxist historians was to explain, and also condemn, their country's actions during and before the war.

The Annales school

The Annales school takes its name from the historical journal *Annales d'histoire économique et sociale* established by French historians Lucien Febvre and Marc Bloch in 1929. However, it is important to note that there is no single Annales approach to the study of history, nor a specific Annales methodology. The cohesive element of Annales historiography is perhaps best described as a shared socio-economic approach focused on the history of ordinary people, and an understanding of history as a social science which could therefore benefit from the adoption and application of anthropological, geographical, economic and sociological theoretical models.

Both Febvre and Bloch were socio-economic historians influenced by the positivism of Comte, who wrote 'history from below' and introduced significant methodological innovations to the discipline. Febvre wrote a history of the Franche Comté region in France which demonstrated the interaction of geographic, political, social, religious and economic factors, but also focused on everyday culture.[17] Bloch, in his work *The Royal Touch*, explored the belief popular in French (and English) society in the early modern period that the king could cure scurvy by touching the afflicted person.[18] One of the greatest contributions of this work was that it explored the *mentalities* of different communities: an approach that subsequently became very popular among Annales historians. Bloch employed a similar procedure in his subsequent work *Feudal Society*, which examines European feudal history from the ninth to the fourteenth centuries. This history does not concentrate on the political or economic aspects of feudalism, instead it explores how medieval people viewed the world around them, what they thought of life and death: it inquired into their mentalities.

Possibly the most famous proponent of the Annales school is Fernand Braudel, best known for his epic work on the Mediterranean in the sixteenth century, *The Mediterranean and the Mediterranean World in the Age of Philip II*, published in 1949. Braudel was influenced by the materialism of Marx's theory, but placed much more emphasis on geographical and environmental factors than just economic ones. Developing the inclusive approach of Febvre and Bloch, Braudel wanted to write a total history of the Mediterranean but, recognising that it would have to be multi-layered, he, again like Febvre and Bloch, moved away from a chronological depiction of events. Instead, he developed three different conceptions of time: the *longue durée* or geographical time, which explores the impact of the environment on human civilisation over millennia where change is very slow; *la moyenne durée*, which focuses on social and cultural history and explores the history of social structures, the rise and fall of dynasties, the development of economic and political systems, and scientific and intellectual changes over the medium term; and *histoire événementielle*, the time of events, the history of individuals and short-term developments common to most historical works. Moreover, Braudel's interest in the history of events or individuals extends only so far as it reveals the existence of the economic, social and intellectual structures that characterise human society. His emphasis on the decisive role the environment plays in determining or influencing the development of human societies, together with his insistence that much of history (particularly that of the *longue durée*) is cyclical, is very reminiscent of Ibn Khaldun's approach to history.

The influence of different disciplines on the Annales school, combined with a desire to transform history into a scientific discipline and the development of new technologies, led to an emphasis among Annales scholars on quantitative history, in particular historical demography and the use of statistical data to investigate price movements, including shifts in food prices and wages. Some historians explored the effect that price movements had on socio-political events such as revolutions or rebellions, and others combined statistical analysis with a study of the mentalities of communities: for example, the analysis of wills to demonstrate the secularisation or dechristianisation of attitudes towards death.[19]

By the 1970s yet another trend could be seen within the very broad Annales approach, that of microhistory. It began with Le Roy Ladurie's painstaking and comprehensive study of a small French village, *Montaillou: village Occitan.* Although, following the Annales tradition, the first few chapters provide detailed information on the geographical, economic and social context of the village, the main part of the book uses inquisitional records to explore the mentalities of the villagers, their views on life and death and their attitudes towards such topics as superstitions and sex. A similar use of inquisitional records was employed by Carlo Ginzberg in his micro-study of the life and outlook of an ordinary Italian miller, *The Cheese and the Worms: The Cosmos of a Sixteenth Century Miller.*[20] As can be seen from these two examples, there was an increasing departure from the study of large-scale structures and long-term developments in favour of a turn towards micro-history and the cultural study of society: that is, an interest in how people constructed their world and how popular ideas influenced a community's ceremonies, rituals and work practices. This does not mean that such histories abandoned the use of laws and generalisations in explaining events, but more that they began to apply them at the micro-level.

Postmodernism, deconstructionism and the re-imagination of history writing

Postmodernism can be a rather problematic word with many, often contested, meanings, but we will use it here as a shorthand way of describing a particular genre of writing history. Postmodernism is a hybridisation of a variety of different intellectual movements from different disciplines which differ in significant aspects, but which have in common the belief that the philosophies, assumptions and theories underpinning post-Enlightenment modernity, in particular empiricist epistemologies, realist ontologies and correspondence theories of truth and language, are no longer useful or relevant for us in continuing to make sense of our world. Such theoretical challenges argue that we cannot use the past as a foundation for historical knowledge as we cannot directly access it in order to check whether there exists a correspondence between this past and our historical narratives. All we have are our interpretations of the sources and, as we cannot escape the cultural frameworks and explanatory concepts that we use to order and make sense of the world, nor distance ourselves from our values, prejudices and assumptions, then our interpretation of these sources will necessarily be subjective and personal. It therefore follows that there is no one, correct, true account of the past that we can reconstruct. There are instead multiple possible accounts of the past written from a variety of perspectives. Consequently, some historians, such as Hayden White, have argued that we can only distinguish between historical accounts on the basis of aesthetic or moral preferences.

As a consequence of postmodernism destabilising the idea that the past can be accurately reconstructed, many postmodern historians have abandoned any attempt to tell *the* story about what happened, and instead focus on exploring how and why different people at different times have variously represented a particular past event. They will perhaps foreground the perspectives of authors of primary and secondary sources; be explicit about the role their own voice plays in the making of their histories; and choose to explore how and why historical accounts have been used, particularly in the context of political legitimisation or identity construction. This is not to say that postmodernist historians do not largely adhere to the protocols of writing history and the historical method, nor that they take an uncritical or cavalier approach to sources. They may use untraditional sources, apply innovative reading strategies often borrowed from other disciplines to these sources, experiment with different ways of writing or presenting their narratives, and argue that their own accounts are to some degree fictive or imaginative, but they do not write fiction, nor do they simply make it up. The aim of postmodernist historians is to narrate a story based upon their understanding of primary and secondary sources according to the protocols or rules of academic history, but which also coheres with and reflects not only their own political, social and aesthetic ideologies, but also their wider beliefs and assumptions about the world.

Postmodernism has changed the way we research and write history: it has changed our understanding of its functions, the topics studied, the sources used and the way it is taught. But what do these new histories look like? How do they differ from their reconstructionist and constructionist counterparts? Postmodernist history is more interdisciplinary, more inclusive and broader in the range of methodologies and sources used. Postmodern historians are self-aware; they foreground the subjective, contested, plural nature of history and try to disrupt the common understanding of history as singular and coterminous; they also reconsider the function of history and the socio-political purposes it serves. They ask ‘why’ questions: why are histories written and read, and what role do they play in our society today?

Voices: whose past is told?

The theoretical challenges raised by postmodernism have challenged the essentialist discourses inherent in much modernist history writing, such as racism and sexism, and have led to an increasing acceptance that socio-political identities are not naturally occurring, but are instead constructed or performed. This in turn has prompted historians to explore the role that narrations of the past have had in such imaginations. Linked to the performance of identities is the enactment or establishment of networks or relationships of power and authority. This concern with questions of authority, together with the interest of postmodern historians in giving voice to marginalised groups, has encouraged an interest in researching and making explicit concealed power relations in society and highlighting how differences of power and privilege were, and are, maintained. Greg Dening has explored how and why the events leading up to, and following, the mutiny on the *Bounty* have been represented in different ways – from the perspectives of the mutineers, Captain Bligh, the British admiralty, the islanders and, later, audiences in Britain. He also considers how these textual, material and physical representations are intimately intertwined with questions about power and authority. Dening is not interested in writing a history that masquerades as a re-enactment of the past, instead he is keen to convey his understanding about the nature of power, symbol making, force, freedom and theatre, while also being explicit about his role in making his story and drawing attention to the 'systems at work in [his] narrative'.[21]

One way of addressing the imbalance of power is to be explicit about the power that the historian possesses by virtue of telling the story, and to try to effectively counter the historian's narrative with the voices of those whose stories are being told. The privileging of archival, institutional and written documents as pre-eminent historical sources in modern academic history, combined with a lack of such sources recording the voice of the marginalised, means it is difficult to adequately narrate the perspectives of the subaltern. In particular, Gayatri Chakravorty Spivak has argued, using the example of Hindu widow immolation, that the speech of the subaltern woman cannot be heard because the socio-historical conditions of representation at the time did not permit her space in which to speak; therefore such examples in effect mark 'the limit of historical knowledge'.[22] It is therefore important to redefine and widen the category of what counts as adequate historical evidence in order that these voices can, if possible, be heard. The use of oral sources provides a possible way of giving a voice, visibility and identity to marginalised communities. Sanjam Ahluwalia attempted to restore the voices of subaltern or marginal groups to the historical record. In researching the debates surrounding the discourse of birth control in nineteenth-century colonial India, she had access to the writings of western elite women, elite Indian men and middle-class Indian women, but the voice of the subaltern women was absent. To remedy this, she utilised conversations (oral interviews) with traditional midwives in order to recover unrecorded memories and experiences of poorer Jaunpur women. It is, however, important to remember that the oral archive that Ahluwalia has created is no less politically charged than imperial archives, and should be subject to the same kind of critical analysis.[23] Likewise, Horacio N. Roque Ramirez wrote about Teresita la Campesina, a male-to-female transgender Latina artist who lived in San Francisco, as representing a living archive of evidence which is absent from the archives of both Latino history and the overwhelmingly white, queer archives.[24] Bain Attwood similarly discusses the use of oral testimony in the case of stolen First Nations children, which not only shifts the power from being exclusively in the hands of the historian, but also helps to produce a more empathetic history and recognises and validates the experiences of First Nations communities.[25]

Dening, in his desire to hear the voices of both sides of the native/stranger encounters in the Sea of Islands (Pacific Ocean), also tries to give equal voice to everyone involved in the encounter. He writes history in a 'double-visioned way', arguing that each side of the native/stranger encounter can only tell their history by also telling that of the other, and that we should, therefore, pay equal attention to the dances, songs, legends, myths, body paint, tattoos, carvings and poetry of the islanders, and not simply privilege the records of the 'strangers'[26]. He notes that it is only in the twenty-first century that the history of the indigenous people living in the Sea of Islands has begun to be taken seriously and be accorded equal *gravitas* as a subject suitable for study. This is a cogent reminder that even today some subjects, some peoples, and some events are deemed more worthy of historical study than others. Dening continues that not only should the voices of the others be heard, but that in important ways the past belongs more to those on whom it impinges today than those in the academy who often narrate it.[27]

Dening also creates a self-reflexive, subjective tone in his *Beach Crossings*. Here he intertwines his chapters on cross-cultural, native/stranger encounters in the Sea of Islands area with reflections on his work as a scholar and storyteller of cross-cultural encounters, and with further discussions about writing history, historical methodology, naming practices, his educational methods, 'ethnogging' and history as performance.[28] These 'crossings', as he calls them, are printed on different-coloured paper and in a different type-face. His aim in these soliloquies is to explicitly situate himself, the story-teller, into his story, challenging the myth that historians can write decontextualised, objective history free from the contamination of the author's interests, assumptions and views.[29]

Anthropologist and historian Richard Price similarly draws attention to his own voice in his histories of the Saramake peoples of Suriname. In *First Time* he transcribes oral histories of the Saramake tribe on the top half of the page and adds his own commentary on the bottom half and, by doing so, destabilises our common assumptions as to whose voice is authorial and authoritative, and challenges the notion of there being a single true account of the past which is necessarily that of the academic historian.[30] In *Alabi's World* (1990) he takes this one stage further and uses four different type-faces to represent the polyvocality of the work: univers 45 for his prose and quoted passages from other academic scholars, bold type for Moravian missionary writings, bold italics for material from predominately the Dutch planters and colonial authorities, and italics for words spoken by Saramakas narrating their history.[31] Rather than privilege the Dutch colonial records, he gives equal respect to the stories, histories and songs of the Saramakas today who are custodians of their past. The inclusion of large sections of primary sources decentres the narrative and to some degree fragments the author's authority, allowing other voices to be heard rather than overwhelmed by the author's interpretation of the sources. This is further assisted by Price's choice to keep much of his commentary and analysis to a long notes section at the end of the book, thereby ensuring that the author's voice is not unduly prioritised in the main body of the narrative.[32]

The linear narrative favoured by most histories by virtue of its form privileges a single narrative, interpretation and perspective – often that embodying the voice of the powerful. So how can one represent, paraphrasing Dening, the native past without the stranger, and the stranger without the native; for no-one can speak just for the one or just for the other?[33] One way deconstructionist or postmodern historians have tried to draw attention to the artificial, constructed and contested nature of historical discourse, and to introduce a degree of polyvocality, is to depict a multiplicity of voices and perspectives through montage. In *Postcolonialism: A Very Short Introduction*, Robert J.C. Young employs the technique of montage, juxtaposing often incompatible photographs, text and testimonials with the aim of capturing the contradictions inherent in 'the history of the present'.[34] Synthia Sydnor has similarly produced a Benjaminian-influenced 'narrative pastiche' of synchronised swimming.[35] Walter Benjamin, writing in the first half of the twentieth century, is the author of *The Arcades Project*, which consists of multiple sections and subsections that include observations, phrases, quotes and references which, in the style of a montage, have no linear sequence. His aim was to provide an impression of the Parisian arcades intertwined with an articulation of his Marxist-inspired philosophy of history.[36] Likewise, rather than present a linear, chronological description of the development of synchronised swimming, Sydnor, under a series of sub-headings, juxtaposes a number of heavily referenced quotations, short passages and word lists to create a 'hybrid text' or tableau of the sport.[37] More specifically she creates *her* tableau, thereby challenging both the dominance of the linear narrative in history and the idea of the historian as a transparent narrator, asking the reader instead to 'dive into *my* narrative tableau of a history of synchronized swimming. You can swim in circles, above and below, without having to gulp a linear argument'.[38] The multiplicity of references and lack of a clear authorial narrative encourages the reader interactively to follow up the references and to create *their* own history. In an epilogue she articulates the philosophy behind her experimental history-as-science-as-art, commenting that she has endeavoured to break up the form of history and to make explicit the artifice of the text and her history's construction.[39]

Jonathan Walker *Pistols! Treason! Murder! The Rise and Fall of a Master Spy*

Walker's history of the first professional Venetian spy, Gerolamo Vano, is not only engaging and informative, but also experimental in form, self-reflexive and explicit about the process by which history is constructed.[40] Walker states that his book is not only about the spy Vano, but also about 'the process whereby historians assemble stories'. He wishes to not only tell stories, but also deconstruct the process of story-telling.[41] In particular, he draws attention to the fact that his sources, primarily the intelligence reports written by Vano, do not organise events into a plot or story or offer interpretations, but that he has had to stitch together the various sources and the information they contain to make a coherent narrative. He wishes to make explicit the manner by which he has pieced together the fragments that make up his story and not imply that his story is somehow *the* version of what happened.[42]

Walker does not present a standard narrative, linear description of Vano's life as a spy, nor the role he played in the execution of the Venetian noble Foscarini. Rather, he employs a number of innovative means of presenting information to the reader, particularly in his use of comic strips and contextual asides in the form of fictional conversations between academics in various Venetian drinking establishments. The comic strips dramatise narratives constructed by the author from primary sources, often using direct quotations from these sources and with the characters dressed in near-contemporary Venetian clothing as illustrated in costume books from the time. The latter 'pseudo-conversations' provide crucial background information on the Venetian economy, average prices and wages; the political tension between Venice and the Habsburg empire; the Council of Ten, and everyday street life and, despite being fictional, they are based on historical facts sourced from real historians.[43] They therefore illustrate the intertextual and dialogic nature of historical narratives. Lastly, where inconsistencies arise in the information derived from the sources, Walker offers a variety of possible interpretations, on one occasion also providing odds on which may be the more likely in his opinion.[44]

Lastly, deconstructionist historians are more likely to acknowledge and celebrate the role that imagination or emplotment plays in the construction of their narratives. Hayden White, unlike reconstructionist historians, has argued that the past does not have an intrinsic story waiting to be discovered; historians subjectively interpret the past and, through the use of literary techniques and their imagination, they create a history. In *Dead Certainties* (1998), a book about the deaths of two very different men, Simon Schama plays with what he calls 'the teasing gap separating a lived event and its subsequent narration'.[45] Schama was not looking to establish with certainty what really happened. Instead he was trying to make explicit the possibilities inherent in the multiple narrations and irreconcilable memories that can exist of a single event. In many ways he plays with the conventions of history writing: he does not tell a story with a beginning, middle and end, but leaps into the action *in medias res* and concludes with many things being unresolved; he does not include footnotes, but provides a note on sources; most crucially, he notes that, although the stories appear to observe the conventions of history writing, they could also be described as historical novellas, because some of the passages are 'purely imagined fiction', despite being closely based on the archival documents.[46] This is not to say that he scorns 'the boundary between fact and fiction', but rather that he draws attention to the fictive, imaginative and inventive nature of history writing inherent in the act of choosing sources, selecting and interpreting facts, commentating on events and passing judgement.

While Dening denies that he writes fiction, he acknowledges that 'to catch the lost passions in places, history will have to be a little more artful than being a "non-fiction" '.[47] He also acknowledges the use of his imagination in writing 'true' stories about the past – history 'begins with the real and enlarges it with imagination'.[48] He uses the term 'historying' to describe what he does, to describe the means by which the past is transformed into words, or dance, or paint or music, to describe the continual process of engaging with and constructing the past.[49] But, for Dening, there is always a factual component to historying, as he says: 'I tell the story with the certainty of my factual knowledge, the probabilities of my understanding and the possibilities of my interpretations'[50]. As Dening notes, such a use of the imagination, 'working the fictions in our non-fictions' allows historians to tell the stories that the words do not say.[51] Robin Bisha combined fictive elements with historical scholarship in her pseudo-biography of Daria Mikhailovna Menshikova: the autobiography Bisha thinks Daria could, or might, have written.[52] Bisha was inspired to adopt this approach because the paucity of sources and studies on elite women in eighteenth century Petrine Russia frequently led historians to resort to legends or rumours to fill in the gaps in their narrative. Rather than quietly rely upon unhistorical rumours, she wrote a fictive autobiography based on extensive reading of memoirs of this era and early Russian women's autobiographies.[53] Events mentioned in the pseudo-autobiography are footnoted and references given to where she obtained the information. While this work is an example of rigorous scholarship, it contains imaginative or fictive elements, but, in doing so, it brings alive and includes in the historical record a little known aspect of Russian history.

Notes

1 Keith Jenkins and Alun Munslow, *The Nature of History Reader* (London: Routledge, 2004) and Alun Munslow, *Deconstructing History* (London: Routledge, 2nd edn 2006). Jenkins in his introduction to *The Postmodern History Reader* (London: Routledge, 1997) describes the reconstructionist and constructionist approach to history respectively as lower-case history and upper-case history.

2 Kristina Spohr Readman, 'Memoranda', in Miriam Dobson and Benjamin Ziemann (eds), *Reading Primary Sources: The Interpretation of Texts from Nineteenth- and Twentieth-Century History* (London: Routledge, 2009) 125.

3 Georg G. Iggers, Q. Edward Wang and Supriya Mukherjee, *A Global History of Modern Historiography* (London: Longman, 2008) 53.

4 J.G. Droysen, *Historik Rekonstruktion der ersten vollständigen Fassung der Vorlesungen (1857). Grundriss der Historik in der ersten handschriftlichen (1857/1858) und in der letzten gedruckten Fassung (1882)* ed. Peter Ley, (Stuttgart-Bad Cannstatt: Fromann-Holzboog, 1977) 128 quoted in Philipp Müller, 'Understanding History: Hermeneutics and Source-criticism in Historical Scholarship', in Dobson and Ziemann (eds), *Reading Primary Sources* 27. Another contemporary, Dilthey, was equally sceptical as to whether objective knowledge was possible and even Ranke himself, while stressing the importance of rigorous source criticism, maintained that intuition was needed to determine the interconnectedness of events and the 'essence' of the age.

5 Müller, 'Understanding History', 22–6.

6 Arthur Marwick, *The Nature of History* (Basingstoke: Macmillan, 3rd edn 1989) 208.

7 Diamond, *Guns, Germs and Steel*; Jack A. Goldstone, *Revolution and Rebellion in the Early Modern World* (Berkeley: University of California Press, 1991).

8 Friedrich Engels and Karl Marx, *The Communist Manifesto* at Project Gutenberg www.gutenberg.org/catalog/world/readfile?fk_files=165453&pageno=2 accessed 16 December 2010.

9 Karl Marx, *Selected Writings* ed. D. McLellan (Oxford: Oxford University Press, 1977) 389 quoted in Hughes-Warrington, *Fifty Key Thinkers* 218.

10 E.P. Thompson, *The Making of the English Working Class* (London: Victor Gollancz, 1963) 12.

11 *Ibid.*

12 *Ibid.*, 9.

13 Harvey J. Kaye, *The British Marxist Historians* (New York: Polity Press, 1984) 140.

14 D.D. Kosambi, *Introduction to the Study of Indian History* (Bombay: Popular Book Depot, 1956).

15 Iggers, Wang and Mukherjee, *A Global History* 241–2.

16 *Ibid.*, 317–320.

17 Lucien Febvre, *Philippe II et la Franche-Comté, etude d'histoire politique, religieuse et morale* (Paris: 1911).

18 Marc Bloch, *The Royal Touch: Sacred Monarchy and Scrofula in England and France* trans. J.E. Anderson (London: Routledge and Kegan Paul, 1973).

19 Ernest Labrousse, *Esquisse des mouvements du prix et des revenues* (Paris: 1933) and Michel Vovelle, *Piété baroque et déchristianisation* (Paris, 1973) and Pierre Chaunu et al. (eds) *La Mort à Paris* (Paris: 1978).

20 Emmanuel Le Roy Ladurie, *Montaillou: village occitan: de 1294 à 1324* translated into English as *Montaillou: Cathars and Catholics in a French Village, 1294–1324* by Barbara Bray (London: Penguin, new edition 2002); Carlo Ginzberg, *The Cheese and the Worms: The Cosmos of a Sixteenth Century Miller* translated by John and Anne Tedeschi (Baltimore, MD: Johns Hopkins University Press, new edition 1992 originally published in Italian in 1976).

21 Greg Dening, *Mr Bligh's Bad Language: Passion, Power and Theatre on the Bounty* (Cambridge: Cambridge University Press, canto edition 1994 first published by CUP 1992) 5, 13.
22 Gyan Prakash, 'Subaltern Studies as Postcolonial Criticism', in Catherine Hall (ed.), *Cultures of Empire: Colonizers in Britain and the Empire in Nineteenth and Twentieth Centuries. A Reader* (New York: Routledge, 2000) 131.
23 Sanjam Ahluwalia and Antoinette Burton, 'Rethinking Boundaries: Feminism and (Inter)Nationalism in Early-Twentieth-Century India', in Morgan (ed.), *Feminist History Reader* 351–359.
24 Horacio N. Roque Ramírez, 'A Living Archive of Desire: Teresita la Capesina and the Embodiment of Queer Latino Community History', in Antoinette Burton (ed.), *Archive Stories: Facts, Fictions and the Writing of History* (Durham: Duke University Press, 2005) 113.
25 Bain Attwood, 'In the Age of Testimony: The Stolen Generations Narrative, "Distance" and Public History', in *Public Culture: Society for Transnational Cultural Studies* 20/1 (2008) *The Public Life of History,* special edition ed. Bain Attwood, Dipesh Chakrabarty and Claudio Lomnitz 75–95. Attwood also draws attention to the problems inherent in relying exclusively on such narrative and ignoring some of the more conventional practices of academic history.
26 Greg Dening, *Beach Crossings: Voyaging Across Times, Cultures, and Self* (Philadelphia: University of Pennsylvania Press, 2004) 13 and 17.
27 *Ibid.*, 1; and Dening 'Performing Cross-culturally', in Keith Jenkins, Sue Morgan and Alun Munslow (eds), *Manifestos for History* (Abingdon: Routledge, 2007) 100.
28 Dening, *Beach Crossings* 17–8. The term Sea of Islands is Dening's in 'Performing Cross-culturally', 103.
29 *Ibid.*, 44.
30 Richard Price, *First-Time: The Historical Vision of an African American People* (Chicago: University of Chicago Press, 2nd edn 2002).
31 Price, *Alabi's World* xx.
32 *Ibid.*, xii.
33 Dening, *Beach Crossings* 11.
34 Robert J.C. Young, *Postcolonialism: A Very Short Introduction* (Oxford: Oxford University Press, 2003) 8.
35 Alun Munslow, *The Future of History* (Basingstoke: Palgrave Macmillan, 2010) 185 uses the term narrative pastiche. Synthia Sydnor, 'A History of Synchronized Swimming', in *Journal of Sport History* 25/2 (1998) 252–67.
36 An extract from *The Arcades Project* is included in Keith Jenkins and Alun Munslow, *The Nature of History Reader* (London: Routledge, 2004) 135–141.
37 Sydnor, 'Synchronized Swimming', 259.
38 *Ibid.*, 254.
39 *Ibid.*, 260.

40 Jonathan Walker, *Pistols! Treason! Murder! The Rise and Fall of a Master Spy* (Baltimore, MD: Johns Hopkins University Press 2007).
41 *Ibid.*, 9 and 11.
42 *Ibid.*, 48.
43 *Ibid.*, 216.
44 *Ibid.*, 116–7.
45 Simon Schama, *Dead Certainties (Unwarranted Speculations)* (London: Granta Books, 1998) 320.
46 *Ibid.*, 327 and 322.
47 Dening, *Beach Crossings* 66.
48 Dening, *Beach Crossings* 12–3.
49 *Ibid.*, 101.
50 Dening, *Beach Crossings* 1.
51 Dening, *Beach Crossings* 328–9.
52 Robin Bisha, 'Reconstructing the Voice of a Noble Woman of the Time of Peter the Great: Daria Mikhailovna Menshikova. An Exercise in (Pseudo)autobiographical Writing', in Munslow and Rosenstone (eds), *Experiments in Rethinking History*.
53 *Ibid.*, n.8 191–2.

Further reading

Jouni-Matti Kuukkanen (ed.), *Philosophy of History: Twenty-First Century Perspectives* (London: Bloomsbury 2020).

Kalle Pihlainen, *History in the World* (Abingdon: Routledge, 2019).

Keith Jenkins and Alun Munslow, *The Nature of History Reader* (London: Routledge, 2004). Contains a variety of extracts from reconstructionist, constructionist and deconstructionist (postmodern) historians which either directly address methodological issues or provide a good example of what history written in each of these paradigms looks like. The last section deals with post-postmodern history in a section entitled 'endisms'.

Keith Jenkins, *The Postmodern History Reader* (London: Routledge, 1997). Includes a variety of extracts focused on the epistemology and methodology of history writing from traditional, postmodern and constructionist historians, although he does not specifically use these terms.

Alun Munslow, *Deconstructing History* (London: Routledge, 1997). A deconstructionist or anti-representationalist argument against realist conceptions of historical knowledge.

Alun Munslow and Robert A. Rosenstone (eds), *Experiments in Rethinking History* (London: Routledge, 2004). An excellent collection of experimental histories which demonstrate how postmodern critiques of the history genre can be integrated into the actual writing of history.

John Tosh, *The Pursuit of History: Aims, Methods and New Directions in the Study of Modern History* (London: Pearson-Longman, 2000). A constructionist argument as to why there is a place for social theory in history.

Rethinking History: The Journal of Theory and Practice, eds. Kalle Pihlainen, Patrick Finney and James Goodman, is the main journal publishing experimental histories.

PART II

WHAT HISTORIANS DO

4

Using sources

What are primary and secondary sources?

For the sake of simplicity, we will begin with the conventional answer to this question. Historians name the various sources they have used to carry out their research by providing a bibliography at the end of their writing. These bibliographies are usually divided into two categories of research materials. Primary sources are listed first, followed by secondary sources. As this ordering suggests, primary sources are regarded as the most important for historical research. These sources might take the form of documents and old texts held in archives and libraries, archaeological remains and old buildings, old newspapers, film footage or recordings of interviews from the period being studied. Secondary sources consist of the writings of other historians about a particular historical topic or event, and they are held to have a different kind of value to original sources. Secondary sources written by historians commonly appear in forms such as monographs, journal articles, popular histories and textbooks.

The privileged status that the raw data in primary sources enjoys among historians has been true since the mid-nineteenth century and the Rankean injunction that to know the past one must first know the archive. This is not to say, of course, that Ranke and his contemporaries invented archival-based history writing. But it was Ranke who inspired modern historians to adopt the critical reading of original documents as the basis for their professional training and scholarly practice. Under Ranke at the University of Berlin, history students attended seminars where they learned to read and analyse medieval documents. Following Ranke's pioneering work in the German archives, historians have long favoured the use of sources that were generated (temporally and geographically) as close as possible to the event that they describe, rather than, for example, a memoir written by an eyewitness years later. Also, for several decades after Ranke's death in 1886, historians were primarily interested in the kind of official documents held in state archives that were the evidence base for writing histories of high politics and diplomacy.

Since the early twentieth century, however, the range of primary sources regarded as legitimate for historical research has expanded greatly. One reason for this is methodological. From the founding of the *Annales* approach to writing history in 1929 onwards, social and cultural historians in particular have gradually become more willing to incorporate almost any available source within their research materials – from the testimony of living witnesses to landscapes and Disney cartoons. This turn towards new kinds of sources is largely a consequence of historians becoming more open-minded about which topics of study they would regard as 'historical' subjects. For example, whereas Ranke had focused on the histories of state politics, historians in the *Annales* school wanted to be able to explain how cultures in particular regions (not necessarily within one country) changed over time and why. They wanted to delineate the economic, psychological, social, intellectual and physical structures of these lived cultures, and to do this they realised that they would need to go beyond the traditional topics of politics and the lives of 'great' individuals. In pursuit of this holistic or 'total' history, *Annales* historians drew freely on the methods and resources of other academic disciplines – geography, sociology, anthropology and economics. And they were similarly pluralistic in their use of non-official sources: ranging from the analysis of tree rings and parish records to the study of manuals on interior decoration and evidence of people's eating habits.[1] Another reason for the proliferation of new sources is technological. From the early printing presses to modern databases and online forums, the ways in which human cultures have generated, preserved, processed and organised data has grown at pace. A problem facing contemporary historians now is the massive volume of data that is potentially available for their research. To borrow an example used by Keith Jenkins, imagine trying to write a history called 'Yesterday in New York'.[2] Consider the potential range and mass of primary sources – qualitative and quantitative – that might be used in such an account: the many millions of events and experiences that people in New York might recall for a researcher, the output of the entire electronic media available in the city that day, the paperwork generated by every civic or community organisation, the combined texts of the print media, the movement of stock prices, the registers of births and deaths, recorded crime statistics, data relating to public health – the list could go on.

A final example we will use to illustrate the broad range of primary sources that historians now consult is taken from Akram Fouad Khater's *Sources in the History of the Modern Middle East* (2004). This book lists 74 different sources that include:

- an Ottoman government decree defining the official notion of the 'modern' citizen, 1870
- the Treaty of Peace and Commerce (Treaty of Turkmanchai) between Iran and Russia, 1828
- *Anis al-Jalis*, an Egyptian magazine on a vision of women and their role in society, 1899
- Shaykh Ben Badis's fatwa against French naturalisation of Algerians in *Al-Basha'ir*, journal of the Association of the *Ulama* of Algeria, 1937
- US President Truman's statement supporting Jewish immigration into Palestine, 1946
- Asadollah Alam's diary entries on some elements of the Shah of Iran's rule in 1976 and 1977
- US consular documents on US diplomats' assessment of the Iranian revolution, 1978
- Internet discussion of marriage and education for Saudi Women, 1996
- article in *Ha'aretz* in which Arab and Israeli soccer players discuss ethnic relations in Israel, 2000
- selection from a roundtable discussion of globalisation and its impact on Arab culture, 2000.

In contrast to the kind of sources listed above, secondary sources are the writings of other historians. Because they are interpretative – and thus likely to be challenged or superseded by later accounts – secondary sources sometimes have only a limited shelf life. By this we mean that, whereas medieval historians will almost certainly continue to read the Domesday Book (a vital resource for scholars of late eleventh-century England) a hundred years from now, it is unlikely that many of today's history books will still be widely read (if at all). With the exception of a few classic texts, most historical accounts eventually pass from being the latest version of some subject to becoming out of date, and thus deleted from the publisher's catalogue and removed from all but the largest libraries' shelves to make space for new material. When we refer to historians' writings in a collective sense we use the term 'historiography'. In addition to their reading of primary sources, a historian working on a particular subject is expected to show a thorough knowledge of the work of other historians in that field. They will be expected to show how their work stands in relation to these other accounts, in terms of their methodology, interpretations and use of sources. This is what tutors mean when they tell students that their own writings should display 'historiographical awareness'.

At the risk of confusing matters, we should note here that the apparently clear division between primary and secondary sources just described does not always apply. What we conventionally regard as secondary sources can in fact be used as primary sources, depending on the nature of the project in which they are put to work. An intellectual history that describes how historians have written about their subjects over time will use historians' accounts as its primary sources. For example, Georg G. Iggers's *Historiography in the Twentieth Century: From Scientific Objectivity to the Postmodern Challenge* (2005) uses the collection of other historians' writings as the primary sources for an intellectual history of modern history writing. This means that a book such as Le Roy Ladurie's *Montaillou* (1975) would usually be regarded as a secondary source for someone studying the Inquisition in southern France in the fourteenth century, but as a primary source for someone writing a history of how *Annales* historians wrote about their subjects. In other cases, historical accounts are a kind of hybrid of primary and secondary source – neither quite one nor the other. We believe that this rather confusing state of affairs suggests two things. The first is the potentially problematic and artificial nature of the primary/secondary source division. The second is that it illustrates how historians have tended to make a fetish of manuscript sources and old documents, while simultaneously assuming that 'proper' secondary sources did not really exist before history as an academic profession came into being in western Europe in the nineteenth century.

Nonetheless, we recognise, of course, that the benchmark of historical research remains tied to the critical use of primary sources. This is not simply a matter of academic prestige: it relates to a set of cultural practices that have material consequences. How far a piece of history writing is based on a systematic study of primary sources is an important consideration for Ph.D. examiners, editorial boards of journals, academic book publishers and research funding councils. For these reasons the 'gold standard' of history writing is still taken to be the research monograph – a detailed study of a subject, based extensively on primary sources, heavily footnoted, finished with a lengthy bibliography and often published by a university press. Below this in the hierarchy come articles in prestigious journals and chapters in edited books. Further down the list are found textbooks or synoptic analyses. These books aim to summarise what historians collectively know about a subject, rather than offer 'new' knowledge based on primary sources. Maintaining that there is a clear distinction between primary and secondary sources (both in terms of their identity and value) is crucial for reconstructionist historians. This is because it helps to support their epistemological explanation of history – that the past is objectively knowable via their selection, verification and critical reading of primary sources. They argue that primary sources are special because they are the original traces or relics of the past. They believe that such sources are unprocessed, authentic and unmediated – in short, free from interpretation. Reconstructionist historians also tend to further classify primary sources into ones that are documents of record and other discursive sources. The former are understood as essentially state documents, largely produced and consumed by the bureaucracy: edicts, laws, treaties, minutes of meetings, memoranda, key state papers, dispatches, telegraphs (more recently emails) and treasury accounts. Discursive primary sources include other people's accounts of what happened, such as reports of meetings, handbooks, guides, diaries, pamphlets, newspaper articles, sermons and literary and artistic sources. They are considered to be inferior to documents of record because they are held to contain various degrees of interpretation, subjectivity and bias. What they tell us is taken to be inseparably linked with the opinions and considerations of the author. Similarly, official sources are seen by some to take precedence over private sources on the grounds that the latter are assumed to be more subjective than the former. The idea here, for example, is that a personal letter will be contaminated by 'opinion', whereas an official government document can be trusted to deliver the 'facts'. Using the same reasoning, secondary sources are considered to be inferior to primary sources (in terms of their evidential value) because of the presence of the author's interpretation.

Not all historians, however, agree with the traditional way of defining and separating out primary and secondary sources that we have described above. Postmodernist historians tend not to see the primary/secondary distinction as crucially important. Instead they focus on a particular source's relevance to their research project. Those sources that are most important to the project – the ones that provide the evidence that forms the basis of their arguments and upon which the quality of their work will be judged – they regard as primary sources. Equally, those sources that provide background information, which inform their theoretical approach and which they use to provide a context, they regard as secondary. The classification for postmodernist historians is less to do with providing epistemological justification for their understanding of the status of historical knowledge and more about providing a bibliographical aid to the reader and making explicit what evidence they have used to justify their arguments. A good example of this is Greg Dening's *Mr Bligh's Bad Language* (1992). Instead of making the conventional distinction between primary and secondary sources in his bibliography, Dening lists all the sources he used in alphabetical order and provides a detailed notes section at the end of the work where he acknowledges the specific sources that he used to make particular arguments. Moreover, the arguments that Dening makes throughout the book to explore why the mutiny on the *Bounty* took place rely on evidence from a variety of traditional and not-so-traditional sources. These include captain's letters, log books, journals, orders from the admiralty, legal decrees, published books, anthropological descriptions of Tahiti, pantomime programmes and feature films about the mutiny.

Postmodernist historians also argue that all sources involve interpretation: they are written from someone's perspective and thus no source should be regarded as objective. One way to illustrate this is by using the example of documents produced in legal proceedings. A reconstructionist like Deborah A. Symonds would argue that such documents of record are largely free from interpretation – they are a true and accurate account of what was said in court. Postmodernists would take a different view, arguing that such records are as positioned (and thus 'subjective') as more obviously personalised or partisan sources. They would say that the contents of records of evidence given in a court of law were framed by the legal framework in place at that time, and the specific expectations of those who were involved in the legal process in question. Those giving evidence would be conscious that they were retelling events not to friends or family but to judges and juries who had power over liberty, life and (sometimes) death. Thus they may have adapted their language or stressed different aspects of the event that they were being asked to recall, depending on how they read the demands of their immediate situation. Moreover, the court's rules of evidence and the prescriptions of the court concerning what can and cannot be said, as well as the questions of the prosecutor or inquisitor, all constrain and shape the evidence a witnesses could give about their experience – in effect, the protocols of the court system can be seen to constitute an already-in-place interpretation of events. It follows from this that what might appear at first to be a transparent recording of events – the transcription of evidence given in court – is in fact an interpretative act.

How do historians use sources?

Historians regard primary sources as the evidence base for their accounts of the past. For those who favour a straightforward empirical and reconstructionist approach to writing history, primary sources are the closest that we have to an encounter with the past itself. According to the genre rules of history writing, the best way to justify a statement relating to the past is by citing an original source as corroborating material – sometimes by quoting that source itself within the account, at other times by referencing the source in the form of a footnote or endnote. This genre rule applies with greater force in the case of original research – such as a historical monograph or journal article – than in synoptic accounts based on other scholars' writings. The convention of citing a primary source in support of a statement also depends on the type of claim that is being made. Statements that refer to common knowledge need no support, but ones that might be contested or are not widely known will need corroboration. So, for example, making a point about population growth in nineteenth-century northern Mexico will require some supporting source material, but stating that Mexico City hosted the Olympic Games in 1968 will not. This way of using sources has been the convention of history writing for some 150 years. The injunction to read, use and cite original sources is still widely observed by historians, even by those who might be described as writing postmodern or deconstructionist histories. The correct use and interpretation of primary sources is a fundamental protocol in the historical method and is a key expectation of the genre of academic history writing. Readers, researchers, historians, journal editors, book publishers and students expect to read academic histories that are grounded on the use of primary sources and that make clear, consistent and intelligible references to them (and in the case of history textbooks – or synoptic analyses – that they integrate material from other historians' primary-source based work). Writing about the past in ways that do not adhere to this convention is usually classified as something other than academic history – such as historical fiction or some other genre of writing about the past. It is also worth acknowledging here that the ways in which we use primary sources as historians has ethical implications. In our selective use of sources we choose to give a voice to some people in the past but to ignore the voices of others; we judge that some people have left us 'reliable' evidence, while others are not to be trusted; we narrate our accounts of the past through the particular perspectives of our chosen sources – which, as

Dominick LaCapra suggests, contributes to the way in which the historian becomes implicated in, identifies with and undergoes forms of 'affective involvement' with their own 'objects' of study.[3]

At an early stage in a research project a historian will need to know what main body of primary sources they intend to use and what kinds of research questions those sources might help them to answer. As the research progresses there is a kind of dialogue between what the historian would like to write about and what the primary sources enable them to justifiably state. Once they have identified and gained access to their primary sources, historians need to know how to make critical use of them. It is important that we do not simply regard primary sources as containers of authenticated facts, but that we consider what they can tell us about identities, mentalities (ways of interpreting the world), and the various (often contested) relationships that exist between individuals on the one hand, and collectives, cultures and societies on the other. For example, letters written by new immigrants to the USA and soldiers in the First World War do not simply provide the historian with data as to what life was like in nineteenth-century America or in the trenches. They can also inform us about how individuals tried to establish and communicate the meanings they attached to their lives, how they used letters to shape their own and their communities' identity, and particularly how in the case of immigrants they were used to shore up a fragile sense of self.[4] However, we should not assume naively that such letters provide a transparent window into the writers' inner lives – their opinions and perceptions. In order to produce a more informed and nuanced reading of these sources we need to recognise that letter writing has always been constrained by societal norms and expectations. For example, letter-writing manuals and editions of published letters have modulated the ways in which people expressed themselves in this format. Returning to our example above, model letters were provided to soldiers in the First World War to give them a 'correct' way of interpreting and communicating their experience. Moreover, the ways in which people express themselves in any given period is always related to prevalent conventions of discourse in society. In some contexts we might also need to be alert to the fact that letters would have been censored according to security, ideological, religious or moral considerations.[5]

In practice, historians make critical use of primary sources by asking certain types of questions about them. We summarise these questions below.

- Is the source in question authentic – that is, is it really from the time, by the author and the type of document that it purports to be?

  - Is it a later inscription of an earlier speech or document?
  - If so, how might this affect the way that we read the document?
- Who wrote or produced the source, and what do we know about them that might help our understanding of it?
- What kind of perspective does the author/producer adopt?
- When was it produced?
- What kind of source material is this, and how does this affect our reading of it?
- What functions did the source originally fulfil?
- How might contemporaries have understood it?
- What does it say (and what doesn't it say)?
- Does it say similar or different things to other sources from the period? Does it cohere with other sources/evidence from the period?
- Does it cohere with information in other histories?
- How have other historians in the field used this source?
- Is it a translation?
  - If so, how might this affect the source? How can we be sure the translation is accurate? But, more importantly, we need to recognise that the translation will be an interpretation of the original by the translator
- Is the source in its original form or is it a reproduction – a transcribed, printed version or a facsimile – and what problems might these pose for a historian? (Transcribed texts are in a fundamental way also translations. The transcriber generally normalises spelling and grammar and interprets unclear words. In so doing, they place their own interpretation on the text.) Edited texts sometimes omit parts of the original. The editor will select those sections that she deems to be important and, as a result, she presents her interpretation of the work to audiences. Moreover, when transcribing handwritten texts to print, some meaning can be lost or changed. For example, handwriting can often reflect the writer's emotional state – particularly useful when reading diaries or personal letters – but this is lost in transcription. Marginalia such as exclamation marks, comments and qualifications by readers or by the author may be omitted as well. Is the spatial placement of texts maintained from the original? For example, when we read a digitised version of a newspaper article we do not always see where this article was originally positioned – the juxtaposition of one text with another can affect how these texts might have been read originally.
  - If it is not in its original form, do we know how the text in question was originally circulated?

We might also add the following considerations from discourse theory:

- We should be alert to the plurality of possible readings for words or phrases
  - Different terms often meant different things to different audiences – that is, words do not necessarily have the same meaning over time and between different interpretative communities
- We should check for the use of binary distinctions in the text as this can tell us a lot about how audiences constructed ideas of self and other.
- We need to think about the use of metaphor to create meanings within texts

In addition to these questions and considerations there are other community-based conventions for using primary sources in history writing. Historians should never deliberately misrepresent the contents of a source in an effort to prop up a line of argument. This means that when they quote from or paraphrase a source they must do so accurately. Moreover, they should not lift fragments of a document out of context in ways that give a false impression of what that whole document might reasonably be taken to mean. However, observing these rules of scholarly etiquette does not necessarily mean that the study of original sources takes us towards the 'reality' of the past. Although historians of all types agree about the necessity of reading texts from the period in question, and also about how to use them, they disagree about their understandings of what type of knowledge these sources might be expected to yield. As we discuss in more detail below, the study of primary sources helps historians to produce more detailed, textured and authoritative pieces of writing. But, however intellectually rewarding such writing might be to read, we should not simply assume that the rigorous use of primary sources provides historians with a way to access to the past on its own terms.

Do primary sources provide access to the past?

We share the view that historians (and history students) should continue to make critical use of primary sources. Reading original sources is an important part of the subject's intellectual and cultural traditions. To borrow a line of thought from Richard Rorty, historians can do no more than make best use of the tools and resources that are available to them to do their work. In this sense, we might regard primary sources as the resources we have for this work and modes of critical reading as our tools for doing it. The more 'old' texts we read, the more we expand our vocabularies for writing history and the more skilled we become at performing our particular 'language game'.

As we have noted already, according to the genre rules of history, primary sources are the final reference point in the procedures that enable historians to make justified statements about the past. If we want an audience to accept the validity of what we write, we will be expected to show that we have used the available evidence in acceptable ways – and to explain why we have declined or neglected to cite sources that might contradict our accounts. Primary sources are the last 'court of appeal' for historians who disagree with each other about how to account for the same set of events. Can both historians in such a dispute substantiate their accounts by referring to original sources? If so, can each of them show that they have used their sources according to the procedural rules of the profession? Have they drawn reasonable conclusions or inferences from the sources, using them to justify their descriptions of part–whole or whole–part relationships in their accounts? If both have done so, we simply have to accept that their different (competing) histories are both equally 'correct' – and conclude that each writer had their own particular reasons for producing the account that they did.

However, some historians bestow much more evidential weight on primary sources than we have in the paragraph above. In some minds, primary sources give historians a kind of access to the past itself, unmediated by the interpretive work of other historians. According to Arthur Marwick, 'the essential concern of history is with the sustainable truth which painstakingly, and often opaquely, emerges from the sources'.[6] By 'sources' here, Marwick was specifically referring to primary sources. In a piece called 'Living in the Scottish Record Office' (1999), American historian Deborah A. Symonds makes a similar point to Marwick as she describes her experience of working with original documents in an Edinburgh archive. For her, reading the manuscripts on eighteenth-century criminal cases was not simply a matter of processing and evaluating data. It was a physical and emotional sensation – a kind of empathetic contact with the past itself. Symonds recalled how she continually lost all sense of present time and her surroundings in the archive, becoming immersed in the other world that she was reading about in the documents. It was this feeling of being transported back in time via the primary sources that led her to state:

> At the risk of arrant romanticisation, I am inclined to argue that historians must hold the original documents of whatever they study, look at the paper, and smell everything. Only by coming face to face with surviving documents, seals, letters, maps, accounts, and receipts

> can one, I believe, fully weigh the meaning of terms like intention, falsification, and truth.[7]

The idea that stores of archival materials are somehow reflective of the past itself has an obvious appeal for some kinds of historian. It enables them to claim that if the sources are in correspondence with the past, and if their historical account of something is in correspondence with those sources, then logically their historical account must be in correspondence with the past. This is the thinking behind the kind of empirical-realist history that seeks to guarantee its knowledge claims about the past.

However, there are several problems with the model that links past-archives-histories together in such a fixed manner. Firstly, the deposits of documents available in archives are highly fragmented, variable, arbitrary and contingent. They are partly the result of accident (what happened to be recorded, what happened to be preserved, what has survived accidental destruction) and partly the product of politics and culture (the editing activities of archivists and librarians, funding decisions by various agencies to catalogue one set of records instead of another, choosing to make particular records available in digital form, releasing some documents to the public but withholding others).[8] Secondly, the ways in which a particular historian might access archival materials depends on any number of external factors. How much research time does she/he have for the archival work involved in her/his current project? Do they require (and can they get) funding to visit distant archives? Do they have the language (or paleographic) skills to read relevant documents? What levels of energy and concentration does the researcher bring to their work in the archive on any given day (which may affect their note-taking and thus citation of sources in the final account)? As Antoinette Burton argued in *Archive Stories: Facts, Fictions, and the Writing of History* (2005), historians have long maintained a relative silence about the 'personal, structural, and political pressures which the archive places on the histories they end up writing – as well as those they do not'.[9] Thirdly, a shift from a correspondence or referential theory of meaning or language use (which conceives of the meaning of a word in terms of its relationship or correspondence to an object or entity in the world) to a use-based theory (which argues that 'the meaning of a word is its use' or that meaning is determined by how a community of language users actually use the term), means that texts can no longer be understood as having fixed, definitive meanings.[10] All texts are open to multiple readings, depending on the context in which they are read, by whom and for what purposes – which is not to say, of course, that texts can mean anything we want them to mean. And if, as a consequence, no text can be given a final authoritative reading (and thus subjected to a 'closure', after which there would be no further ways of interpreting or re-describing it), then we must let go of the idea that primary sources are simply reflective of the time and place in which they were produced. They can always be read in subtly (but importantly) different ways, according to the needs of the researcher and his/her research question.

Fourthly, beyond the level of corroborating a simple factual claim, primary sources do not simply tell historians what they want to know about the past. For example, Hansard *Parliamentary Debates* provides a transcript of Winston Churchill's first speech to the House of Commons as British Prime Minister on 13 May 1940. We can therefore be reasonably sure about what he said – allowing for the fact that speakers can correct the transcripts of what they say, and that 'errs' and 'ums' and other verbal slips are excised. But in order to evaluate the speech, to make a judgement about why he said those words in that particular way, or to make some points about the speech's political importance, we have to use inferential reasoning. This means we move from particular data (the speech) to general conclusions (about its various functions and levels of meaning). In practice, this means that we use our knowledge of context (recognising that this is itself based on reading other texts) – the speech was made just three days after Churchill became Prime Minister, it followed a recent British military defeat in Norway, Churchill was Prime Minister but not yet the leader of a political party, his predecessor had been deposed partly because he seemed to want to conciliate rather than fight the enemy, and Germany had just launched its offensive on Western Europe. We apply our knowledge of mid-twentieth-century British parliamentary customs – its debating procedures, its traditions of adversarial exchange, the conventions governing language use and modes of address. We use what we know about Churchill as an orator, politician and minister. And we use our knowledge of other sources (such as John Colville's and Hugh Dalton's diaries) to make the point that with this speech Churchill passed his first public test as Prime Minister. We can see why it was widely agreed that Churchill had said the right things at the right time, by politicians, newspaper commentators, civil servants and the public. Put this way, inferential reasoning looks like a useful way of working. But we should not mistake it for a way of guaranteeing historians' judgements. Inferential reasoning is not a 'reliable' methodology as such. It is largely a matter of intuition and experience, a 'feel' about what the sources might yield, with the important procedural decisions left in the hands of the historian (which of the available contexts will they decide to employ?, what other corroborating sources are available and will they cite?; what will they do about those other sources that they haven't yet read, but which might cause problems for their argument? – and how will they signal to the reader which sources they have yet to consult?). Finally, there is the problem of the relationship between the sources and the written account. How will the primary sources be deployed, combined and weighted in the historian's text? When and where will the historian quote directly from the source(s)? What governs their choice about the length of any given quote? When will they paraphrase part of a document, or perhaps simply cite a source in a footnote to support a claim? In other words, instead of regarding sources as data that give us access to the past, we should see them as resources that historians deploy figuratively to justify their statements and ensure that their work qualifies as 'history'.

Example of primary source analysis

Fethname (victory letter)

Ottoman *fethnames* (victory letters) provide an interesting example of the potential complexities inherent in source analysis. *Fethnames* are early modern Ottoman state documents that record and celebrate Ottoman victories and conquests. Such documents were variously sent to Ottoman state officials and governors; read aloud in Ottoman towns and cities; sent to foreign rulers; incorporated into Ottoman histories; and included in other literary collections. Such a *fethname* was written to celebrate the Ottoman conquest of Eger castle in today's Hungary in 1596. There are a number of versions of this *fethname* in existence today. One was sent to the English Queen Elizabeth I and is in the National Archive. Another was copied by the sixteenth-century Ottoman historian Selaniki into his history of the Ottoman Empire. Selaniki also notes that the *fethname* he copied was originally sent to the chief judge of Istanbul and was intended to be read aloud on the streets of the city to inform the population of the great victory. A third version was included in a nineteenth-century Ottoman printed edition of a collection of Ottoman cultural writings. And lastly, there exists an English translation of an Arabic version of the *fethname* sent to a Yemeni emir. These four extant versions of the Eger *fethname* are commonly assumed to be essentially the same as they all describe the capture of the castle in basically the same way. However, the small textual differences, together with the re-inscription of the *fethname* in different textual contexts, provide evidence that the Eger *fethname*(s) had diverse functions and audiences and are not therefore simply the same source copied in different documents.[11]

The implied *fethname* that Selaniki describes in his history as being read aloud on the streets of Istanbul was ostensibly intended to communicate news of the conquest to the Ottoman people. However, it may also have been designed to convince the Ottoman population of the validity of a long and costly war and of the greatness and magnificence of the empire. In doing so, it helped to create public memories which in turn served as a form of social cohesion and provided a sense of identity.

In contrast, the inclusion of the *fethname* in Selaniki's history serves a very different function. Although it provides information about the victory, Selaniki had already provided a full description of the capture of the castle. Therefore the inclusion of the document at the end of his narrative appears to serve a similar function to a modern historian's quotation and citation of primary sources: that is, it serves to validate and authorise his work as a true and accurate history and himself as a respected historian because his history is based upon official documents. Moreover, Selaniki's *fethname* includes an additional section defending the actions and eulogising the grand vizier which was not included in that sent to Queen Elizabeth nor in the nineteenth-century printed version. The inclusion of this section in Selaniki's version of the *fethname* is perhaps not surprising given that he was employed by the grand vizier soon after the latter was appointed to his post.

The *fethname* sent to Queen Elizabeth, although largely similar to the others, does include a number of small lexical differences which indicate that it served another purpose in addition to that of providing information about an Ottoman victory. These differences mainly concern the religious terminology used, which suggests that the Ottomans specifically re-wrote the *fethname* to take account of Queen Elizabeth's Christian faith. While not all Qur'anic references are removed, those that remain refer to events also found in the Bible. Specific references to Allah are replaced with the phrase 'the supreme sovereign'. Moreover, the concluding section of the English *fethname* differs from the others by mentioning the role of the English ambassador in that year's Ottoman military campaign and offering hope for the success of the English fleet which had been sent against the common enemy of the English and the Ottomans, the Spanish Habsburgs. The inclusion of these last comments provides evidence that one of the functions of this *fethname* was to be a tool of diplomacy and to maintain and reaffirm the cordial Anglo-Ottoman relationship.

The English translation of the Arabic-language *fethname* sent to the Yemeni emir has also been rewritten to account for the religious beliefs of its recipient. This version employs a more pronounced Islamic framework and, in particular, exploits the rhetoric of antagonistic religious difference to narrate events with numerous references to the sultan as an exemplary Muslim waging jihad against the infidel. This *fethname* seems to have been sent with the hope of reinforcing the loyalty of the Ottoman's representative in the Yemen to the Ottoman Empire, as well as reminding him of the power and strength of the empire. However, the fact that we only have available the English translation of the Arabic original means that we have to be very careful in drawing conclusions as we do not know how accurate a translation it is.

The last example is a nineteenth-century printed edition of a much earlier manuscript collection of examples of Ottoman cultural writings. While in the early modern period such collections would have been used by scribes, secretaries and bureaucrats as style and protocol templates, it is very unlikely that this would have been the function of the nineteenth-century printed version. It is far more likely that it, just like the printing of a number of Ottoman 'classic' histories at this time, was intended to establish a particular set of shared social memories of an Ottoman golden age that would help to create a proto-national sense of Ottoman identity. Therefore we cannot read this version of the *fethname* unproblematically as an exact copy of an earlier sixteenth-century *fethname*. Many nineteenth-century printed editions of earlier manuscript versions of Ottoman histories demonstrate differences in vocabulary and also omit some sections of text. For example, this *fethname* is much shorter than the other versions. Unlike the others, it only describes the capture of Eger castle and not the subsequent battle of Mezokeresztes, which the Ottomans only just managed to win. It therefore acts as a powerful iconograph of a golden age of Ottoman victory and success, which contrasts significantly with the military and economic problems that the Ottoman Empire suffered in the nineteenth century.

As we have seen, the various extant versions of the Eger *fethname* served different functions and allowed different potential meanings to be created by different audiences. Source analysis is therefore not simply a matter of extracting 'facts' or documentary evidence about a particular event, in this case the capture of a castle. We also need to ask who each particular version was written for and why. We need to pay close attention to seemingly insignificant differences, as well as the textual framing of the document. And we must therefore be very cautious about uncritically relying on copies of primary sources in collected source books, edited editions, transcriptions and translations and printed versions of originally manuscript texts.

Notes

1 Georg G. Iggers, *Historiography in the Twentieth Century: From Scientific Objectivity to the Postmodern Challenge* (Middletown CT: Wesleyan University Press, 2005 edn) 57–60.

2 Keith Jenkins, *At the Limits of History: Essays on Theory and Practice* (London: Routledge, 2009) 5–6.

3 This is a familiar theme in LaCapra's writing. For a recent example see Dominick LaCapra, *History and its Limits: Human: Animal, Violence* (Ithaca: Cornell University Press, 2009) 16, 198.

4 Miriam Dobson and Benjamin Ziemann (eds), *Reading Primary Sources: The Interpretation of Texts from Nineteenth- and Twentieth-Century History* (London: Routledge, 2009) 60–1.

5 *Ibid.*, 63.

6 Arthur Marwick, '"A Fetishism of Documents"? The Salience of Source-based History,' in *Developments in Modern Historiography* ed. H. Kozicki (London: Macmillan, 1993) 116.

7 Deborah A. Symonds, 'Living in the Scottish Record Office', in *Reconstructing History* E. Fox-Genovese and E. Lasch-Quinn (eds), (New York: Routledge, 1999) cited in Keith Jenkins and Alun Munslow (eds), *The Nature of History Reader* (London: Routledge, 2004) 25.

8 For further discussion of this see Gesa E. Kirsch and Liz Rohan (eds), *Beyond the Archives: Research as a Lived Process* (Carbondale: Southern Illinois University Press, 2008).

9 Antoinette Burton (ed.), *Archive Stories: Facts, Fictions, and the Writing of History* (Durham and London: Duke University Press, 2005) 9.

10 Ludwig Wittgenstein, *Philosophical Investigations* (New Jersey: Prentice Hall, 1973) 43.

11 For more on *fethnames* see Claire Norton, '"The Lords of Lewdness": Imagining the "Other", in Ottoman *Fethnames*', in Robert Born and Andreas Puth (eds), *Osmanischer Orient und Ostmitteleuropa. Perzeptionen und Interaktionaen in den Grenzzonen zwischen dem 16. Und 18. Jahrundert* (Stuttgart: Franz Steiner Verlag, 2014) 281–299.

Further reading

Catherine Armstrong, *Using Non-textual Sources: A Historian's Guide* (London: Bloomsbury Academic, 2016). This book combines theory and practice, guiding students in the use of sources such as film, cartoons, photographs, music, pottery and artefacts. Detailed analytical readings of non-textual sources include the Hereford Mappa Mundi (*c.*1300), a Tudor religious propaganda painting and John Ford's 1954 Western film *The Searchers.*

Antoinette Burton (ed.), *Archive Stories: Facts, Fictions, and the Writing of History* (Durham and London: Duke University Press, 2005). Contains a range of personalised reflections from scholars about their experiences of working in archives. The testimonies collected are a useful reminder that, while archives remain central to historians' work, they are anything but neutral repositories of information.

Miriam Dobson and Benjamin Ziemann (eds), *Reading Primary Sources: The Interpretation of Texts from Nineteenth- and Twentieth-Century History* (London: Routledge, 2009). A good introduction to interpreting and using a variety of primary sources with chapters on the use of novels, autobiography, speeches, court files, letters newspapers and diaries among others. It also includes an introduction which discusses some general approaches to textual analysis and interpreting primary sources.

Suraiya Faroqhi, *Approaching Ottoman History: An Introduction to the Sources* (Cambridge: Cambridge University Press, 1999). A very useful introduction to both European and Ottoman archival and narrative sources on Ottoman history, which discusses the sources in the context of current research questions, issues and projects.

Gesa E. Kirsch and Liz Rohan (eds), *Beyond the Archives: Research as a Lived Process* (Carbondale: Southern Illinois University Press, 2008). These essays argue that archival collections of materials are always the product of an interested perspective, and that the materials they contain are always read from an interested perspective. The importance of serendipity, chance discoveries and personal connections with archival documents is a theme that links the various contributions.

5

Creating historical knowledge

What is the historical method?

Academic histories are produced by writers who put the historical method to use. This method is the generally agreed set of rules that constitute historians' professional code of conduct. It should not be confused with the various methodologies that historians use to address different types of research question. The core rules that constitute the historical method as it is today relate back to the empiricism of the Enlightenment and the nineteenth-century development of history as an academic subject as it was taught in European universities. These rules reflect the ways in which history was initially modelled on the natural sciences – and therefore seen to be capable of producing 'hard', rational and verifiable knowledge. Historians now disagree (sometimes sharply) about the kind of knowledge that the historical method is capable of producing. But all agree about the need to observe its protocols, and for one simple reason. All academic historians, by definition, employ the historical method in their work – because anyone who writes about the past without using these methods is regarded as having produced work that is something other than academic 'history'. This is not necessarily a question of value (historians are not guaranteed to produce better accounts of the past than anyone else), but it is a matter of categorisation. In other words, it is adherence to the protocols of the historical method that defines what it is to 'do' history. For this reason, part of your challenge as a history student is to be able to recognise and follow the protocols of the historical method in your own work.

What are these protocols? Historians have to base their accounts on source materials. In order to make a statement about the past they need to be able to produce a corroborating reference to justify it. This means that historians need to be able to locate and organise the relevant sources (the traces left behind from the past and the works of historians) on which they will base their account. They need to be able to verify sources, to date them, locate their place of origin and identify their intended functions. They need to show that they have read them with close attention and demonstrate how they have been used to answer the research question under discussion. Historians need to make accurate notes from their sources, taking care to distinguish between quotes and parts that are paraphrased, noting page numbers where available, checking dates, checking whose views are being presented at particular points in the text – is it the actual author or are they relaying someone else's views in that passage? Also, they need to be careful not to mislead by strategically lifting small parts of a text from the whole in order to deliberately change the meaning of that text. Historians need to be able to distinguish between how they use sources to support a simple factual claim and how they use them to infer things about the past. Historians also need to be able to show how their hypotheses relate to the available source materials.

The historical method

The 'rules' for writing history are socially determined and contingent. This means that they are not fixed but could be subject to change. In fact, many of the postmodern histories discussed throughout this book do not physically frame their texts as histories and are not written using the 'impersonal' voice. This suggests that adherence to these rules does not need to be comprehensive, but rather that it is sufficient for one to adhere to a majority of them. In practice there is a degree of flexibility. The rules or practices for writing history contained under the term 'the historical method' can be described as the following:

- the use of standard models for the ascription of cause, effect and contingency
- the use of generally accepted or recognised interpretative models
- critical appraisal of primary and archival sources, which includes an assessment of the reliability and authenticity of the documents
- the physical framing of the work as history through the employment of a critical apparatus including acknowledgements, explanatory

introduction, footnotes, bibliographical references, appendices and indexes
- invocations of authority such as the identification of the narratorial voice with the known author and the attribution of information to cited sources
- Intra- and inter-textual coherence – that is, internal coherence within the work and coherence or agreement between the work and other sources
- inclusiveness – that is, the work should explain coherently all the evidence available
- the acquisition of substantiating and countervailing evidence
- the establishment of facts from this evidence
- a decontextualised tone and the use of expository prose – the incorporation of the facts into a narrative in an objective, disinterested manner
- an explicit explanatory purpose or function
- the diachronic situation of the narrative within the discourse of history through citations of other accepted histories
- if controversial interpretative models are to be utilised, or established facts are to be challenged, a coherent explanation/defence of this should be provided.

Does the historical method ensure that our knowledge of the past is objective and true?

The most powerful rejection of the belief that historians have ever known about the past objectively or 'as it happened' has come from forms of postmodernist thinking (alternative terms for this are poststructuralist or postfoundational thinking). In a general sense, postmodernist thought has focused attention on the ways in which our knowledge about the past is generated by the use of language in texts. It holds that there are no ready-made meanings in the past itself: meaning is instead generated by the linguistic descriptions that are marshalled and produced by historians. Hence postmodernist ways of thinking are also associated with 'the linguistic turn'. This phrase is generally used to describe a philosophical shift in how language has been understood to function. Rather than see language as a transparent and neutral vehicle that can unproblematically represent or describe the real, proponents of the linguistic turn acknowledge the key role of language in creating meaning and constituting our world as we perceive it. The linguistic turn has its origins in turn-of-the-twentieth-century linguistic and philosophical developments. In the specific context of historical writing, probably the two most influential thinkers are Hayden White and Frank Ankersmit. They argue that the language we use when writing historical narratives does not simply reflect meaning, but that its figurative nature is what ultimately leads to the creation of meaning. They propose that turning facts extracted from primary sources into a historical narrative requires a considerable degree of subjective interpretation. We first have to select the facts that we will include. We never include in our narrative all the possible true facts that we could construct from the sources, so we choose only those facts which have relevance for the story we want to tell. Moreover, the facts that we categorise as significant will partly depend on the research questions we ask and the explanatory models and frameworks we use to interpret the sources. We then have to organise the facts into a historical narrative. Rather than simply chronicle past events in a linear fashion, historical narratives attempt to explain the past, and this involves making interpretative and narrative decisions. For example, to impose a beginning, middle and end on one's narrative involves a degree of interpretation and an imaginative element. Events have a beginning and end only from a human perspective.

White argued that the past itself does not have a story: we impose one on it and we can choose different types of story to emplot our facts. He outlines four main generic story types: comedy, tragedy, romance and satire.[1] The first stresses the temporary triumph of man and the conservation of shared human values against the threat of disruption. The second emphasises that affairs can and do go wrong, values will always collide and tension will always exist in society. The third tells of the heroic struggle of individuals or groups – of good over evil. And the last emplots events in a story of unending human suffering. Thus the history of Christian–Muslim interactions in the Mediterranean could be emplotted as a comedy: as a story of common values and shared responses to similar environmental conditions. Alternatively, it could be narrated as a tragedy, as an unending clash of civilisations between two very different communities who hold opposing and unreconcilable values. Or, if plotted as a romance, it may tell the story of Christian triumph over the Islamic threat to Europe and the heroic sacrifice of individuals and states who bravely withstood the infidel onslaught. Lastly, if plotted as a satire, the history of this encounter may be situated within a broader narrative which argues that the history of humanity is one of eternal conflict, antagonism and violence, of which this is simply one more example. While White's model is more complex than outlined here and there have been some criticisms of it, it is an interesting example of how the same events can be narrated in radically different ways.

Both White and Ankersmit argue that, while statements or individual facts can be verified as true or false by checking whether they cohere with the evidence in the primary sources, at the level of historical narrative such verification is impossible. The selection of facts, emplotment strategy, figurative styles and rhetorical tropes all require the historian to make subjective judgements and interpretations based upon their interests, opinions and conceptual schemas. Because historians' accounts are so suffused with subjectivity, it is impossible to determine whether they are true or false, accurate or inaccurate. In other words, histories cannot correspond to the past as it happened because the past has no intrinsic story of its own.

White and Ankersmit are not anti-realists. That is, they do not fundamentally challenge realist models of the world. White believes that events did happen, while Ankersmit claims to be an adherent of empiricist accounts of historical writing at the level of statements about the past, but not for the text as a whole.[2] However, they do problematise the extent to which we can acquire or represent objective, true knowledge of the world in a narrative form. Other philosophers and historians have more directly challenged realist models and argued that knowledge of the world (past or present) 'as it is in itself' is impossible, which therefore undermines realist historians' claims to be able to provide true, objective accounts of the past. These challenges generally focus on the reality–appearance distinction, which is integral to realist and empiricist theories. Very few philosophers or historians argue for naïve or direct realism anymore – that is, the theory that we perceive the world actually as it is in itself, free from human classificatory frameworks and interpretative schemes. Instead, it is acknowledged that 'the world is presented in a kaleidoscopic flux of impressions which has to be organized by our minds… We *cut nature up* and *organize* it into concepts, and ascribe significance…'[3] Reality is far more complex than we can deal with, so our minds sift, organise and categorise our experience in order to simplify our experiences and give them some kind of order. Reality is thus always apprehended through human interpretative frameworks, which are constrained by biology, but also by culturally determined structures and categories of analysis. Our ways of apprehending, engaging with and thinking about the world are therefore not neutral, naturally given and universally shared, but are culturally determined, contingent and subject to change. John Beattie argued that 'people see what they expect to see, and that the categories of their perception are largely if not wholly determined by their social and cultural background. So members of different cultures may see the world they live in very differently. And it is not just a matter of reaching different conclusions about the world from the same evidence; the very evidence which is given to them as members of different cultures may be different'.[4]

Even if we could somehow access the past free from our interests and assumptions, we could not adequately represent it in a narrative form that somehow corresponds to the past because the past is just too big to describe. It exists as an infinity of events and the historian has to decide (on the basis of their own interests and cultural needs) which aspects are of significance. Moreover, we can only ever access the past indirectly through textual or material remains. Thus, as Ankersmit has argued, evidence from primary sources does 'not point towards the *past* but to other *interpretations* of the past', which therefore further problematises the notion of there being a correspondence between the past itself and historical narratives.[5]

Responses to postmodern challenges

There was always an asymmetrical character to history's internal arguments about the status of the knowledge that the discipline claimed to produce. Only a very few historians took seriously the linguistic turn's wider undermining of epistemic certainties across all fields of knowledge production and sought to use it as a set of tools for critiquing the genre of academic history. Felipe Fernàndez-Armesto probably expressed the prevailing view of the history profession when he dismissed postmodern epistemological scepticism for having turned out to be a 'paper tiger'.[6] The editor of a collection of essays about the state of the discipline made the same point fairly recently: 'by and large, practicing historians have rejected the nihilistic tendencies of postmodernism in favor of a commonsensical approach to their craft… they do not lose sleep over epistemological matters'.[7] For writers like these, the epistemological instability generated by postmodern challenges went beyond a threat to academic standards. They saw history as a guarantor of social meaning, morality and ethical norms. In *Telling the Truth About History,* Appleby, Jacob and Hunt sought to defuse postmodern critiques by peeling off those parts of it that they could accept and discarding the rest. They conceded that the act of representing the past makes the historian complicit in shaping how it is seen. They agreed that it is possible to have many different accounts of any given event, all of which are equally valid. They also acknowledged that representations of the past are always bound up with present concerns, which means that they will be read differently from one generation to another.[8] However, despite embracing a postmodernism-influenced 'healthy scepticism' towards our construction of knowledge, they take a firm stand against what they perceive to be the cynicism and nihilism of contemporary relativism or postmodernism.[9] They argue that a belief in the reality of the past and its knowability is a fundamental component of what constitutes the genre of history. They describe their position as one of practical realism, which they present as a more nuanced, less absolute kind of realism, but one which still allows people's perceptions of the world to have some correspondence to it. In other words, the past dimly corresponds to what the historian says about it.[10] Therefore truths about the past are possible, they say, even if they are not absolute.[11]

Richard Evans holds a similar view, arguing that few historians would defend a 'hard-line concept of historical objectivity' anymore.[12] He acknowledges that literary models, social science theories, as well as our moral and political beliefs, all play a role in guiding our selection and interpretation of sources. Moreover, he discusses how postmodernism has opened up new areas of historical research and encouraged historians to re-examine old topics in new ways; he concedes that it has encouraged historians to examine texts more closely and to think about them in a different fashion; and he recognises that it has spurred historians to think about their own methods and procedures in more detail. However, he still adheres to a realist ontology and empiricist epistemology and insists that 'we can, if we are very careful and thorough, approach a reconstruction of past reality that may be partial and provisional, and certainly will not be objective, but is nevertheless true'.[13]

Evans argues that history is essentially a practical discipline and that historians should be more concerned with the content rather than the nature of historical knowledge. He likes some of what postmodernism can do, but is not prepared to abandon the supposed security of a mind-independent foundation for our knowledge claims about the past. One of the main reasons for this is a moral desire not to assist those who wish to 'suppress, distort or cover up the past,' particularly Holocaust deniers. However, this desire does not effectively rebut the philosophical challenges raised by postmodernism to traditional empiricist theories of historical knowledge. Evans' other main arguments against postmodernism are also contentious. He accuses postmodernists of using excessive jargon and obscure vocabularies, and of being narcissistic and elitist. He adds that they want to abandon the notion of historical truth and objectivity not because these ideas are philosophically problematic, but because such concepts do not suit their political or personal purposes.[14] However, historians who wish to retain an empiricist epistemology need to discuss and refute the philosophical challenges made against it in detail. Ignoring questions about the nature of historical knowledge because they are anxious about where those enquiries might lead is not a good enough response. Where Evans does attempt a philosophical critique of postmodernism, he seems to misunderstand the problems raised by it. He argues that postmodernists hold their own theories about knowledge to be true, while at the same time they tell historians that there are always multiple perspectives on the past, never one that is singularly true. This, says Evans, is self-refuting. If there are many different but equally valid ways of thinking about the past, he argues, then postmodernists also have to accept that they cannot claim special status for their ideas about knowledge and meaning. But, as we will discuss below, postmodernists do not argue for the objective truth of their theories. Nor do they believe that any one account of the past is as good as any other. While they may accept that all such accounts are equal in terms of their shared non-correspondence with a mind-independent reality, they point out that there are other ways of discriminating between them.

Evans's *In Defence of History* has been a highly influential book. It is regularly reissued and it continues to advertise itself as a 'classic explanation of the craft of history' that 'demolishes the wilder claims of postmodern historians'. But the book has many shortcomings, so it is useful to know that more thoughtful and nuanced responses to the linguistic turn in history are available to read. William Sewell's *Logics of History*, for example, can be read as a response to postmodernism that describes how the author moved away from writing quantitative social history to embrace the linguistic turn as a cultural historian from the 1980s onwards, and then developed reservations about where this new approach was being taken. As Sewell explains, the 'new cultural history' that he and others produced drew extensively on the anthropology of scholars such as Clifford Geertz, as well as the poststructuralist theories of the likes of Derrida, Foucault and Lacan. The field that best exemplified the new approach was feminist history. Here, the linguistic turn provided the conceptual tools that pioneers such as Joan Scott and Denise Riley could use to show that existing social categories were discursively produced, not objective or fixed realities of social life. These conceptual tools led to 'tremendous intellectual gains',[15] wrote Sewell, but they also came at a price. In his view, by making discourse and textuality their central concerns, cultural historians became reluctant to talk about 'social structures, social forces, modes of production, or class relations as facts standing outside of textual logics'.[16] Sewell, therefore, sought an approach to writing about the past that reconciled his intellectual commitment to the linguistic turn with a belief that socio-economic structures and forces could and should be analysed. He wanted to pay close attention to language, discourse and text, but he also wanted to take account of the effects of economic development, demographic trends, employment patterns, geographic concentrations and dispersals and so forth. We can see how Sewell put this approach to work in his essay on Marseille dockworkers between 1814 and 1870.[17] His objective was to explain how these workers were able to retain a privileged position in the labour force at a time when other groups were suffering the effects of economic change, both within France and across Europe more generally. In order to do this, Sewell combines quantitative research (on wage rates, employment rates, Marseille's growing population, volumes of trade going through the docks), empirical work on the dockers' labour association, analysis of the complex organisational ecology and daily routines of Marseilles dockers, and interpretive work on the growing political militancy of these workers from 1848 onwards. Sewell concludes that economic and political temporalities diverged in the case of the Marseilles dockworkers. His study, he argues, shows how particular cases can be used to question general theories about labour relations in nineteenth-century France. But equally, he writes, it shows how a narrative account of the Marseille dockers, with its concern for sequence, contingency and agency, also needs to draw on the theoretical vocabularies of social science.

Paul Roth's work on narrative explanation is also worth noting here, because it engages with the same questions of reference, meaning and truth in history writing that preoccupied White and Ankersmit. Along with White – and against the later work of Ankersmit – Roth rejects as philosophically untenable any proposition that there is such a thing as 'historical truth' that exists prior to representation.[18] He also dismisses as naïve any discussion about whether narratives correspond to what it is that they refer to. These are by now familiar positions. Roth's work is distinctive in the way that it argues at a high level of abstraction that historical narrative is crucial to specifically historical explanations of events.[19] History for Roth does not possess any special explanatory power, but neither does it suffer from deficiencies that are not also shared by other empirical disciplines. Drawing on the work of Arthur Danto, Roth argues that historians search for antecedents that help to explain the event that is the particular object of their enquiry. So, when a historian states that 1618 was the beginning of the Thirty Years' War in Europe, they are making a retrospective point about a sequence of occurrences that could not have been known to an observer who was present in 1618, but which can only be described as significant years afterwards. Historians convey this knowledge, he argues, with the use of narrative sentences (which have epistemic and cognitive value). In fact, he says, it is impossible to detach a historical explanation of any given event from the narrative in which it is constituted and organised as an object of knowledge. History, in this sense, is more a matter of classifying past events rather than perceiving them. And because there is nothing that limits ways of classifying things beyond social agreement among communities of practitioners, says Roth, we have to talk about plural pasts rather than a singular past.

> Given alternative modes for structuring what happens, changes in descriptions can alter relations among events imputed to a past, and so how a past thus structured impacts what becomes possible going forward. A plurality of pasts results because constituting a past depends to some degree on socially mediated negotiations of a fit between descriptions and experience. Even what we take to mark what can change and what cannot itself depends on the descriptions deployed. Unless for reasons now unknown there ceases to be a possibility of descriptive change or reclassification, human histories will continue to reveal a multiplicity of pasts.[20]

Plural pasts and Rortian pragmatism: an alternative view of historical knowledge

Richard Rorty argues that we should abandon a realist model of the world, which differentiates between the existence of a mind-independent reality free from value judgements and human interests, and our perception of this reality, where the former acts as a foundation for knowledge in the latter.[21] In other words, he does not think that it is useful to continue to make the distinction between what exists in itself (reality) and what exists in relation to human minds (appearance). He argues for a different model, one in which we no longer perceive our relationship with the world in representational terms – that is, we should stop thinking that what we perceive is a representation of what is actually there. Instead, he argues, we should think about our relationship in causal terms. This means that we should accept that the world causes our perceptions and that these perceptions are all we can have knowledge of. Therefore we should stop speculating about what the world is really like in itself.[22] With such a model there will no longer be any need to distinguish between appearance and reality, there will only be reality as perceived by human observers. This is not to deny that reality (both past and present) exists. Rorty's point is that employing a model of the world that distinguishes between a fixed, singular, true, mind-independent reality and our perception of such a reality causes considerable problems which would be eliminated, or cease to have such significance, with the adoption of a different model.

This shift in epistemic models has a number of implications for history writing. Rather than there being one, determinate 'past reality' hidden somewhere behind our representations of it, there will be a potentially endless number of plural past realities which will reflect the various viewpoints of the communities and individuals perceiving them.[23] The employment of different norms and ways of interpreting the world, together with the different needs of communities, will result in the construction, remembrance or narration of a variety of alternative, plural pasts, none of which can be adjudicated as *the* true past outside of institutional or cultural structures. Secondly, it means that historical knowledge can no longer be justified, or corroborated as true, by reference to its correspondence with a past reality independent of our perception of it. History writing is therefore epistemologically no different to other genres of writing about the 'before now' or other literary genres, if by this we mean that it is true because it corresponds to the world as it is in itself.

If history writing is no longer epistemologically different (meaning that it does not constitute a different type of knowledge) from other types of literature, then can we still talk of history being a separate genre of writing? Can it still be considered different from literature? We think that there is no doubt that history is a culturally, (but not epistemologically) distinct genre of writing. We have no trouble identifying histories and historians, although of course at the edges of the discipline there may be some blurring and disagreement. History is different from other forms of literature and also from other mnemonic practices or narratives of the 'before now' and we need to be able to explain what makes academic history different from popular history, heritage, historical fiction, period dramas, films and other accounts of the 'before now' such as those expressed in song, in comic books, museum displays, websites, art and dance.[24] It is important to bear in mind that, in the future, these distinctions between academic history and other historical cultures might become much more blurred. So what makes history different, if we can no longer argue that it is its referential relationship with the past that gives it a special status as a distinct type of knowledge? We argue that history is characterised and defined by the protocols, rules or practices to which its practitioners adhere. In effect, what defines history as history is the historian's use of a set of critical, interpretative and analytical practices that are referred to as the historical method. A narrative of the 'before now' can therefore be considered as history if the author has constructed their account using the protocols that we described earlier in this chapter. It is thus possible to separate the two strands of empiricist thought. We can retain the empirical methodology by which one can acquire and test knowledge through observation, but discard the empiricist theory of knowledge which argues that this methodology guarantees direct access to reality. Therefore the actual practice of history essentially remains the same for everyone, despite their epistemological preferences. That this is the case is corroborated by Nancy Partner's argument that, despite the language-based and philosophical challenges to realist history writing, historians (particularly postmodern historians) still largely continue to adhere to the integrity of method manifested through disciplinary protocols which govern the finding and handling of evidence and the methods of argumentation.[25] They do this, not because it ensures correspondence with a real past, nor because it enables the historian to narrate the past free from subjective influence, but because this is what writing history consists of. Non-adherence to these protocols opens historians to professional criticism and potentially to charges of fraud and the exclusion of their work from the genre of history.

However, David Harlan has challenged the arguments put forward by Hollinger and Haskell that this 'professionalism' or adherence to the protocols inherent in the historical method can provide a foundation for historical knowledge.[26] We would agree with Harlan that professionalism cannot provide an independent epistemological foundation for historical knowledge, but adherence to such protocols can be seen as defining history as a genre and giving it a particular cultural status. While historical narratives are no more accurate, reliable or true in terms of a correspondence with the past as it really happened than other accounts, they might be deemed to be more socially useful in certain circumstances. Harlan also identifies a further problem, noting that there does not exist a shared set of practices common to all historians. This is certainly true, but historians do not need to agree *exactly* on which practices and rules must be followed to 'do history'. A cluster theory approach could be adopted where the set of practices that constitute history is understood to be very broad, incorporating not only the basic skills of source analysis and interpretation, but also the variety of interpretative models employed by different historians, as well as the different forms that history writing takes. Writers would be considered to be doing history if they adhered to particular core principles as well as a subset of other practices. The example of a history department in a university illustrates this well. Most university history departments are made up of historians who specialise in different time periods and geographical and cultural areas, who write different types of history, use different interpretative strategies and reading practices, and hold different epistemological understandings of history, yet they all generally recognise and acknowledge each other as historians. Just as we recognise a plurality of types of history including economic, social, military, cultural, intellectual, and political, there is no reason why 'methodological pluralism' should not also be encouraged and embraced.[27]

How can we distinguish between good and bad history?

Rortian-influenced postmodern history may well look and feel very similar to traditional history, but if the referential link between historians' accounts of the past and the past itself are severed, how will we be able to distinguish between good and bad histories, between true, factual accounts of the past and more fictional, less accurate accounts? Does this mean that the term 'true' will become redundant, that all accounts of the past must be seen as equally true? Does it mean we can just 'make up' the past as we see fit to suit our needs and political or ideological desires? Rorty argues we could use agreement or congruence with socially agreed upon norms, practices or standards to differentiate between our beliefs or histories. It is possible to justify historical knowledge by asking whether it adheres to the collective norms and practices of the community: that is, does it cohere with the practices set out in the historical method? Paraphrasing Kuhn and applying his thoughts in a historical rather than a scientific context, we might argue that a historical narrative or statement can be considered valid when a majority of the most learned practitioners agree that it explains all available evidence in a coherent manner. Thus when we describe a historical account or fact as true we are not commentating on its relationship to past reality as it is in itself, but we are instead endorsing it within a particular framework – we are recommending it and acknowledging that it was produced in accordance with particular guidelines and practices. Specifically, we are stating that it coheres with the relevant primary and secondary sources: truth is therefore located not in correspondence with a past reality but in inter-textual coherence. To put it another way, and borrowing an analogy from Munslow, just as we do not judge art in purely representational terms and distinguish between good and bad art in terms of how realistically graphic it is, similarly we can use a variety of contingent guidelines or criteria to categorise histories.[28]

Likewise, objectivity could be redefined not as correspondence with the past as it actually happened, but as systematic knowledge acquired through the application of community-agreed rules or practices. A benefit of this model is that it mirrors actual praxis. When we critically review a history book or article, we do not check whether it corresponds to the past, we instead examine the degree to which it adheres to disciplinary protocols. For example, Paul A. David et al's criticism of Fogel and Engerman's controversial study of slavery, *Time on the Cross*, focuses on the 'dubious and largely unexplained models of market behaviour, economic dynamics, socialization, sexual behaviour, fertility determinations and genetics' that the authors used.[29] This illustrates how important it is for historians to use community-accepted interpretative models or, if they use new models, that they adequately explain and justify their use.

Of course, even if we accept that we cannot compare histories in terms of their faithfulness to the 'past as it happened', we still have ways of discriminating between one history book and another. All kinds of acceptable histories on a variety of topics are written within the conventions of the profession, yet we still make judgements about them, praising some and criticising others. This suggests that, to some extent, we differentiate between histories on aesthetic, ideological or moral grounds: we prefer particular histories over others because, in Harlan's words, 'we like what we can do with them'.[30] For example, Richard Evans's negative review of *The Annales School: An Intellectual History* by André Burguière and of the Annales approach to history writing in general reflects his rather hostile position towards social-science based history.[31]

Although we have emphasised the significance of the protocols and practices that constitute the historical method, it is important to remember that these are not fixed or timeless. As we discussed earlier, such protocols are socially determined historical products which have themselves developed over time. As such they are subject to modification and change. For example, although many of the practices of ancient and pre-modern historians are still considered to be part of the historical method, Thucydides's use of evidence from the oracles and Naima's use of astrology are not. In a more up-to-date context, some historians have become less inclined to mask their own voice in their work. Historians such as Richard Price are increasingly playing with making their voice and the voices of others explicit in their work.[32] Similarly, fictional invention in the form of anecdotes, scenes taken from other books, the inclusion of miracles and verbatim renditions of secret conversations is commonly assumed to belong to the protocols and practices of ancient and pre-modern historical communities and not twenty-first century western academic history writing.[33] But, increasingly, historians are incorporating imaginative reconstructions of conversations and other fictive elements within their writing. It is therefore possible for historians to modify the genre conventions of history, to introduce new ways of narrating the past and to adapt or discard existing conventions. If there is resistance to them doing so, it comes from the conservatism of their fellow historians, not because the past itself demands that they use a particular mode of writing to represent it.

What does the adoption of a pragmatist model of knowledge acquisition mean for history?

We will have to:

- abandon the idea of a singular past that can be used as a foundation for the truth claims of our histories
- acknowledge the existence of plural pasts that reflect not only the interpretative frameworks of those narrating them, but the multiple functions that such pasts serve
- Recognise history as a literary genre of writing about pasts that is different from other narratives of the 'before now', not because it corresponds to a foundational past out there, but because it adheres to socially accepted and determined genre conventions or protocols
- accept that we distinguish between good and bad histories not by comparing them to what actually happened, but by asking how well they adhere to these protocols
- acknowledge that these protocols are socially determined and are thus subject to change in accordance with the community's needs and agreement.

For postmodernists it is these contingent, fluid norms of the historical profession, together with historians' different interests and ways of interpreting the world, that help to explain changes in historical narrations over time and disagreements between historians. History-making for postmodernists is a presentist activity – that is, the past is rewritten by every generation or community to reflect its interests, identities and needs. As the identities of communities and societies shift over time, as different values are seen to be important, then older histories no longer do their job of reflecting and reinforcing the identity of the community as effectively. Therefore, new histories come to be written.

The understanding of history writing and the contingency of its disciplinary protocols outlined above allow us to see different accounts of the same event for what they are: accounts written for different purposes and from different perspectives. The realist model of historical knowledge has in effect elided the subjectivity, ideologies and diverse functions inherent in all histories. The myth of studying the past for its own sake to achieve an objective, accurate and true account of it is no longer a useful or coherent model. Rather than worry about how well historical accounts correspond to the past, we should concentrate on asking who was this history written for, whose interests does it represent and what functions does it serve? We should enquire about the types of history we as individuals or as a society want or need, and we should scrutinise history for what it really is – an often fascinating genre of literary writing which is ideologically motivated, which helps construct our worlds and identities, and which can be used to teach, encourage, illuminate or entertain.

Notes

1 Hayden White, 'Interpretation in History', in *Tropics of Discourse: Essays in Cultural Criticism* (Baltimore, MD: Johns Hopkins University Press, 1978) 51–80, 70.
2 F.R. Ankersmit, *Sublime Historical Experience* (Stanford: Stanford University Press, 2005) xiv.
3 Benjamin Lee Whorf, *Language. Thought and Reality* (Cambridge: M.I.T. Press, 1956) 213–4. Quoted in Chris Swoyer, 'Relativism', in *The Stanford Encyclopedia of Philosophy* (Winter 2010 Edition), Edward N. Zalta (ed.), forthcoming URL = http://plato.stanford.edu/archives/win2010/entries/relativism/> accessed 13 May 2010.
4 John Beattie, *Other Cultures: Aims, Methods, and Achievements in Social Anthropology* (London: Cohen & West, 1964) 75. Quoted in Swoyer, 'Relativism', in *The Stanford Encyclopedia of Philosophy.* For an example, see Segall, Campbell and Herskovitz's cross-cultural studies on interpreting the Müller-Lyer and Sander Parallelogram perspective illusions in Marshall H. Segal, Donald T. Campbell, and Melville J. Herskovits, *The Influence of Culture on Visual Perception* (Indianapolis, IN: In: Bobbs-Merrill, 1966) and the discussion of relativism and perception at Swoyer, 'Relativism', in *The Stanford Encyclopedia of Philosophy.*
5 F. R. Ankersmit, 'Historiography and Postmodernism', in *The Postmodern History Reader* ed. K. Jenkins (London: Routledge, originally published in 1997, reprint 1998) 287.
6 Felipe Fernàndez-Armesto, 'Epilogue: What is History *Now*,' in *What is History Now?,* ed. David Cannadine (Houndmills, Basingstoke: Palgrave Macmillan, 2002) 155.
7 Donald A. Yerxa ed., *Recent Themes in Historical Thinking: Historians in Conversation* (Columbia: University of South Carolina Press, 2008) 3.
8 Joyce Appleby, Lynn Hunt and Margaret Jacob, *Telling the Truth About History* (London: W.W. Norton and Company 1994) 249, 254, 256, 262, 265.

9 *Ibid.*, 4.

10 *Ibid.*, 283 and 247–8.

11 *Ibid.*, 7.

12 Richard J. Evans, *In Defence of History* (London: Granta, 1997) 3.

13 *Ibid.*, 249.

14 *Ibid.*, 200. He argues that Paul de Man was only in favour of postmodernism as a means of exculpating his responsibility for his earlier writing for a Nazi-controlled journal during the occupation of Belgium. Ibid., 234.

15 William H. Sewell, *Logics of History: Social Theory and Social Transformation* (Chicago: University of Chicago Press, 2005) 23, 44.

16 Sewell, *Logics of History*, 51.

17 Sewell, *Logics of History*, 271–317.

18 Paul Roth, 'Whistling History: Ankersmit's neo-Tractarian Theory of Historical Representation', in *Rethinking History*, 17/4 (2013) 548–69.

19 Paul Roth, *The Philosophical Structure of Historical Explanation* (Evanston, IN: Northwestern University Press, 2019).

20 Paul Roth, 'The Pasts', in *History and Theory*, 51/3 (2012) 339.

21 For a good definition and introduction to pragmatism see Christopher Hookway, 'Pragmatism', in *The Stanford Encyclopedia of Philosophy (Spring 2010 Edition)*, Edward N. Zalta (ed.), URL = http://plato.stanford.edu/archives/spr2010/entries/pragmatism/>

22 Richard Rorty, *Truth and Progress: Philosophical Papers*, (Cambridge: Cambridge University Press, 1998) 49.

23 Our position here echoes that of Robert Braun, 'The Holocaust and Problems of Representation', in *The Postmodern History Reader* ed. K. Jenkins, (London: Routledge, originally published in 1997, reprint 1998) 418–425, 421.

24 The phrase 'mnemonic practices' is from Ann Rigney, 'Being an Improper Historian', in Keith Jenkins, Sue Morgan, Alun Munslow (eds), *Manifestos for History* (London: Routledge, 2007) 152. By this phrase she means a publicly expressed reflection on the difference between past and present.

25 Nancy Partner, 'Historicity in an Age of Reality-Fictions', in *A New Philosophy of History* eds F. Ankersmit and H. Kellner, (London: Reaktion Books, 1995) 22.

26 David Harlan, *The Degradation of American History* (Chicago: University of Chicago Press, 1997) chapter 4.

27 The phrase is from Joanna Bourke, 'Foreword', in Keith Jenkins, Sue Morgan, Alun Munslow (eds), *Manifestos for History* (London: Routledge, 2007) xii.

28 Alun Munslow, *The Future of History* (Basingstoke: Palgrave Macmillan, 2010) 206.

29 Paul A. David et al. *Reckoning with Slavery: A Critical Study in the Quantitative History of American Negro Slavery* (New York: 1976) cited in Evans, *In Defence* 42.

30 David Harlan, *The Degradation of American History* (Chicago: University of Chicago Press, 1997) 54.
31 Richard J. Evans, 'Cite Ourselves!', in *London Review of Books* 1/23 (3 December 2009) 12–14.
32 Richard Price, *Alabi's World* (Johns Hopkins University Press, 1990).
33 Nancy Partner, 'Historicity in an Age of Reality-Fictions' 24.

Further reading

Elizabeth Deeds Ermarth, *History in the Discursive Condition: Reconsidering the Tools of Thought* (Abingdon: Routledge, 2011). Ermarth describes a shift from the modern condition (the term she uses to characterise certain Euro-Atlantic cultures for six centuries from the Quattrocento onwards) to the discursive condition (characterised by the systemic and relational understandings of knowledge that were developed across various intellectual fields in the twentieth century). She examines the implications for writing history in conditions where no signifying practices or codes can claim epistemic authority outside of the discursive system in which they are situated.

Richard J. Evans, *In Defence of History* (London: Granta, 2018 edn). A key neo-realist book which notes the advantages of a postmodern approach while still desiring to ultimately retain realist and empiricist epistemologies.

Keith Jenkins, *Rethinking History*, with a new preface and conversation with the author by Alun Munslow 2nd edition (London: Routledge Classics, 2003). A very short book, first published in 1991, which played a key role in popularising the postmodern challenge to history by challenging the idea that historical narratives in some way correspond to, or unproblematically represent, the past.

Alun Munslow, *Narrative and History* (Basingstoke: Palgrave Macmillan, 2007). An accessible introduction to the work of key narrative theorists and a clear discussion of how various narrative techniques affect the potential meanings of the text.

Richard Rorty, *Truth and Progress: Philosophical Papers* (Cambridge University Press, Cambridge, 1998). A collection of some of the most important papers of this seminal pragmatist philosopher.

William H. Sewell, *Logics of History: Social Theory and Social Transformation* (Chicago: University of Chicago Press, 2005). This book attempts to show how two different intellectual approaches to thinking about the past can be made to work together. On one side, approaches to writing cultural history that draw on the insights of the linguistic turn; on the other, approaches to writing about the social that recognise the value of quantitative methods (stripped of their old naïve objectivism), and which take seriously the effects of socio-economic structures and processes.

6

Writing histories

Historical interpretations and imagination

What kinds of questions do historians answer?

The starting point for any piece of historical writing is a research question. One of the genre rules that permits a piece of writing to qualify as history is that it answers a 'proper' research question. Such questions define the boundaries of a discussion in terms of time and space. They position it as belonging to a particular category of history (such as social, ethnographic, cultural, political, diplomatic, intellectual). And they bring a set of research materials into play (historians' writings and contemporary sources). Instead of thinking that the kind of history we read is shaped by the characteristics of a singular past (how it was back then), it is more useful to think of it as being determined by the interaction between historians, their research materials and their research question. Instead of thinking that historians offer us different perspectives on the past, it might be better to think that they offer us different perspectives on how to answer questions using their research materials – or, indeed, different perspectives on what kinds of questions are worth asking in the first place. This is why we need to pay attention to the types of question historians ask and answer. History teachers think carefully about the questions they set for students – or they insist on having final approval of questions that students set themselves. There are two main reasons for this. Firstly, they know that generalised or fuzzy questions tend to produce generalised or fuzzy answers. Secondly, they know that historical questions are never neutral or innocent – they all carry assumptions about what historians are able to know and what they can claim to explain and resolve. As Hannah Arendt wrote in 'The Concept of History, Ancient and Modern', the kinds of answers that we find in any form of human enquiry are always dependent on the questions asked – and the questions that we ask are always *our* questions.[1]

It might help here to divide historical questions into two general categories. The most common category assumes that the object of enquiry is some aspect of 'the past itself' that requires explanation or interpretation. This produces questions that ask about events, what happened and why, or ask about long-term changes in society, politics or economic practices. Such questions invoke the concepts of chronology, causation, continuity, similarity and difference. And they relate to a hypothesis that a historian has in mind. So, for example, asking a question about the importance of public debt as a cause of the French Revolution suggests a hypothesis that will be tested. If, in practice, a question turns out to be largely unanswerable (and the hypothesis breaks down), the historian usually changes their question for one that works better. Significantly, however, what remain intact here are the assumptions that the French Revolution is a singular object that we can study and that historians have the tools and methods for making judgements about why it happened. Similarly, a question that asks whether a particular period was marked by continuity or change assumes that such terms are valid analytical categories and that historians know how to weigh them up against each other.

A different category of questions makes history writing itself (discourse) the object of enquiry. Probably the most common form of these in higher education is the type that asks about historians' differing interpretations of something – for example, 'Why do historians disagree about the reasons for the collapse of the Soviet Union and which interpretation do you find most persuasive?' Alternatively, we might ask about the relationships between written histories and other ways of producing narratives about the past. 'Is Joe Sacco's graphic novel *Footnotes in Gaza* a history?' This category also includes questions that ask historians to think about their own practices. The issues at stake here are the kinds of claims that historians have made about the past, how they have validated those claims and what we as readers make of those claims. An example of this in practice is the work of Saul Friedländer and others on representing the Holocaust. Friedländer posed the question of how – indeed whether – it could be possible adequately to represent the Holocaust according to the genre conventions of history.[2]

This line of questioning raises a number of questions about history writing. Using what narrative forms and with what vocabulary could historians write about the events of the Holocaust without trivialising what happened? In attempting to represent the Holocaust, do traditional forms of history writing (particular genres of books, articles and essays) reduce it to a set of statistics, documented claims and explanatory schemes? Is there a danger that this kind of shaping work by historians – however well intentioned – makes the chaotic events of the Holocaust intelligible and, as a consequence, rational? Moreover, what kinds of issues are raised by historians' preferences for using certain primary sources rather than others in their accounts of the Holocaust – for example, Nazi documents rather than survivor testimonies? In fact, questions like these can be applied to historical writing on any event –it is simply that in the context of the Holocaust they have a particular import and resonance

Are there 'right answers' to historical questions?

History quizzes and multiple-choice tests for history students depend upon the assumption that some statements about the past can be regarded as right and others as wrong, and that we have ways of telling one from the other. If we were asked where Captain James Cook's ship *Endeavour* landed on 29 April 1770 and we replied 'Brazil', we would have given a wrong answer. Let us say, for the sake of argument, that the 'right' answer is Botany Bay in Sydney, Australia. Separating right from wrong statements about the past at this level of knowledge is usually a simple procedure. We can use different types of texts (reference books, historical accounts, primary sources) to help us decide whether a particular proposition about the past is right or wrong, true or false. In the end, this method for establishing correct facts about the past depends on whether we can corroborate those facts by citing observable data – in other words, empiricism. If we want to confirm where *Endeavour* landed on 29 April 1770, we can read Captain Cook's journals of his voyage and put the matter seemingly beyond doubt.

We say 'seemingly beyond doubt' because sometimes even apparently straightforward, corroborated factual claims can turn out to be problematic. The inlet where Cook landed was given the name 'Botany Bay' in the official published edition of his journals. This name was a reference to the wide range of plant specimens that was collected by the ship's resident botanists, Joseph Banks and Daniel Solander. But in previous logs – that is, written before publication of his journals – Cook and others had called the inlet 'Sting-Ray Harbour'. Furthermore, the indigenous Bidjigal and Geawegal people who lived on the inlet's northern and southern shores would have used their own place names. So we might say that Botany Bay in Sydney, Australia, is one right answer to the question about where Cook landed on 29 April 1770. Or that this is the answer that certain historians are most likely to give. But the answer is not 'right' in a kind of pure or absolute sense. Its 'rightness' cannot be cleanly separated from issues of power, culture and language – in this case, how did one group of people take naming rights over a territory away from others and then maintain those rights for over 200 years? 'Botany Bay' is the right answer to the question when viewed from a European perspective. But viewed from another perspective – say, that of the colonised rather than the colonisers – the right answer would be different. The point that we are making here is that finding a corroborating source is only the first step in the procedure that makes an answer to a historical question the 'right' one. The second stage is to persuade various audiences (historians, history students, readers of history books, commissioning editors, journalists and so on) of its 'rightness'. And here it is useful to think of these audiences as being tied to specific times, places and cultures – not as being timeless, universal or in some other ways ahistorical.

All of these difficulties are multiplied when we think about questions that call for some kind of commentary about the past. History students spend much of their time dealing with these matters of interpretation. Instead of writing simple descriptions of some aspect of the past, you will normally be expected to organise history essays around an answer to a specific 'historical question'. As we previously noted, definitions of what constitutes a 'historical question' are in the end self-referencing. Historical questions are the kinds of ones that historians have become accustomed to asking, the ones that they like to set for themselves (or for their students). We previously divided these questions into two related types (see Chapter 1). The first asks about things such as events, phenomena, processes, concepts or personalities in the past. Why was the French monarchy overthrown in 1789? What were the main consequences of the 1789 revolution for Anglo-French relations in the nineteenth century? Was Napoleon Bonaparte a great French leader? The second type explicitly asks about the ways in which historians have written about a particular subject. Which recent accounts of the origins of the French Revolution do you find most persuasive and why? How do you explain historians' changing approaches to writing about the French Revolution since the 1950s? Both types of question are difficult to handle because they can be answered in a number of different ways. Their openness is, in fact, one of the reasons why tutors set these kinds of questions in the first place. Part of what students learn from degree-level study is that knowledge is contested, provisional and constructed for particular purposes. So, asking a question that can only be answered in one possible way is insufficiently difficult for a degree course.

But these questions also take us back to an epistemological issue – one that concerns what it is that historians can know about the past.

Historians can make justified, rational, evidence-based, even brilliant attempts to explain why something once happened. But of course this is a long way short of stating that they might one day arrive at the 'right' answer to a question like 'Why was there revolution in France in 1789?' Different historians will always have their preferred ways of nominating and weighting causal factors within their accounts. Some will prefer class-based explanations of revolution (the rise of the French bourgeoisie, the failure of the aristocracy to make political or economic concessions to this rising class). Others will focus on the importance of ideas (Enlightenment rationalism, modern political ideologies). Historians who like to cite economic factors as agents of change will stress the crisis in the French public finances of the late eighteenth century, caused in part by the state's regular involvement in wars. Perhaps others will interpret the revolution as being the product of interlocking contingencies – a matter of chance and chaos. Also, there is nothing in the archives, published accounts or implicit within their methodologies that tells a historian how far back they need to go in search of the long-term causes of the revolution – ten years, 50 years, a century or more?[3] In the end, a historian's choice about when to begin their explanation of why revolution occurred will always be a matter of personal preference – shaped of course by reading and rational thinking, but personalised nonetheless. This helps us to understand M.C. Lemon's argument that historians can only 'explain' something in the sense that they can 'explicate' it. By this, he means that historians can make something clear or intelligible with detailed information, usually by putting it in a sequence with other events or phenomena. But they cannot *account* for events as such.[4] Even theorists who are largely optimistic about historians' ability to explain change over time accept that no scholar can provide a wholly satisfactory account of why something happened. This is why they tell us that historians can give us only 'provisional answers', 'tentative conclusions' or 'plausible hypotheses' in relation to the past. Moreover, they say that historians' explanations have to rely on the secondary justifications of 'warranted assertability' or 'indirect confirmation', but they cannot be *proven* as such.[5]

All of this raises an obvious difficulty for history students. If working historians are unable to provide 'right' answers to questions about their specialist subjects, what are students meant to do when faced with those same questions? In *Historiography: An Introduction*, Roger Spalding and Christopher Parker offer some sensible advice on this issue. Their broad point is that there are right *ways* to answer historical questions rather than right *answers* as such. As they point out, in most cases – with the obvious exception of an extended research project – students will answer historical questions using secondary sources. The answer to the question (the essay), therefore, involves a historiographical discussion: that is, an assessment of the available historical interpretations. They advise students to identify several of the most important interpretations in the field and then to read these accounts critically. It is not enough, they advise, simply to summarise the various interpretations – 'historian *x* argued this, but historian *y* argued that'. Students need to make a judgement about the merits of the different accounts they read. This might involve reading academic reviews of the works in question (usually found in journals), and it will certainly involve thinking about the ways in which the account has made use of an evidence base (particularly primary sources) and the reasoning behind its line of argument. It will involve considering how the historian imposed a shape on their account, and what kind of perspective they brought to their work. This kind of critical reading will enable you to go beyond making a straightforward précis of how a particular collection of historians have explained or interpreted something in the past. It will put you in a position to justify why you think that certain answers to the question at hand are more persuasive (but not necessarily more 'right') than others.

What is the role of imagination in history writing?

For historians who wanted to model their work on the 'objective' natural sciences, any contention that the imagination played a role in history writing was troubling. After all, in *The Republic*, Plato in had written that imagination was inferior to – and potentially in conflict with – rationality. Nineteenth-century German historians, who were central to history's formation as an academic discipline, were similarly suspicious. As Herman Paul has described, these historians commonly made sense of their approach to academic work by invoking types of scholarly personae as guides for professional conduct. When they listed the 'virtues' that should guide the work of the scholar-historian, imagination was not among them. Instead, they typically referred to values like impartiality, honesty, accuracy, industry, patriotism and loyalty. There were disagreements about the relative weighting that should be given to each virtue on the list. Was patriotism more important than impartiality? How should one negotiate the sometimes competing demands of accuracy and loyalty? As these discussions played out, influential historians such as

Leopold von Ranke, Georg Waitz and Heinrich von Treitschke were used by different sides in the debate as exemplars of contending ways of ordering the list, and thus as embodiments of certain types of scholarly personae.[6] But what all these historians agreed upon was that their work should be described as a rigorous and evidence-based pursuit of truth.

Making concepts such as impartiality and objectivity into scholarly ideals perhaps made sense in the nineteenth and early twentieth centuries, when the historical profession itself was a largely homogenous community: bourgeois, white, 'western' and predominantly male. These scholars could at least agree about what, for them, constituted 'proper' history, what were legitimate sources and how they should write their accounts. It was this homogeneity that enabled Lord Acton to tell contributors to *The Cambridge Modern History* in 1898 that they should work with such impartiality 'that nobody can tell, without examining the list of authors, where the Bishop of Oxford laid down the pen, and whether Fairbairn or Gasquet, Liebermann or Harrison took it up'.[7] But the profession's narrow social base – and thereafter its shared understandings of what historians should study – broke apart from the 1960s onwards. Academic historians collectively became more diversified in terms of their gender, ethnic and social class identities. The number of subjects that they wrote about and the perspectives that historians brought to their writing proliferated – 'history from below', 'black' history, feminist history, post-colonial history, non-Eurocentric history and more besides. And with this proliferation of research interests, the notion that all historians should share a kind of neutral or 'centrist' space when they worked no longer made sense. Of course there were (and still are) female historians who defined themselves as 'historians who happened to be female', just as they were (and are) black historians who defined themselves as 'historians who happened to be black'. But there were also those who defined themselves as specifically *feminist* or *black* historians with their own agendas to pursue on behalf of the collectives that were so central to their sense of self. In their eyes, Lord Acton's 'impartiality' was no more than an attempt to pass off *his* own particular western, andro-centric values, agenda and world-view as universal.

It was against such a changing background in the second half of the twentieth century that Peter Novick's *That Noble Dream* demonstrated how long-standing ideas about historical objectivity were so confused that they were in effect redundant. Novick was neither 'for' nor 'against' objectivity. His argument was rather that present-day historians would be better served by abandoning the concept as a guiding aspiration in their work. 'It seems to me that to say of a work of history that it is or isn't objective is to make an *empty* observation; to say something neither interesting nor useful', he wrote.[8] David Harlan put it more starkly: 'A full-fledged theory of objectivity is about as useful to a historian as antlers would be to a duck'.[9] As older notions of historians' scholarly virtues were undermined politically (by new social movements) and epistemologically (by the linguistic turn), it was easier to make the point that literary, fictive and imaginative aspects of history writing had a long lineage. In fact, viewed against the longer tradition of history writing, nineteenth-century academic attempts to remodel the discipline along 'scientific' lines might be seen as a brief (and unsuccessful) attempt to sever historiography from its literary or rhetorical roots. For example, Herodotus's *Histories,* the multi-volumed epic narrative of the growth of the Persian Empire and the Greek states of Athens and Sparta (*c.*430–424 BCE), acknowledged the poetic influences of Homer and Hesiod in its composition.[10] Although Herodotus often used evidence in a critical manner that we would now regard as conventional, he also occasionally employed imaginative excesses in his story-telling. In Book Three of the *Histories*, for example, we read about giant ants that were 'in size smaller than dogs but larger than foxes' and 'winged serpents' which guarded the trees that produced frankincense.[11]

In Hayden White's view, the works of the nineteenth-century 'masters' of historiography – Michelet, Ranke, Tocqueville and Burckhardt – are to be revered more for their literary and artistic qualities, and for the powers of their 'constructive imagination', than for the specific explanations they offer for the 'facts'.[12] In recent times, historians have used imagined passages within their work as a device for signalling their self-awareness of the ways in which they are implicated in the creation of their historical accounts. Natalie Zemon Davis in *Society and Culture in Early Modern France: Eight Essays* (1975) and *Women on the Margins: Three Seventeenth-Century Lives* (1995) created imaginary dialogues between herself and the historical subjects of her research. Simon Schama's *Dead Certainties* (1991) provides two complementary novellas in which evidence-based and purely imagined accounts relating to the deaths of General James Wolfe in 1759 and the murder of George Parkman in 1849 are combined as a way of exploring the gap that necessarily exists between an event and its descriptions. And Jonathan Spence's *The Question of Hu* (1988) similarly blurs the conventional distinctions between history and the historical novel in its tale of how a Chinese man, John Hu, was brought to Paris in 1722 by a Jesuit missionary to help edit and translate the huge volume of Chinese texts he had acquired on his travels. Spence wrote this account as an imaginary log narrated in the present tense. The text itself is not furnished with footnotes, but there are 36 pages of notes at the end of the book that readers can use to see how and where Spence based this imagined log on primary sources.[13]

Martha Hodes also acknowledged the importance of the relationship between imagination and archival research when writing her multi-perspectival account of a New York City race riot from 1900. Her story began with an incident on 12 August 1900 (at around 2am) when a white, plain-clothes cop called Robert Thorpe was stabbed by a black man named Arthur 'Kid' Harris following an altercation over a woman, May Enoch. Thorpe died of his injuries, and the night before his funeral a crowd gathered outside the building where he had been living. Two men, one black and one white, got into a fight. With tensions already running high, this fight sparked a riot on 15 and 16 August in which 'thousands of white New Yorkers turned on black New Yorkers, and the mostly Irish American police force did not stop anybody. In fact, the police joined in with all their might'.[14] No officers were prosecuted for their role in the riot. Instead, the police were able to use their institutional power to establish a dominant story about what had happened, one which blamed Kid Harris for the riot (he was eventually sentenced to life imprisonment for the second-degree murder of Robert Thorpe). Police Commissioner President Bernard York accepted that his officers had clubbed 'many people' during the disturbances, but he said that the situation had been 'very serious' and that the use of police force had been necessary to 'restore order'.[15]

Hodes's account of this incident probes the complexities of telling the story from the victims' perspectives. The main part of her text is written in short-story format not as a conventional history. She narrates Kid Harris stabbing Robert Thorpe from the viewpoints of nine different witnesses, none of which match any other. Similarly, her account of the two-day riot uses multiple sources, including extracts from a compilation of nearly 80 statements from victims. These testimonies had been compiled by the Citizens' Protective League and were published as *Story of the Riot* a few weeks after the violence. Again, Hodes brings out the different perspectives of those involved in the events, using the headings 'the mob', 'the police', 'the victims', 'William Elliott' and 'white witnesses'. Each produce a different description of what happened. In a reflective postscript to her story, Hodes discusses her ambition to write a longer account of the New York riot. She explains: 'There are many ways to write stories, and the kind I would most like to write here is a truly multi-vocal and multi-version narrative constructed with both rigorous research and historical imagination'[16]. In saying this, Hodes was recognising that the events that took place over a few short days in New York in 1900 did not happen *as if they were a story.* In order to make those events intelligible as a narrative, Hodes had to make creative decisions about the form and content of the story she wished to tell. Archival research was a vital feature of her work, but the material in the archives by itself did not determine what story she should write. Much evidence was missing and the evidence that was available showed that there were many ways of narrating the events in question. Therefore, in order to convey the plurality of voices and points-of-view that she found in the archives, rather than create a singular story that smoothed out differences and contradictions, Hodes had to imaginatively create a form for her account that emphasised multiplicities.

Davis, Schama, Spence and Hodes each have their way of modifying some of the conventions of the genre of scholarly history writing. But all share the view that historians do not (and cannot) simply transcribe the past by applying a methodology to the extant primary sources. They each make meticulous use of primary sources, but they also acknowledge that making these sources intelligible and then selectively integrating them into an historical account is an exercise in imagination as well as inferential reasoning. Of course, the requirement that a historical account stands in relation to the sources sets boundaries on the imaginative possibilities open to the historian. But as R.G. Collingwood argued in *The Idea of History* (1946), historians ultimately exercise autonomy in the construction of their accounts. He makes the point by way of analogy: a landscape painter might think that he (*sic*) is copying nature, but in the end it is the artist and not nature that dictates what goes into the picture.[17] Collingwood was in no way stating that historians were free to say whatever they wished and still have that regarded as history. His position was that a form of truthful historical knowledge was possible, but in the sense that a historian could imagine the past as an object of thought rather than as an object of perception.[18] For Collingwood, in fact, historians could only explain the actions of a person (agent) in the past if they were able to re-enact in their own minds the thought of what that act had meant to that agent. History was therefore a form of imaginative identification with people in the past.[19] Collingwood freely acknowledged the mediating force of the historian's imagination in this procedure. But what set the historian apart from the historical novelist was that each act of the former's imagination had to be justified by valid reasons – not simply the internal coherence of the story.

Collingwood also wrote that 'all history is an attempt to understand the present by reconstructing its determining conditions'.[20] Niall Ferguson argued in *Virtual History: Alternatives and Counterfactuals* (1997) that we might imagine the present not as the only possible (pre-determined) outcome of history, but as the result of chaos or contingency. Perhaps, he wrote, the present could be thought about as being the one scenario among a set of plausible alternatives that just happened to play out in practice. We mention this mode of thinking here not because we endorse it, but because Ferguson and his contributors used it to construct imaginary alternative histories – not, they maintain, completely fanciful or speculative histories, but limited to '*those alternatives which we can show on the basis of contemporary evidence that contemporaries actually considered*' (original italics).[21] So, for example, the essays include: 'What if there had been no American Revolution?', 'What if Nazi Germany had defeated the Soviet Union?', and 'What if John F. Kennedy had lived?'.

Why do historians disagree with each other?

Pieter Geyl argued in *Napoleon: For and Against* (1949) that 'it is impossible that two historians, especially two historians living in different periods, should see any historical personality in the same light'.[22] In fact, history writing on all subjects is marked by disputes and controversies. We argue throughout this book that historical accounts are shaped more by the organising and figurative work of historians than by how the past itself once looked. The governing relationships in history writing are those between historians' perspectives, their research questions, their sources and the genre conventions that set the boundaries for how they present their writing. We expect historians to disagree with each other about how they interpret the world around them – in their attitudes to politics, private morality, social values, religion, climate change and so forth. And given that they feature so heavily in the construction of their accounts – remember Collingwood's point that the painter controls what goes on the canvas – we should expect them to disagree about how they choose to write about their subjects.

We should also acknowledge here that academic historians are professionally obliged to create disagreements with each other. Aspiring historians gain entry into the profession and build their careers by showing that they are different from others writing in the same field. The most prestigious rewards for practising historians are granted for 'original' work. 'But we already know all this' are dreaded words for historians to read or hear when they receive peer feedback on their research. There are two main ways to be original. One way is to say new things about an old subject, perhaps by citing previously unused primary sources as an evidence base, or else applying a different interpretative template to familiar material to produce an unexpected thesis. Historians sometimes make a name for themselves by overturning previously held assumptions about a historical subject. John Horne and Alan Kramer, for example, successfully challenged the belief that stories about German atrocities during the Great War were fabricated as part of the Allied propaganda campaign. In *German Atrocities, 1914: A History of Denial* (2001) their research confirmed that German troops killed thousands of Belgian and French civilians between August and October 1914.[23] A second way is to write about previously ignored subjects – such as marginalised groups, cultures regarded as peripheral or narrowly specialised topics. In either case, the historian will be expected to discuss directly how their account relates to – and differs from – previous work.

It is common to think about disagreements between historians as forming part of a progressive narrative of history writing. That is, we think about historical knowledge as being cumulative – with each generation of historians building on (and refining and correcting) the work of their predecessors.[24] In this progressive view, older historical accounts of something are seen as eventually giving way to newer and therefore improved accounts. Historians (and equally publishers) encourage us to imagine that historians' collective writings are leading towards an end-point – a more complete account of the past. In the meantime, readers of history books will be familiar with the marketing quotes that tell them how some or other of these books should be regarded as now 'definitive' or 'unlikely to be bettered'. These claims are most likely to be made on behalf of accounts based on newly available or previously unread primary sources. A simple equation is suggested: new sources equals new knowledge, equals more knowledge, equals a better account of the past. Behind this is the commonly invoked trope of the historian as a discoverer, better allowing the past through the sources to speak to us. But, in our view, it is more useful to explain historiographical disagreements without recourse to the assumption that historians are collectively becoming better at what they do. Instead, as the case study below suggests, historians disagree with each other because they bring an individual – but not unique or context-free – perspective to their work.

Case study

The American Revolution, *c.*1763–*c.*1783

Gwenda Morgan's *The Debate on the American Revolution* (2007) discusses in detail how historians have disagreed about the causes, consequences and meanings of the revolution, and about which people's experiences of the revolutionary period can be regarded as legitimate subjects to be studied. In some cases these disagreements are matters of debate between individual historians. In other cases they are interpretative disputes between historians who can be grouped into different 'schools'. In her review of the debate about the causes of the revolution, for example, Morgan examines the contending interpretations of 'imperialist' and 'progressive' historians. Imperialists such as Charles Andrews, Herbert Levi Osgood and George Beer wrote about the American colonies in the broader context of the British empire. They argued that from the late seventeenth century onwards there was an incremental increase in the political powers of colonial assemblies – in North America and elsewhere – at the expense of royal (British) authority. Thus Charles Andrews argued in *The Colonial Background of the American Revolution* (1924) that the rejection of British authority in the American colonies was a consequence of a 'silent revolution' that had transformed relations between the imperial centre and parts of the periphery in the previous hundred years. Rather than repeat familiar denunciations of British tyranny and oppression in the American colonies, imperialist historians argued that the British had devolved a substantial degree of political and economic autonomy to the colonies by the 1760s. In their mind, revolution was the final stage of a century-long journey towards full political independence.[25]

In contrast, 'progressive' historians such as Carl Becker, Arthur Schlesinger and Frederick Jackson Turner thought that the best way to understand the causes of the American Revolution was to see them as being in symmetry with the causes of the 1789 French Revolution. In short, they argued that revolution in the colonies was driven by internal conflict between social classes and various sectional interests. Revolution in this sense was a dual contest. As well as being a fight against British control in America, it was simultaneously a struggle for power between rival interest groups inside the colonies. Thus Carl Becker's *The History of Political Parties in the Province of New York, 1760–1776* (1909) described how common freeholders and unfranchised mechanics and artisans forced their way into the political arena at this time, much to the annoyance of the landowning and merchant aristocracy who had hoped to dominate politics in the wake of the British being expelled from the colonies.[26]

How might we explain these different readings of the causes of the revolution? Morgan does so by pointing to the vantage points from which the contending accounts were written. Imperialists, she states, wrote from the vantage point of Britain's political centre – Westminster and Whitehall. These histories were written through the lens (and sources) of colonisers who were confronted with the practical political challenge of maintaining control of a widely dispersed empire on limited resources. Moreover, they were largely written at a time when the United States of America was building an empire of its own, and when there were improved diplomatic ties between the USA and Britain. In such a context, histories that helped to rehabilitate the reputations of imperialism and British rule in America served contemporary (conservative) political ends. Progressives – as the label implies – wrote histories from a different perspective. These were liberals who were inspired by the values of 1789. Comparing the American and French revolutions was a way of associating liberal ideals with the very foundation of the modern United States of America. Also, progressives wrote about the American Revolution at a time when the nation was confronting the modern challenges of urbanisation, industrialisation and immigration.[27] Their reading of their present, in other words, gave them a modern conceptual framework which they could use to produce intelligible accounts of the causes of the revolution. As we have argued throughout this book, historians always write about the past from a present perspective and in service of their current needs.

There have been other attempts to account for the revolution besides those offered by imperialists and progressives. In the nineteenth century, for example, George Bancroft believed that American independence was part of a divinely ordained plan thus reflecting the religious context of much of nineteenth-century American life. In the 1960s, Bernard Bailyn used a particular set of primary sources – over 400 revolutionary pamphlets – to justify a different way of thinking about the revolution's origins. Instead of focusing on the social and economic conditions in which revolution fomented, Bailyn analysed the language in which revolutionary thinking was communicated. In particular, he was interested in how the libertarian rhetoric of early eighteenth-century English radicals re-emerged in the pamphlets of American revolutionaries. This reading of sources confirmed his 'old fashioned view' that the revolution was primarily a struggle for political and constitutional ideals rather than a competition for power between social groups.

We should note at this point that male historians who were primarily interested in male colonisers or revolutionaries wrote all the accounts discussed above. Women were at best marginal or at worst negligible figures in these histories. It was only after the 1960s – following the 'culture wars' over identities, the rise of second wave feminism, the growth of social history and an increase in numbers of female students and staff within universities – that studies of women and the American revolution began to appear. The first of these was Joan Hoff Wilson's essay 'The Illusion of Change' (1976), which argued that the revolution had been a step forwards for men but a step backwards for women. Mary Beth Norton's *Liberty's Daughters: The Revolutionary Experience of American Women 1750–1800* (1980) took a more optimistic view, arguing that revolutionary times saw the development of (some) women's political consciousness in America. Linda Kerber's *Women of the Republic* (1980) focused on the activities of the Philadelphia Female Academy and argued that in the revolution women devised a new role for themselves. This new role was 'republican motherhood', based on the service of civic virtue and the orientation of the family unit towards 'appropriate' political values.[28]

Notes

1 Hannah Arendt, 'The Concept of History, Ancient and Modern', in *Between Past and Future: Eight Exercises in Political Thought* (Harmondsworth: Penguin, 1977, first published 1954) 41–90.

2 Saul Friedländer (ed.), *Probing the Limits of Representation: Nazism and the Final Solution* (Cambridge, MA: Harvard University Press, 1992).

3 Keith Jenkins, *Re-thinking History* (London: Routledge, 1991) 62.

4 M.C. Lemon, *The Discipline of History and the History of Thought* (London: Routledge, 1995) 144–50.

5 See, for example, works by writers such as C. Behan McCullagh; Joyce Appleby, Lynn Hunt and Margaret Jacob; Stefan Berger, Heiko Feldner and Kevin Passmore.

6 Herman Paul (ed.), *How to be a Historian: Scholarly Personae in Historical Studies, 1800–2000* (Manchester: Manchester University Press) 2019.

7 (Lord) John Emerich Edward Dahlberg Acton, 'Letter to Contributors to the Cambridge History,' 12 March 1898, in *Lectures on Modern History* (London: Macmillan, 1906) 315–18.

8 *Ibid.*, 6.

9 David Harlan, *The Degradation of American History* (Chicago: University of Chicago Press, 1997) 75.

10 Marnie Hughes-Warrington, 'Herodotus' in *Fifty Key Thinkers on History* (London: Routledge, 2nd edn 2008) 172.

11 G.C. Macaulay (trans.), *The History of Herodotus: The Third Book of the Histories, Called Thaleia,* 3.102 and 3.107, http://ebooks.adelaide.edu.au/h/herodotus/h4m/index.html.

12 Hayden White, 'Historicism, History, and the Imagination,' in *Tropics of Discourse: Essays in Cultural Criticism* (Baltimore, MD: Johns Hopkins University Press, 1978) 119.

13 Jonathan D. Spence, *The Question of Hu* (London: Faber and Faber, 1989 first published 1988). See also B. Mazlish, 'The Question of *The Question of Hu*', in *History and Theory,* 31/2 (1992) 143–52. Mazlish concluded that *The Question of Hu* was neither historical narrative nor historical novel.

14 Martha Hodes, 'Knowledge and Indifference in the New York City Race Riot of 1900: An Argument in Search of a Story, *Rethinking History*, 15/1 (2011) 62.
15 Hodes, *Knowledge and Indifference*, 75–6.
16 Hodes, *Knowledge and Indifference*, 82.
17 R.G. Collingwood, *The Idea of History: With Lectures 1926–28*, 1946, ed. Jan Van Der Dussen (Oxford: Oxford University Press, revised edn 1993) 236.
18 *Ibid.*, 242.
19 Stefan Collini and Bernard Williams, 'Collingwood, Robin George (1889–1943)', *Oxford Dictionary of National Biography*, Oxford University Press, September 2004; online edn, October 2008, www.oxforddnb.com/view/article/32503, accessed 9 June 2010.
20 R.G. Collingwood, 'Lectures on the Philosophy of History (1926)', in *The Idea of History*, 420.
21 Niall Ferguson (ed.), *Virtual History: Alternatives and Counterfactuals* (London: Picador, 1997) 86.
22 Pieter Geyl, *Napoleon, For and Against*, trans. O Renier (London: Cape, 1949) 15.
23 John Horne and Alan Kramer, *German Atrocities, 1914: A History of Denial* (New Haven and London: Yale University Press, 2001).
24 Arthur Marwick, *The New Nature of History: Knowledge, Evidence, Language* (Basingstoke: Palgrave, 2001) 40, 43.
25 Charles M. Andrews, *The Colonial Background of the American Revolution: Four Essays in American Colonial History* (New Haven: Yale University Press, 1924) cited in Gwenda Morgan, *The Debate on the American Revolution* (Manchester: Manchester University Press, 2007) 51–3.
26 Carl Becker, *The History of Political Parties in the Province of New York, 1760–1776* (Madison: University of Wisconsin, 1909) cited in Morgan *Debate on the American Revolution*, 54–5.
27 Morgan, *Debate on the American Revolution*, 52–3.
28 *Ibid.*, 231–2.

Further reading

Byron Hollinshead and Theodore K. Rabb (eds), *I Wish I'd Been There: Twenty Historians Revisit Key Moments in History* (London: Macmillan, 2008). Asks scholars to choose a moment in the past that they believe they can (imaginatively) inhabit.

Tracey Loughran (ed.), *A Practical Guide to Studying History: Skills and Approaches* (London: Bloomsbury, 2017). This collection uses the idea of the 'historian's craft' to examine various ways in which historians conceptualise and carry out their research. This is combined with practical advice to students about writing their own essays and projects.

Gwenda Morgan, *The Debate on the American Revolution* (Manchester: Manchester University Press, 2007). Part of MUP's 'Issues in Historiography' series. It provides a good example of how to write a detailed historiographical review of the literature in a field. Morgan organises the analysis of texts under headings that include the pioneers, the making of the constitution, slavery, African-American resistance and the 'new era' in female history.

Peter Novick, *That Noble Dream: The 'Objectivity Question' and the American Historical Profession* (Cambridge: Cambridge University Press, 1988). Part of CUP's 'Ideas in Context' series. This is a very detailed and lengthy study of American historians and historiography, and how they relate to the rise and fall of 'objectivity' as a professional aspiration. Novick hoped to provoke historians to greater self-consciousness about their work and to outline alternative ways of thinking about what historians do.

Kalle Pihlainen, *The Work of History: Constructivism and a Politics of the Past* (Abingdon: Routledge, 2017). This is a sophisticated and challenging collection of previously published articles. Pihlainen is the best guide to the legacy of Hayden White's work on historiography and narrative constructivism, particularly its ethico-political implications.

PART III

WHOSE HISTORY?

7

The power of history

It has been argued by realist or reconstructionist historians that history, if done properly, should simply be concerned with finding out what happened. Historians should divorce themselves from any subjective, political or ideological interests that they may have, and research and write history 'for its own sake'. However, as we saw in Chapters 5 and 6 many historians now believe that it is impossible for a historian to completely remove herself from her own personal interests and concerns and the wider socio-cultural framework, theories, models, and classificatory systems she uses to make sense of, or interpret, the world. For such historians, therefore, historical narratives always reflect to some degree the ideological or political perspective of the historian. The question is not then whether a particular narrative is ideologically motivated, but rather whether it consciously acknowledges the viewpoint from which it is written and the functions it hopes to have. The argument that we study and write history for its own sake and do not use it for political, social or cultural ends is further undermined by the vast sum of money that is spent worldwide each year on providing history education in schools and universities, organising conferences and subsidising the publication of books. If history has no socio-political function, then why do governments invest all this money in it?

The link between history and politics is perhaps most clearly demonstrated by the fact that so many historians across the world have been intimately involved with the governing or administration of states and empires. We saw in Chapter 2 how in China and the Ottoman Empire government bureaucrats were employed to write histories of the state, for example Sima Qian and Mustafa Naima. Ibn Khaldun and Macaulay also had political careers, with Ibn Khaldun employed as prime minister for the Hafsid ruler and Macaulay being elected to parliament and playing a role in the Whig administration. In the later nineteenth century, with the development of nationalism and the geo-political division of territory into nation states, the political role of historians became even more pronounced, not simply with historians writing histories which contributed to the imagination and development of national identities, but also with their direct involvement in political life. In Egypt, Taha Husayn and Muhammad Rif'at Bey were not only among the founding fathers of the Egyptian historical profession, but both served as Minister of Education. In Turkey, Mehmed Fuat Köprülü, one of the Republic's leading historians, was also a member of the Turkish parliament, and the first Prime Minister of India, Jawaharlal Nehru, was a renowned historian.[1] In a British context, the Prime Minister Winston Churchill was awarded the Nobel prize for literature for his history of the Second World War and, more recently, the modern British historian Tristram Hunt was elected as Labour member of parliament for Stoke-on-Trent in the May 2010 general election. Similarly, the historian Andrew Roberts works for two centre-right think-tanks (The Centre for Policy Studies and the Centre for Social Cohesion) and was an adviser to the Conservative-Liberal Coalition government on revising the school history curriculum. In America, Bernard Lewis is a right-wing historian of early modern Islam who advised the Bush administration in America concerning its goals of regime change in south-west Asia.[2]

In this chapter we will argue that history as taught in schools and universities and as manifested in academic histories plays a crucial socio-political role. It has been, and is, used to imagine or reinforce communal identities, particularly national identities; to promote particular political or social systems; to legitimise claims to nation-state status; to facilitate or justify the expansion of empire; as a means of social control; and as a guide to morality. We will therefore take a brief look at the power that history can wield in an imperial and nationalist context, in secondary level and higher education, and in the archives.

Colonial history

Colonial and imperial states have often used history as a means of justifying their rule over their colonies and asserting a colonial identity. It is no coincidence that orientalism (the imagination of the east – or Afro-Asian societies and cultures – through academic discourse as qualitatively different from and inferior to the West) developed as an academic subject in European universities at the same time as European colonial expansion occurred. The case of British colonial writings clearly illustrates the political aspect inherent in such histories. Early British colonial histories of India were written by administrative historians employed by the East India Company and were intended to gather information on local customs and practices that could help facilitate company rule and the collection of revenue.[3] As the company grew in power and confidence, it began to justify its rule in India by arguing that it was part of a wider effort to civilise the country and people. History was used to support the idea that British rule in India was beneficial to the population, in that it brought civilisation, good government and a competent administration to a 'backward, stagnant, lethargic' country.[4] To do this it had to contrast British rule favourably with the pre-colonial Indian past, which was consequently depicted as inferior, despotic and in need of British guidance. The eighteenth-century Indologist Sir William Jones argued that ancient India had as great a civilisation as ancient Greece, but that it had declined during the time of Muslim rule in the early modern period, thus necessitating the protection and help of the British. In contrast, James Stuart Mill, who never visited India but wrote his *History of British India* (1817) solely using the East India Company archives in London, argued that Indians were, and always had been, low down on the evolutionary path and that it was British rule that had freed them from their primitive state and in doing so had brought them into history.[5] British rule would therefore 'emancipate India from its own culture'. For Mill, however, it was not Muslim governance that was to blame, but the rule of earlier Hindu states.[6]

Colonial economic historians similarly asserted, in contrast to Indian nationalist economic histories, that the economy in pre-colonial India was small, underdeveloped and lacked the substantial infrastructure needed for growth, such as good road networks. Of course they argued that the British changed all of this and not only improved the infrastructure, but also the economy, thereby 'helping' the Indians to enter the modern world.[7] Colonial history was not only taught and read in Britain, but was taught in the missionary and vernacular schools which trained Indian clerks and civil servants in India. By emphasising the exemplary achievements of the British and other Europeans, and simultaneously downplaying the achievements of Indian societies, they aimed to create a compliant population who were convinced of the benefits that British rule could bring to India.[8] In this way, British histories of India were a key aspect of cultural domination and control and had a lasting effect on the self-esteem of Indians and their identity.

This perception of India, and Asian societies in general, as stagnant, unchanging and isolated from the progressive development found in western societies was prevalent among nineteenth-century western thinkers, including Hegel, Marx and Ranke, and also continued into the twentieth century, when, in the light of increasing nationalist action, histories such as Vincent Smith's *Oxford History of India* (1919) and the six-volume *Cambridge History of India* (1922–32) became even more strident in their assumptions of Indian backwardness as they attempted to continue to justify colonial rule.[9] The view of the 'East' as stagnant and despotic is still to be found in Eurocentric histories.

Just as British historians of India stressed the backwardness of India in order to legitimise their colonial rule, Japanese scholars of Korean history similarly emphasised the inferiority and stagnation of Korean civilisation in order to legitimise the Japanese annexation of Korea in the early twentieth century. They argued that China had dominated Korea for much of its past and that it was only with Japanese rule in the fourth and seventh centuries that Korea was 'liberated' from this oppression. Shiratori Kurakichi went one stage further and developed a historical thesis that argued for the shared racial origins of the Japanese and Korean people, which was intended to further legitimise Japanese rule over Korea. This thesis of shared racial origins was later extended to include the Manchus, presaging Japan's interest in annexing Manchuria.[10]

Nationalist history

The geo-political division of territory into nation states has had a profound influence both directly and indirectly on history writing. And history writing has played a significant role in the establishment of nation states. Despite the increased professionalisation of history and the commitment of historians to scientific objectivity and the quest for truth, historians have used their supposedly neutral research techniques and practices to both justify the existence of particular nations and to help create national identities. As Eric Hobsbawm has noted: 'history is the raw material for nationalist or ethnic or fundamentalist ideologies [...] The Past is [...] perhaps the essential element, in these ideologies. If there is no suitable past, it can always be invented'.[11] History in all communities is used or abused, depending on your perspective, for nationalist purposes. Such a use can be seen in the establishment of national archives, museums and monuments, in the development of school curricula and the writing of popular and academic histories. While some authors and historians have explicitly written histories which contribute to a national cause, all historians, to some extent, find themselves influenced in terms of scope and subject matter by the nation as a means of dividing up geo-political space and by the organisation of primary sources into national state archives. The concomitant rise of modern nation-states and the professionalisation of history facilitated the development of the nation as a key framework for comprehending and understanding the past. For example, historians generally describe their field of expertise in nation-state terms: they are experts in British, Italian, German or American history, and modules offered at school and university level are typically organised around the nation: Society and Politics in Tudor England, Twentieth-Century Britain, Economy and Society in Weimar Germany, Revolutionary America and Democracy in Russia. Moreover, the notion of the modern nation-state is teleologically projected back in time in order to make manifest the forces which have (inevitably) led to its evolution. As Morris-Suzuki has noted, modern historians of all persuasions write history that essentially presents a vision of the forces that have made national society. Thus we find monographs on modern Greek history which include chapters on the Byzantine Empire, histories of Thailand since the tenth century and of the Soviet Union since Paleolithic times.[12]

At times of intense nation building, when new nations are working both to define their identity and to legitimise their existence to their own people and other nations, historians and their histories are often co-opted to help in the endeavour. Determining the longevity, integrity and uniqueness of one's national community is seen as critical for establishing a right to nation-state status. This can be expressed by demonstrating that the community in question shared a common language, religion, ethnicity or culture, and has existed as a distinct collectivity for hundreds, if not thousands, of years. Historical narratives therefore play a critical role in establishing the 'credentials' of a nation. Indeed Renan argued that a common heroic past was more important as a constituent ingredient for a nation than a common race, language or religion.[13] But nationalist histories do more than simply legitimise claims to nation status, they can also have a therapeutic and ideological function in that they help develop a shared national identity and in doing so encourage people to take pride in their nation and to develop a collective sense of self-esteem and dignity.

In order to establish the continuous existence, and development, of the nation, periods of colonial rule or occupation have to be interpreted as of limited significance and as having no influence on the cultural and ethnic integrity of the nation. Nations frequently gloss over such periods and instead look back to a time of florescence, a golden age. Thus Greek nationalist histories look back to the achievements of ancient Greece and the Byzantine Empire as evidence of the uniqueness and longevity of their 'nation', and gloss over the period of Ottoman rule during which they assert that the Greek nation lay dormant, but not forgotten.

Likewise, Indian nationalist writing developed alongside the radicalisation of Indian politics during the last years of British colonial rule. In order to confront the negative accounts of Indian society and culture, and to compete with the discourse of western superiority and dominance, nationalist historians searched their past for inspiring examples of Indian civilisation or examples of modern elements present in pre-colonial Indian society. Ancient Indian civilisations, particularly that of the Gupta Empire (320–540 CE), were often depicted as golden ages for Indian society and culture and presented as proof that Indians were capable of establishing unified, prosperous and successful states. Alternatively, some Hindu nationalists argued that contemporary Indian society was underdeveloped and impoverished, but this was not the result of a flawed Indian culture *per se,* but was rather a consequence of centuries of Islamic corruption, despotism and misrule.[14] To this extent they agreed with the narrative of British colonial Indologists such as Sir William Jones, but used their histories for a very different purpose. This approach was favoured by Hindu nationalists such as V.D. Savarkar, who was a historian and hero to the Indian Hindu right. Savarkar attempted to construct a Hindu ethnic identity for India through his sectarian, anti-colonial, Hindu nationalist history, which conceptualised a glorious Hindu past and future for India and was subsequently seen as providing a master-narrative for the new nation-state.[15] Savarkar used history not only to challenge the western stereotype of Indian passivity and to construct a Hindu nationalism, he also used the memory of the past to encourage resistance to British rule. On the fiftieth anniversary of the 1857 conflict that British historians called the Indian Mutiny, he presented an account of events entitled *The Indian War of Independence*.[16]

After Indian independence, the new governing leadership preferred to stress the multicultural rather than Hindu character of India. Therefore there was a need for histories that would not only correct the colonial narratives and record the freedom struggle against the British, but which would also unite the various different peoples of India. Jawaharlal Nehru, the first Prime Minister of India, wrote the *Discovery of India* and proposed a definition of India and Indianness that was complex, fluid and multi-layered – a fusion culture comprised of many communities which retained their distinctiveness, but who also engaged with each other.[17] This was a vision of the past that could be used to embrace the new multi-lingual, poly-ethnic, pluralistic, religiously diverse India. Historians researching and teaching within the state sector were therefore required to emphasise the 'communal harmony' of India's past.[18] This is evidenced in the selection of author chosen to write the semi-official *History of the Freedom Movement in India*. Originally R.C. Majumdar had been chosen to write it, but his draft deviated from the official government attitude of 'unity in diversity' and furthermore he argued that the idea of Hindu–Muslim fraternity was not only not in line with the available evidence, but was a politically motivated fabrication and that Hindu–Muslim conflict had in effect characterised relations between the two major religious communities in India over the past seven centuries. In contrast, Tara Chand, who actually wrote the book, foregrounded evidence which pointed to communal harmony.[19] Majumdar went on to edit *The History and Culture of the Indian People,* which, like the earlier work of Savarkar, argued that India was, and should continue to be, culturally and ethnically primarily Hindu, and that, despite the many invasions from outsiders, Hindu culture had been preserved.[20]

As we will see in Chapter 9, the past can also be articulated in non-textual ways through monuments, museums and other heritage sites. The political use of such places plays a critical role in imagining, projecting and maintaining the identity of the nation and the values deemed to be important. Joshua Arthurs explores how the Roman past has been used ideologically in a nationalist and imperialist context in the three incarnations of the Museo della Civiltà Romana (Museum of Roman Civilisation). The first archaeological exhibition was organised in 1911 to celebrate the fiftieth anniversary of Italian unification and was intended to demonstrate Italian technology, civilisation and accomplishments. It consisted of scale models, casts, photographs and reconstructions of Roman objects and monuments displayed in a series of pavilions that geographically represented the Roman Empire. The exhibition reconstructed a picture of imperial Roman society that not only demonstrated how the Romans brought civilisation to Europe, but reified the connection between the Roman Empire and modern Italy, finally reunited after centuries of conflict and foreign rule, but now ready to resume its civilising mission.[21] It presented the Roman Empire as a logical precursor to Italian liberal bourgeois internationalism, while at the same time justifying and legitimising Italian colonial exploits in North Africa.[22] In the 1930s under the Fascist government, the archaeological exhibition was resurrected and reorganised for an exhibition that would celebrate the bi-millenary of the emperor Augustus's birth. In this reincarnation, the exhibition was reorganised into three sections.

The first traced the development of Roman civilisation up until Mussolini's Italy, stressing the need for strong authoritarian leaders and constantly reinforcing the links between Augustus and Mussolini. The other two sections concentrated on public works and everyday life. The exhibition presented the Roman world as a disciplined martial state and as a 'blueprint for Fascist modernity'.[23] It also worked to legitimise Mussolini's rule by directly comparing him to the Emperor Augustus. Moreover, the state took great pains to ensure that as many people as possible visited the exhibition by advertising on film and radio and organising special package tours and discounted train fares.[24]

Museums and memorials that present a particular vision or interpretation of the past and hope for the future have similarly been used for political ends in South Africa. Flynn and King discuss how, in post-apartheid South Africa, the public commemoration of the past has been used as part of the government's policy of non-racist, inclusive, civic nation-building. Existing apartheid-era museums and monuments that celebrate white Afrikaner South Africa have been largely left untouched, but a Legacy Project has undertaken the development of new heritage sites which celebrate the history of *all* South Africans. The two Afrikaner monuments that Flynn and King discuss are the bronze ox-wagon laager on the Ncome River, which celebrates the Afrikaner victory over the Zulus in 1838 at the Battle of Blood River, and the Voortrekker Monument overlooking central Pretoria, which celebrates white Afrikaner subjugation of the interior. Both monuments are the focus of pilgrimages and celebrations by white Afrikaners. However, a new Zulu museum opposite the ox-wagon laager has recently been built which pays tribute to the Zulus who died during the battle, and in Pretoria work has begun on the development of Freedom Park. This park is on a neighbouring hill to the Voortrekker monument, and crucially, when viewing the memorial in Freedom Park, one's back is towards the Voortrekker monument, thereby physically symbolising its representation of a divided past whereas the Freedom memorial symbolises a united, inclusive future.[25] Thus, these two new monuments, without erasing the colonial era, act as a counterpoint to a narration of a solely white Afrikaner past.

The history curriculum – who decides what is taught and why?

> The great thing is that you don't need to teach patriotism. All you need to do is teach a completely objective, accurate account and the outcome is naturally patriotic because it is such a great story.
>
> Andrew Roberts[26]

> *The bankruptcy of history teaching in our schools has become a national danger .... A people who loses its memory, loses its identity.*
> Francois Mitterand[27]

Who should decide the history curriculum: the government, historians, schools, parents, examination boards? Whose views and values will it foreground? Should history taught in schools stress national endeavour, solidarity and achievements? Should it acknowledge the negative as well as positive aspects of a nation's past? Or should it be a neutral enquiry into the past for its own sake? Is an 'objective, accurate account' of a nation's past naturally patriotic as Roberts's claims?

As the above quote by former French President Francois Mitterand implies, the history taught in schools plays an integral part in the dissemination and reinforcement of national identities. It provides students with a sense of self, an idea of where they came from and of the values of their nation. This is most obviously evidenced by the fact that the history curriculum of a country focuses almost exclusively on the history of that state. Thus the history taught in the UK focuses on the Tudors, the Victorian Age and Britain's role in the two World Wars. History in US schools looks at the colonisation of America by Europeans, the War of Independence, the Civil War and the civil rights movement. School textbooks and curricula provide further evidence as to how nation-states project themselves to their citizens. The post-1974 Greek history curriculum states that there are three objectives to the teaching of history at the level of secondary education: it should cultivate national sentiments and democratic ideas; it should facilitate the acquisition of historical knowledge and techniques; and it should promote the Greek nation's historical continuity and its role in the development of global civilisation. The post-1985 Turkish history curriculum is very similar in its goals, and aims to inform Turkish school-children of the place of the Turkish nation in world history and the contribution that Turks have made to humanity and world civilisation; to strengthen national feelings; to foster an appreciation of the distinctiveness and aptitude of the Turkish nation; and to nourish the values of national independence and democracy.[28]

Key therefore among the aims in teaching history to Greek and Turkish school-children is a desire to promote a sense of national identity and pride. Moreover, it can also be argued that both education systems are using history education as a means of legitimising Greek and Turkish claims to national status. By emphasising the longevity of both cultures, the contribution that they have made to the world, and stressing the importance of democracy, they are in effect presenting an argument for their status as natural nation-states. These aims are reinforced by the subjects covered in the curriculum. History teaching in Greece stresses the longevity of the Greek 'nation' beginning with ancient Greece, continuing through the Byzantine Empire, glossing over the period of Ottoman rule and culminating with the modern Greek nation-state. The emphasis on the role that ancient Greece played in the foundation of a wider European culture also re-situates Greek national identity firmly in Europe. The period of Ottoman rule is given proportionally less space and is depicted as a negative period in the history of Greece. The Ottoman Turks are depicted as uniformly aggressive towards Greeks, first destroying their empire and occupying 'their' land, and then stealing their children, all of which ultimately led to the temporary alienation of Greece from the path of western European development and thus its underdevelopment. This narrative of [Ottoman] Turkish aggression is continued into the present day, culminating in the 1974 Turkish invasion of Cyprus.[29] Through all this the Greeks are presented as resisting Ottoman rule and ensuring that their ethno-cultural identity remained intact.

Similarly, in France the teaching of French history is explicitly acknowledged as a fundamental means by which Frenchness is transmitted. It is a primary means of acquiring ideological integration and social order, instilling a love of the institutions and values of the Republic and cultivating a shared sense of belonging in students.[30] Since the 1890s, school textbooks have, by foregrounding the lives of French heroes, achievements and culture, articulated a vision of France as unified, indestructible, enduring, unique and exemplary.

James W Loewen has argued that American history textbooks similarly present mythologised and ideologically distorted depictions of American history.[31] In a study of 12 American history textbooks he concludes that most of them depict an American past as being one full of challenges and difficulties that Americans heroically overcame in order to build a great and promising nation of unity which should make contemporary Americans proud and give them hope for the future. The titles of these textbooks exemplify this meta-narrative: *The American Adventure; Life and Liberty; The Challenge of Freedom; Triumph of the American Nation;* and *Land of Promise.*[32] However, Loewen argues that non-white American students do not seem to feel included in this patriotic vision of the past because they view history classes with a special dislike and comparatively do far worse in them than in other subjects.[33] This may be because much American history in textbooks is narrated from a white American perspective, and non-white (particularly black) Americans are frequently depicted as helpless or primitive and their voices are silenced by the exclusion of relevant primary sources.[34] Similarly, while history textbooks do discuss the brutality of black slavery in the United States, they minimise white complicity in it, presenting it as a national tragedy that was finally overcome, rather than as a moral wrong.[35] Moreover, they tend to ignore (or not discuss at any length) the racism that was behind both black slavery and the rampant discrimination against non-white Americans that still continues today. This depiction of slavery also contributes to the depiction of US history as one of continual progress and advancement: there used to be slavery and lynchings, but now there aren't.[36] This, Loewen argues, is part of a general trend to erase or gloss over anything bad in America's past, in favour of a focus on American 'heroes', who are portrayed in an exclusively positive light. For example, half of the textbooks omit to mention that Jefferson owned slaves, and those that do stress that he believed it to be wrong. As such, US textbooks ignore the fact that Jefferson was an advocate of the expansion of slavery into the western territory, that he owned 267 slaves, whom he treated inhumanely, and that he only freed eight of his slaves, who were all blood relatives.[37]

We could equally cite other similar ways in which textbooks discuss aspects of US history – most obviously the Vietnam War.[38] The point is that a self-congratulatory depiction of American history creates an impression among American students that their country is the home of human rights and democratic values, and that over the past few centuries Americans have continuously striven to make their nation and the world a better place, something that they are still continuing to do in the present day. Such a depiction of American history is ideological and politically motivated. It is, in Loewen's words, simply ethnocentric cheerleading, designed to make Americans feel good about themselves and their government and its actions. The emphasis on the continual progress of the nation as an explanatory frame for understanding American history has a number of political consequences. It stifles criticism of institutions and practices and it tends to reinforce the status quo. After all, if America is seen as having been a beacon in the past for social and economic progress, and as the champion of freedom, democracy, tolerance and diversity, then why question its authority in the present? History in this sense functions as a force for conservatism. These textbooks are essentially 'handbooks for acquiescence'.[39]

Although Loewen wrote his book in the 1990s, the politicisation of American history teaching in schools continues. A recent example of this is the controversy surrounding the Texas Board of Education's vote to make a number of key amendments to the history curriculum, ostensibly with the intention of correcting the liberal bias thought to exist in the American education system. The amendments reflected a right-wing, religious bias and stipulated that the Founding Fathers' commitment to Christian values should be stressed, while their dedication to the separation of church and state should be questioned; that the new secular dating system of BCE and CE should not be introduced; that the superiority of American capitalism should be emphasised; and Republican policies should be presented in a more favourable light. The board, which is made up of 15 elected officials, ten of whom are Republicans and five are Democrats, voted along party lines and passed the amendments.[40]

History education in the UK is not free from such political or ideological elements either. In 1988, Kenneth Baker, the then Secretary of State for Education, argued that school pupils should be taught about 'the spread of Britain's influence for good throughout the world'.[41] This understanding of history education as a means of instilling national pride was echoed by the Conservative Shadow Minister for Education, Michael Gove, in 2009, when he argued that 'there is no better way of building a modern, inclusive, patriotism than by teaching all British citizens to take pride in this country's historic achievements'.[42] He developed this theme in interviews leading up to the 2010 general election, arguing that school history lessons should focus on Britain's achievements – particularly those of the British Empire – and that 'guilt about Britain's past is misplaced'.[43] As Secretary of State for Education in the 2010 Conservative-Liberal Coalition government Gove continued to make similar statements. Most recently, during a discussion at the Hay Festival, he praised and offered a job redesigning the history curriculum to right-wing historian Niall Ferguson. Ferguson, who is the author of a controversial pro-imperial history of the British Empire entitled *Empire: How Britain Made the Modern World,* has plans to develop a four-year history syllabus on the 'rise of western domination of the world' which is '*the*' story of the past 500 years.[44] On his website, Gove praises Ferguson for taking 'a degree of pride in his country' and for his 'balanced approach' to the British Empire, in contrast to many other historians who want 'to put Britain in the dock for its past actions'.[45] While Ferguson does at times note in passing some of the negative aspects of British imperialism, his book, as the title suggests, essentially celebrates the British Empire. Ferguson argues that the economic and civilisational improvements that the empire achieved – such as the triumph of capitalism, the internationalisation of the English language, the influence of Protestantism, the Anglicisation of North America and Australasia and the spread of parliamentary institutions – outweigh the negative aspects of slavery, genocide and colonial occupation.[46] Ferguson's history is a Eurocentric, teleological, celebratory model that conveniently devalues the contribution that other states and peoples have made to the modern world. It is therefore ideological, like all other histories. Its particular ideology reflects a politically right-wing, pro-capitalist, free-market perspective, which makes its appeal to Conservative politicians understandable. Not everyone, however, believes that the function of history education should be to uncritically celebrate a nation's history. Some argue instead that it should encourage students to question and engage with their own and others' pasts in a thoughtful manner – as can be seen from the lively debate that Gove and Ferguson's interaction ignited in the columns and letters page of various newspapers.[47]

The power of the professional historian

> *It seems rather obvious that, seen in a wider cultural and 'historical' perspective, multi-million pound institutional investments such as our national universities are integral to the reproduction of the ongoing social formation and are thus at the forefront of cultural guardianship (academic standards) and ideological control; it would be somewhat careless if they were not.*
>
> Keith Jenkins[48]

As the quote by Jenkins suggests, despite historians' protestations that they are above the ideological fray and are writing objective history for its own sake, the history written and taught in a university context is just as politicised as that taught in schools. Jenkins goes so far as to argue that professional histories can be understood as expressions of how the dominant ideologies currently articulate history 'academically'.[49] Just as school curricula reflect the dominance of the nation-state, so too does the work of professional historians. This can manifest itself indirectly in the choice of research topics and sources, or in the explanatory frameworks and assumptions used to interpret the evidence. Alternatively, it can be seen as a more overt commitment to a nationalist narrative.

Geza Dávid, Pal Fodor, Klara Hegyi and Lajos Fekete are respected Hungarian historians of the Ottoman–Habsburg borderlands in sixteenth- and seventeenth-century Ottoman Hungary who are known for their thoughtful, well-researched articles and books. However, while in theory they acknowledge that borders are places of interaction, acculturation, migration and technological and cultural transmission, they deny that this was the case along the Hungarian-Ottoman–Habsburg borderlands. Instead, they claim that there was no long-lasting interaction between the Hungarian civilian population and the Ottomans; Ottoman rule amounted to nothing more than a military occupation and Hungarian society and culture remained intact and unpolluted by the Ottoman invasion. Furthermore, they argue that Christians who converted to Islam or who worked for the Ottoman military-administrative structure were not 'proper' Hungarians, but were Slavs. This insistence on the cultural, ethnic and religious preservation of a pre-Ottoman Hungarian community through the entire period of Ottoman rule, despite evidence of a degree of interaction and acculturation between the communities, could be interpreted as being a response to the power of the nation-state paradigm which encourages historians to stress the longevity and cohesiveness as well as the achievements of 'nations'. Such a depiction of the past helps create and maintain a sense of Hungarian-ness and also validates the relatively recent Hungarian nation-state.[50] Hungarian scholars are not alone in narrating the past from a present nation-state perspective. Such cultural chauvinism is apparent in Braudel's very nationalistic and conservative *The Identity of France*, which claims that French borders have not changed significantly since the thirteenth century and that French blood has not been diluted since prehistory, thus providing geographical and racial evidence of a continuous French identity.[51] It is also evident in Niall Ferguson's narration of the 'superior' achievements of Britain and her apparently incomparable contribution to the making of the modern world.

The political paradigm of the nation-state is so ubiquitous, and so rarely explicitly interrogated, that it is able to influence our constructions of the past in very subtle (and in some much less subtle) ways. Examples of the less subtle ways include a number of university press-published histories of South-West Asia in the early twentieth century, which aim either to exonerate western imperialism in that region or to justify Zionist territorial claims. Charles D. Smith cites the example of Bernard Lewis's *What Went Wrong: Western Impact and Middle Eastern Response* as an example of an account that exonerates western imperialism for the political and economic problems faced in the Arab world today.[52] Smith also discusses the work of Isaiah Friedman and Elie Kedourie. Both writers, he argues, misrepresent sources in order to support their claims that the British in no way misled the Arabs about their prospects of independence after the First World War, and that furthermore, because the Arabs agreed to the principles of Zionism at that time, they therefore have no historical basis for challenging it now. Such scholarship is intended to legitimise Zionism while simultaneously delegitimising Arab (and particularly Palestinian) national claims, and is common not only in Israel but also in America (see, for example, the work of David Fromkin and Efraim Karsh).[53] Ann Curthoys has similarly demonstrated how a conservative Australian academic Keith Windschuttle has selectively interpreted sources to construct a version of the past that draws into question the genocidal practices of the 'white' Australian state against its First Nations people and posits European colonisation as an example of morally justified human progress.[54] Such 'denialist' accounts therefore become a political resource for undermining indigenous populations' claims for reparations for past injustices at the hands of the colonisers. Moreover, they also help maintain a particular Anglo-centric form of Australian nationalism which has no place for genocidal impulses in its narrative of identity. Dirk Moses has noted that the genocide debate in Australia also has a political dimension and constitutes part of its 'culture wars', with a collective of conservative, right-wing politicians, media pundits and academics believing that these claims of genocide are being enflamed and exaggerated by left-liberal intellectuals keen to establish or reinforce their own cultural hegemony.[55]

The power of the archive

Archives are very powerful institutions. Rather than transparently making accessible traces of the past for historians to study and analyse, by virtue of their selective process in acquiring, collating and maintaining documents they play a significant role in determining what can and cannot be written. Only traces from the past deemed legitimate, or of value by the bureaucratic administration that established the archive in the first place, will find a place in the archive.[56] Moreover, further interpretative filtering occurs when private individuals or institutions donate material to archives, as they often select the letters and documents that best represent their interests and agendas. Similarly, sensitive or classified government material might be kept closed for up to 30 years and some documents related to defence, security or foreign relations may remain closed indefinitely.

State archives, libraries and museums often have specific political agendas and in particular work to articulate the identity of the state and nation and to preserve and project particular memories. They are often housed in imposing buildings, located centrally and near to other architectural projections of state power. A national story can be implicitly suggested by the ways in which particular documents, individuals or topics are prioritised within an archive. Tony Ballantyne describes how the national archive in New Zealand consciously promotes the state ideology of biculturalism: a policy that imagines New Zealand as containing two distinct populations who have essentially harmoniously co-existed since the Treaty of Waitangi in 1840. Biculturalism functions as a framework for narrating the state's history, and the architecture of the national archives as well as their layout reflects this – signage is in both languages and artwork represents both cultures. The organisation of documents in the archive also reflects this biculturalism, and sub-collections of documents that do not easily fit into this framework are distributed in a rather chaotic fashion around the library.[57] As Ballantyne argues, although the National Library does not preclude heterodox readings of the material held there, 'it does provide a series of powerful ideological statements about the kind of visions of the nation and its past that library users should produce'.[58]

To further complicate matters, archives and guides to archival material are often organised in ways that direct researchers to particular material or which encourage the formulation of particular questions. Jeff Sahadeo describes how the Soviet-era published guides for the Central State Archive of the Republic of Uzbekistan promoted a particular vision of politics and society through their categorisation of documents. The division of the guides and the archive itself into historical and revolutionary sections makes locating continuities across regimes difficult, and thus further directs the type of history that can be (manageably) written. Published guides also do not necessarily mention all available or relevant sources – for example, the above-mentioned guide to the Uzbek archives excludes a significant amount of the archive's holdings.[59]

More problematically, some states restrict access to documents that deal with sensitive issues or exclude certain people from accessing them on a variety of grounds. Craig Robertson, in an article describing his work in the National Archives and Records Administration in the USA, mentions that he was denied access to documents relating to the development of the passport in the USA through a combination of bureaucratic entanglements, respect for personal privacy and national security considerations, and the personal power of the man responsible for the documents who had already written a history on the subject himself.

The sympathies and interests of archival staff to a particular project can further facilitate or hinder a researcher's access to documents, either formally or informally. If the topic seems to be counter to nationally acceptable narratives then staff may not directly hinder access or exert active censorship (although in some countries they do), but they may be less willing to search out or to suggest documents that could facilitate the project. For example, Durba Ghosh recounts how archival staff in India tried to control and mediate her work in the archives and were particularly resistant to her investigation into the extent of personal and sexual relations between British men and local women in India. The dominant national narrative in India currently argues that such miscegenation did not occur and when British men did form sexual relations with local women it was with Muslim rather than Hindu women: Hindu culture is therefore seen to be preserved from contamination by the 'occupying' power. In contrast, evidence of sexual interaction between British men and Indian women serves a positive role within the framework of the postcolonial agenda in Britain. As Ghosh argues, it enables racial tensions to be overwritten by narratives of familial sentiment and thus presents the colonial encounter in a far more positive light.[60] To this extent she found the archival staff in the UK to be far more helpful. Ghosh also notes that primary sources can reflect the political agendas of their authors and subsequent historians or archivists. For example, it is extremely hard to find any evidence of native Indian women in eighteenth-century British colonial documents because they were either renamed or left out of baptismal records, a practice that continued into the twentieth century, when the names of mixed race children in baptismal and marriage records were omitted when these primary sources were published in the academic journal *Bengal Past and Present*.[61]

Lastly, communities, nations or peoples without states also lack the infrastructure that can facilitate the writing of their history. The Palestinian state lacks official museums and archives within which documentary evidence could be stored, kept safe and made available to historians. In order to write the history of the 1948 war between Palestine and Israel, the ethnic dislocation of Palestinians from their homes and the subsequent obliteration of their villages, historians have generally had to rely upon the archives of the Israeli state and the Israeli Defence Force, which, despite the claims of some historians, are not ideologically and empirically impartial, but instead reflect the perspectives and broader political aims of the Israeli state. For example, Palestinian villages physically destroyed in the conflict have subsequently been textually erased from official Israeli maps so there is therefore very little documentary evidence of their existence. Moreover, where documentary evidence does exist that could be used to tell the story of the *Nakba* ('catastrophe') – the 1948 expulsion of Palestinians from their homes – from a Palestinian perspective, it generally reflects the voices of the male elite. In the 1940s, 66 per cent of the Palestinian population were agrarian peasants, with a literacy rate of about 15 per cent. The majority therefore were not in a position to document their experiences or view of the war. One means to overcome this archival bias is to utilise oral testimony from Palestinians. For example, Walid Kahlidi's *All That Remains* is an encyclopedic work which aims to recover and document memories of inhabitants of more than 400 Palestinian villages that were destroyed or depopulated in the 1948 Arab–Israeli war. Because there is very little material or textual evidence attesting to the previous existence of these villages, Khalidi and his team of researchers relied upon the oral testimony of former residents and local guides as well as other Arab and western sources, in order to compile an economic, topographical, architectural, social and cultural picture of each village.[62]

The myth of history for its own sake

Following Jenkins, we should perhaps not waste time trying to prove that history can be objective, neutral and is written for its own sake, but instead inquire of individual histories who it is written for and why.[63] The dominated and the dominant will both have different histories of an event, histories that legitimise their actions and practices, and that reinforce their identities.[64] Histories will therefore always be contested. The histories we write and the histories we approve of generally reflect our broad political or ideological positions. While histories can obviously be more or less politically motivated, those who argue that some academic histories are neutral and objective, whereas others are politically motivated and biased, are being rather disingenuous. It is too easy to dismiss opposing views to our own as biased or ideological, and to mistake those viewpoints that we happen to share as being universal, 'common sense' and objective. As we have seen in this chapter, history is, and always has been, used for political and ideological purposes. As historians, we need to be honest and open about our use and interpretation of sources. But we also need to be explicit about our own biases, presumptions and viewpoints, and about the interpretative models we employ and the reasons why we use them.

All history writing relates to questions of power. A historical account written by a professional historian and published by a reputable press conveys a veneer of authority and legitimisation on the people or event described and the viewpoint from which it is narrated. Some subjects and theoretical approaches are still considered to be more appropriate than others for historians. While it is not true to say that all history reflects the dominant discourses of a society or that it represents the concerns and interests of the elite, it is probably reasonable to claim that much of the history taught in schools does to some extent reflect these discourses and serves to reinforce the views of those in positions of power. Jenkins has noted that in schools, and also to a large extent in universities, we do not see a black, Marxist, feminist perspective in subject matter and methodological approach in the teaching of history. This is not because such an approach is any more biased or subjective than standard traditional, reconstructive history, but rather that those who tend to write such history are not generally in positions of power and so cannot significantly influence curricula.[65]

Similarly, Dening has pointed out that it is only now, at the beginning of the twenty-first century, that the study of indigenous people from their perspective, using their sources and featuring their voices, has begun to be accepted as legitimate and interesting – both within the academy and the wider public sphere. But he argues that a massacre of FIrst Nations people defending their land is still not accorded the same *gravitas* or historical significance as an armed rising of miners against what they perceived to be unjust taxation.[66] In the next chapter we will look in more detail at how and why historians have gradually started to write the histories of those traditionally excluded from the dominant western historical narrative, and the impact this has for our discussions about histories, ideologies and identities.

Notes

1 Georg G. Iggers, Q. Edward Wang and Supriya Mukherjee, *A Global History of Modern Historiography* (Harlow: Pearson, Longman, 2008) 204, 237.

2 Charles D. Smith, 'Historiography of World War I', in Israel Gershoni, Amy Singer, and Y. Hakan Erdem (eds), *Middle East Historiographies: Narrating the Twentieth Century* (Seattle: University of Washington Press, 2006) 41.

3 Iggers, Wang and Mukherjee, *A Global History* 99.

4 Q Edward Wang, 'Cross-Cultural Developments of Modern Historiography: Examples from East Asia, the Middle East, and India', in Q Edward Wang and Franz L. Fillafer (eds), *The Many Faces of Clio: Cross-cultural Approaches to Historiography, Essays in Honor of Georg G. Iggers* (New York: Berghahn Books, 2007) 2001.

5 *Ibid.*, 103, 39–40.

6 Michael Gottlob (ed.), *Historical Thinking in South Asia: A Handbook of Sources from Colonial Times to the Present* (Oxford: Oxford University Press, 2003) 7–8.

7 *Ibid.*, 233.

8 *Ibid.*, 101.

9 *Ibid.*, 232.

10 *Ibid.*, 218 and 221.

11 Eric Hobsbawm, *On History* (London: Abacus, 1998) 6.

12 Tessa Morris-Suzuki, 'The Frontiers of Japanese Identity', in Stein Tonneson and Hans Antlöv (eds), *Asian Forms of the Nation* (Richmond, 1996) 41–66, 42 quoted in Daniel Woolf, 'Of Nations, Nationalism and National Identity: Reflections on the Historiographic Organization of the Past', in Wang and Fillafer (eds), *The Many Faces of Clio,* 71–103, 74.
13 E Renan, 'What is a Nation?', in Homi Bhabbu (ed.) *Nation and Narration* (London: Routledge, 1990), 19 cited in Umit Özkirimli, *Theories of Nationalism: A Critical Introduction* (Basingstoke: Palgrave, 2000) 35.
14 Iggers, Wang and Mukherjee, *A Global History,* 232 and Wang, 'Cross-Cultural Developments of Modern Historiography', 203.
15 Iggers et al., *Global History* 231.
16 Gottlob (ed.), *Historical Thinking* 34.
17 *Ibid.,* 238.
18 Gottlob (ed.), *Historical Thinking* 69–70.
19 *Ibid.,* 69–70.
20 *Ibid.,* 240.
21 Joshua W. Arthurs, '(Re)presenting Roman History in Italy, 1911–1955', in Claire Norton (ed.), *Nationalism, Historiography and the (Re)construction of the Past* (Washington: New Academia Publishing, 2007) 32–3.
22 *Ibid.,* 39.
23 *Ibid.,* 39.
24 *Ibid.,* 36–7.
25 M.K. Flynn and Tony King, 'Renovating the Public Past: Nation-building, Symbolic Reparation and the Politics of Heritage in Post-Apartheid South Africa', in Norton (ed.), *Nationalism* 45–60.
26 Andrew Roberts quoted in *The Independent,* 4 October 2008 www.independent.co.uk/news/education/schools/how-should-we-teach-british-history-950804.html accessed 2 July 2010.
27 Mitterand quoted in Jean-François Fayard, *Des enfants sans histoire* (Paris, 1984), 9, quoted in Ann-Louise Shapiro, 'Fixing History: Narratives of World War I in France', in *History and Theory: Studies in the Philosophy of History,* Theme Issue 36, 'Producing the Past: Making Histories Inside and Outside the Academy' 112.
28 Vasilia Lilian Antoniou and Yasemin Nuhoglu Soysal, 'Nation and the Other in Greek and Turkish History Textbooks', in Hanna Schissler and Yasemin Nuhoglu Soysal (eds), *The Nation, Europe, and the World: Textbooks and Curricula in Transition* (New York: Berghahn Books, 2005) 108–9.
29 *Ibid.,* 115–6.
30 Shapiro, 'Fixing History', 115.
31 James W. Loewen, *Lies My Teacher Told Me: Everything Your American History Textbook got Wrong* (New York: Simon and Schuster, 1995).
32 *Ibid.,* appendix, not paginated.

33 *Ibid.*, 12.

34 *Ibid.*, 157, 168, 301–2.

35 *Ibid.*,

36 *Ibid.*, 169. See also chapter ten for a longer discussion of the archetype of progress.

37 *Ibid.*, 147–8

38 *Ibid.*, 244–9.

39 *Ibid.*, 258 and 216.

40 See Texas Board of Education website with minutes of meetings and details of board members www.tea.state.tx.us/index3.aspx?id=1156 accessed 27 July 2010; *New York Times*, www.nytimes.com/2010/03/13/education/13texas.html accessed 27 July 2010; and *The Guardian*, www.guardian.co.uk/world/2010/may/16/texas-schools-rewrites-us-history accessed 27 July 2010.

41 Quoted in Aldrich (ed.), *National Curriculum* 95, and again by Beverley Southgate *History: What and Why? Ancient, Modern, and Postmodern Perspectives* (London: Routledge, 1996) 53.

42 Quoted in *Evening Standard,* 7 October 2009 http://waugh.standard.co.uk/2009/10/michael-goves-history-list.html accessed 2 July 2010.

43 Quoted in *The Times,* 6 March 2010 www.timesonline.co.uk/tol/news/politics/article7052010.ece accessed 2 July 2010.

44 *The Guardian,* 30 May 2010 www.guardian.co.uk/politics/2010/may/30/niall-ferguson-school-curriculum-role accessed 2 July 2010.

45 www.michaelgove.com/content/theres-only-one-fergie-history-game accessed 2 July 2010.

46 Niall Ferguson, *Empire: How Britain Made the Modern World* (London: Penguin, 2004, first published by Allen Lane in 2003) xxvii.

47 For examples of the debate Gove and Ferguson's conversation engendered see www.newstatesman.com/blogs/the-staggers/2010/06/history-british-ferguson, www.guardian.co.uk/commentisfree/2010/jun/10/british-empire-michael-gove-history-teaching and www.guardian.co.uk/books/2010/jun/12/facts-and-figures-of-empire.

48 Keith Jenkins, *Re-thinking History* (London: Routledge Classics 2003, first published in 1991) 25.

49 *Ibid.*

50 Claire Norton, 'Narrating the "Yoke of Oppression": Twentieth Century Hungarian Scholarship of the Ottoman-Hungarian Borderlands', in Claire Norton (ed.), *Nationalism, Historiography and the (Re)construction of the Past* (Washington: New Academia Publishing, 2007) 187–200

51 Richard J. Evans, *In Defence of History* (London: Granta Books, 1997) 192–4.

52 Smith, 'Historiography' 40–1.

53 *Ibid.*, 43.

54 Ann Curthoys, 'The History of Killing and the Killing of History', in Antoinette Burton (ed.), *Archive Stories: Facts, Fictions, and the Writing of History*

(Durham: Duke University Press, 2005) 367. See also the articles in the special edition of the journal *Aboriginal History* 21 (2001). We thank Dan Stone for making us aware of this special edition.

55 A. Dirk Moses, 'Coming to Terms with Genocidal Pasts in Comparative Perspective: Germany and Australia', in *Aboriginal History* 21 (2001) 91–115, 92.

56 Ann Curthoys, 'The History of Killing' 363, notes the supposed destruction of the papers of the first lieutenant governor of Van Diemen's Land by two leading officers of the government. Southgate also comments that the Nazis eliminated records with regard to their killing of the Jews and others, as did those involved with the bureaucracy of slavery. Beverley Southgate, *History Meets Fiction* (Harlow: Longman, 2009) 191.

57 Tony Ballantyne, 'Mr Peal's Archive: Mobility and Exchange in Histories of Empire', in Burton (ed.) *Archive Stories* 87–110, 89–90.

58 *Ibid.*, 102–3.

59 Jeff Sahadeo, '"Without the Past There is No Future": Archives, History, and Authority in Uzbekistan', in Burton (ed.) *Archive Stories* 55.

60 Durba Ghosh, 'National Narratives and the Politics of Miscegenation', in Burton (ed.) *Archive Stories* 31.

61 *Ibid.*, 34

62 Walid Khalidi, *All That Remains: The Palestinian Villages Occupied and Depopulated by Israel in 1948* (Beirut: Institute for Palestine Studies, 1992) quoted in Nur Masalha, *The Palestine Nakba: Decolonising History and Reclaiming Memory* (London: Zed Books, 2011) chapter four 'Palestinian Oral History and Indigenous Memory: The Historian's Methodology'. We thank the author for allowing us to read a draft copy of this chapter.

63 Jenkins, *Re-thinking History* 22.

64 *Ibid.*, 21.

65 *Ibid.*, 20.

66 Greg Dening, 'Performing Cross-culturally' in Jenkins et al. (eds), *Manifestos for History* (London: Routledge, 2007) 99.

Further reading

Antoinette Burton (ed.), *Archive Stories: Facts, Fictions, and the Writing of History* (Durham and London: Duke University Press, 2005). Contains a range of personalised reflections from scholars about their experiences of working in archives. The testimonies collected are a useful reminder that, while archives remain central to historians' work, they are anything but neutral repositories of information.

Georg G. Iggers and Q. Edward Wang, with contributions from Supriya Mukherjee, *A Global History of Modern Historiography* (Harlow: Pearson, Longman, 2008) An insightful and very detailed exploration of Afro-Asian historiography.

James W. Loewen, *Lies My Teacher Told Me: Everything Your American History Textbook got Wrong* (New York: Simon and Schuster, 1995). A critical examination of US history textbooks.

Claire Norton (ed.), *Nationalism, Historiography and the (Re)construction of the Past* (Washington: New Academia Publishing, 2007). An edited collection of essays that examine the myriad ways in which nationalism has impinged on the narration of the past.

Q Edward Wang and Franz L. Fillafer (eds), *The Many Faces of Clio: Cross-cultural Approaches to Historiography, Essays in Honor of Georg G. Iggers* (New York: Berghahn Books, 2007). A collection of essays taking a comparative approach to the study of historiography.

8

Histories from another perspective

Introduction

In this book we have argued that many historians currently understand history writing to be a situated, perspectival practice unavoidably influenced or affected by the assumptions of the author, their preferred theoretical models and the wider socio-political context in which they conduct their research and write their books. In the last chapter we discussed how, despite historians' claims to objectivity and neutrality, history teaching and writing is an inextricably political or ideological undertaking. History is never studied for its own sake, consciously or unconsciously it is always written with a particular objective in mind. Many, if not most, historians do not explicitly discuss or acknowledge the ideological dimension of their work. Indeed, as Said notes, 'the adjective "political" is used as a label to discredit any work for daring to violate the protocol of pretended suprapolitical objectivity'.[1] However, in recent years this has begun to change. Some historians, understanding the transformative power inherent in historical narratives, have begun not only explicitly to acknowledge the perspective from which they are writing, but also to write histories that are intended to have practical political effects. In particular, they seek to make the silent voices of dispossessed, marginalised, subaltern peoples heard. This chapter will explore how non-Eurocentric, postcolonial, feminist, queer and black historians have challenged the traditionally very white, andro-centric character of modern academic historical writing and what this means for the history profession.

As we saw in Chapter 7, Niall Ferguson's *Empire: How Britain Made the Modern World* depicts the past 500 years as one of predominantly white European male agency: as the title suggests, he argues that it was essentially Britain that was responsible for making the modern world. In this manner he erases the contributions, challenges and actions of the majority of the world: he writes them out of history. Such a Eurocentric view is relatively common in historical discourse. Landes and Jones, in their histories of the 'the rise of the West', similarly foreground the activities and achievements of Europeans, while ignoring or denigrating the contribution made by Afro-Asians and other non-European peoples.[2] Such histories are teleological, that is, they assume there is an end-point to history which provides meaning for all that happened before. Eurocentric histories are teleological because they assert that the inevitable end-point of historical development is the domination of the West and its culture, systems of governance and economic practices. The past becomes the story of the inevitable progress of western civilisation (progressive and nationalistic histories are nearly always teleological). Moreover, such histories explain what they consider to be the advance of European culture in terms of permanent and unique cultural or geographical advantages which led them to be in some ways superior to other peoples and cultures. They interpret the West and East as two distinct separate entities: westerners or Europeans are depicted as dynamic, curious about the world, interested in commerce, motivated by a desire to gain control over raw materials and trade routes, as developing sophisticated governmental and economic practices and as loving freedom and liberty. In contrast, the non-West or Afro-Asia is depicted as stagnant, against innovation and trade, irrational, motivated by religion and superstition and as preferring rule by despotic sultans or bureaucrats. Landes argues that 'the Chinese lacked range, focus, and above all, curiosity. [...] Unlike the Europeans they were not motivated by greed and passion', they abhorred mercantile success and, believing in their own superiority, they isolated themselves from the rest of the world.[3] Similarly Jones argues that the Ottomans encouraged obscurantist thought and 'were against the borrowing of western techniques and against native inventiveness'. Instead, he presents the Ottoman Empire as 'a plunder machine which needed booty or land to fuel itself, to pay its way, to reward its officer class'.[4] Such histories can also be read as apologies for colonialism, as they argue that the colonised countries and peoples were already suffering developmentally before colonialism happened, so their current underdevelopment is not a consequence of colonialism but a result of their environment or culture not providing the conditions necessary for modernisation. As Jones argues:

> The Ottoman, Mughal and Manchu systems were all alien, imposed military despotisms: revenue pumps. They were primarily responsible for the blighted developmental prospects of their subjects: prospects already dimming independently of the colonialism, treaty ports, unequal trade agreements, and indemnities with which Europe was to beset them in the nineteenth century.[5]

Non-Eurocentric history

Eurocentric versions of the past and the belief in European exceptionalism have been challenged by non-Eurocentric historians such as Hobson, Blaut, Goody and Frank, among others, who argue that the caricature of Afro-Asian civilisations and peoples portrayed in Eurocentric histories is contradicted by the available evidence. Non-Eurocentric historians argue that we cannot really talk about the rise of the West, or how the West made the modern world, because for hundreds, if not thousands, of years there has been close cultural, economic and political interaction between states and peoples in both the West and the East. Easterners have not passively sat by and watched the West invent modernity and accepted their role as victims or subjects of western power. Instead, they have been active participants in modern developments and have contested and challenged western power in many ways. Many inventions or discoveries that we assume are unique European inventions have non-European antecedents. For example, see Hobson's discussion of the eleventh-century Chinese 'industrial miracle', in which many of the developments that we associate with the eighteenth-century British Industrial Revolution occurred, such as massive growth in iron and steel output, the mass production of cast-iron implements, the use of blast furnaces and piston bellows in smelting, the substitution of coke for charcoal, water-powered spinning machines, canals and pound locks.[6] See also Goody's discussion of the development of banking and accountancy practices such as double-entry book keeping, bills of exchange and the formation of joint-stock companies in South-West Asia and China years before they were transmitted to Europe.[7]

Furthermore, Eurocentric history only makes sense, that is, we can only write a narrative of linear European progress and domination, if we take the current politico-economic situation as the finishing point of history. If 250–300 years ago, we had decided to write an account of the development of the world up to that point, then a very different story would have been told, one which would have focused on explaining the dominance of China, the

Ottoman Empire and Mughal India. Similarly, with the recent exponential development of India and China, if in 100 or 200 years we were to look back at the past millennium, we might again tell a different story from that of inexorable European progress and domination of the world. We might instead interpret the nineteenth and twentieth centuries as a brief period of European cultural, political and economic florescence before power reverted back to its previous centres in Asia.

Non-Eurocentric historians restore agency to non-western cultures. Hobson, for example, challenges the idea that Europeans had a monopoly on long-distance travelling and exploration, scientific curiosity and economic adventures in his discussion of Chinese and Islamic technological and navigational developments. Goody similarly demonstrates the eastern origin of many inventions and practices that we consider to be quintessentially European, such as banking, various commercial practices, rational systems of thought and the structure of the family. Frank challenges the linear narrative of western European economic progression, development and dominance through his 'global perspective on early modern economic history', in which he replaces the Eurocentric paradigms that have been used to interpret the evidence with 'a more humanocentric global paradigm'.[8] He argues that the linear 'rise of the West' narrative might be more usefully replaced by a cyclical model which sees the world as a global, economically interrelated system within which areas of the world oscillate between economic and cultural hegemony and relative 'decline', which in turn allows other areas to advance. He argues that only in the nineteenth century did the locus of economic and political power previously primarily centred on India and China definitively shift to Europe, and that this was largely as a result of late eighteenth-century economic decline in Mughal India, the Ottoman Empire and Qing China.[9]

The discovery of the smallpox vaccine

The late eighteenth-century British scientist and doctor Edward Jenner is generally recognised as the inventor of the smallpox vaccine and father of immunology.[10] Jenner's 'invention' is most frequently interpreted within a broader Eurocentric narrative of European progress and development, even when the Chinese and Islamic antecedents of smallpox vaccination are acknowledged. It is understood as another example of curious Europeans instigating scientific discoveries, exerting control over their environment and bringing benefits to the world. However, the development of the smallpox vaccine could be interpreted differently. Rather than being used as an argument for European knowledge and superiority, it could instead be read as an example of the trans-global exchange of knowledge and as evidence of how different communities interacted with each other and have contributed to the making of the modern world.

Although Jenner is credited with developing a vaccine for smallpox, there is evidence that inoculation against the disease was widespread in China in the sixteenth century, but had been known in both China and India many centuries previously. In China, inoculation against the disease was not done with the cowpox virus, but with powdered scabs inhaled up the nose from people who had either already been inoculated or who only had a mild case of the disease *variola minor*. Moreover, the scabs were often kept in a vial close to the body for up to 30 days depending on the season. This had the effect of rendering 80 per cent of the living virus particles inactive so they could therefore not give anyone smallpox, but, like vaccination, they would stimulate the body to make antibodies.[11] In the eighteenth century, when Lady Mary Wortley Montagu visited the Ottoman Empire, inoculation against smallpox was widely practised (powdered scabs were scratched into the skin), and she provided a detailed account of it and the inoculation of her own children in her letters.[12] She also actively promoted the procedure upon her return to Britain. There is also evidence of the practice occurring in America in the early eighteenth century. The first recorded instance of inoculation in America is by Zabdiel Boyleston, who was told about the technique by Cotton Mather, who learnt it from his Guramantese slave Onesimus and had it confirmed by other African and Levantine sources.[13] The story of the eradication of smallpox is therefore more complicated than simply being another case of scientific discovery by a white European man. By shifting the interpretative stress, we can write a different story of the past 1,000 years, one where Afro-Asian peoples are not portrayed as passive and backward, but are credited for developing and innovating ideas and technologies. The transmission of smallpox inoculation practices between India and China, and then to the Ottoman Empire and Africa, also challenges the Eurocentric notion that it was Europeans who discovered or opened up the world to globalisation. If we tell the story of the development of the smallpox vaccine by focusing mainly on the actions of Jenner, we erase the contributions of Chinese, African and Islamic cultures and erroneously depict Europeans as being somehow different and special.

Postcolonial history

Postcolonialism is a general term used to describe a body of interdisciplinary scholarship that seeks to analyse and critique colonial and neo-colonial relationships. We saw in Chapter 7 that history was used as an important means of legitimising the colonial enterprise and controlling subject peoples. Historical narratives are crucial to identity – they help to validate a sense of communal self – but colonial and Eurocentric histories do not acknowledge the achievements, struggles and experiences of tricontinental and other indigenous people.[14] Postcolonial history attempts to redress this balance. It does not privilege the activities, beliefs and culture of the colonists or imperialists, but seeks to re-instate people previously relegated to the footnotes of academic texts and depicted as passive recipients of colonial violence or beneficence. However, postcolonialism is not only about telling the stories of the colonised, it also seeks to make explicit the means by which colonial powers dominated, exploited and oppressed their colonial subjects, as well as examining the various means by which colonial power was contested, mediated and overcome. While still acknowledging the achievements of western Europeans, postcolonialism seeks to tell a story of the past 2,000 or more years without presenting western cultures as superior and without eliding the achievements of non-western cultures and disregarding the viewpoint of the colonised. It seeks to foreground the fact that many of the so-called economic and political successes of the modern world were achieved at the expense of indigenous and First Nations people, who were decimated, enslaved, forcibly dislocated and whose cultures were destroyed. For example, although Niall Ferguson's *Empire* stresses the benefit of the spread of the English language and British religious and legal practices to the colonised, he fails to realise, or acknowledge, the negative effects that the imposition of western forms of knowing had on indigenous cultures. Moreover, he spends less than ten pages discussing slavery, and much of these ten pages is consumed with the narrative of a white abolitionist. The horrific impact of slavery is thus glossed over and examined largely from a white western European perspective – no attempt is made to convey the viewpoint of the enslaved because they are not important in this nationalistic tale of British dominance and 'success'. Postcolonialism, on the other hand, seeks to make explicit the violence inherent in the colonial venture, and also to analyse why and how it is erased from later histories and memories.

In terms of scope, postcolonial scholarship engages with issues of cultural and ethnic diversity and the power relations that surround such constructions in a historical, anthropological, literary, economic and sociological context. It explores issues of race and how it was instrumental in legitimising the colonial enterprise and in dominating subject populations; analyses the politics of settler societies, the environment, globalism, migration, slavery and diasporas; and considers how and why difference was, and is still, constructed.

Postcolonial writing does not pretend to be neutral, objective and disinterested. Instead it outlines a politics of the subaltern or the dispossessed. It is a form of activist writing, and it focuses not simply on the oppression of the colonial past, but also on the forces of coercive domination that are the inheritance of colonialism. It seeks to articulate a form of emancipatory politics and works to not only give a voice to subordinated peoples, but to correct injustice, erase current inequalities and provide equal access to resources for everyone.[15] It aims to empower the dispossessed, promote toleration of diversity and difference, and refuses to impose western ways of thinking on tricontinental societies. Postcolonialism has had a close association with Marxist critiques of past and present inequities, and its proponents are generally politically left wing. However, while it often interprets the past from such a perspective, the Marxism it employs is flexible and transforms itself to respond to different local and historical conditions.

Postcolonial histories challenge mainstream Eurocentric meta-narratives, including the 'rise of the West' narrative. Writing the history of tricontinental states and peoples from the perspective of the 'rise of the West' meta-narrative means that these histories become essentially about Europe: such a history of India or of South-West Asia will always position itself comparatively in relation to the progress and development of the West – it becomes simply a variant of the master narrative of the history of Europe.[16]

Lastly, postcolonial writing challenges the representation of tricontinental peoples within the interpretative framework of westerners. It argues that, rather than impose western European interpretations onto the subaltern, they should be allowed to speak for themselves. For example, anthropological, historical and social discussions in western discourse of the veiling by some Muslim women is frequently (mis)interpreted within a western analytical framework which positions it as an example of female oppression, and as a sign of the despotic and backward nature of societies in which it is practised. The veiled woman is the archetypal passive subject of the western gaze: a woman who needs to be freed by the enlightened, civilised West. Such an interpretation imposes the social practices and assumptions of the observer onto the women. But, is it less oppressive to demand that a woman *not* cover her head than to demand that she should? The Shah of Iran, as part of his efforts to westernise the country in the 1970s, banned the black *chador* often worn by rural and traditional urban Iranian women. France and Turkey similarly ban women from veiling their head in certain public spaces. In contrast in Saudi Arabia and in post-revolution Iran, all women are required to cover themselves. Which is more oppressive? Moreover, in the months leading up to the revolution and the Shah's deposition, politically active secular women in Iran frequently took to the streets wearing the *chador* alongside their more religious compatriots as a sign of protest against the Shah and his regime. The veil thus became a symbol of agency and opposition.[17] Furthermore, following the revolution during the Iran–Iraq war, stamps and posters were produced by the Iranian government that depicted militant, veiled women bearing arms, conveying the message that the *chador* does not and should not hamper a woman's activities either at home or in serving her country – it is simply an expression of her chastity.[18] Similarly, the choice today by many Muslim women to cover their head is an active symbol of their identity and their political and religious beliefs. Postcolonial scholars argue that events and practices should be interpreted in terms of what they mean for the people involved and not what outside observers assume them to mean.

Subaltern studies

The journal *Subaltern Studies* was founded in 1982. According to its editor, Ranajit Guha, it was established in order to challenge the dominant historiography of India, which, he argued, was elitist in that it portrayed the independence movement and Indian nationalism as the work of key bourgeois political figures. Instead, he wanted articles in the journal to explore the histories of the lower castes and peasants, the ordinary people who had been left out of the standard modern Indian historical narrative. In particular, one of the key assumptions of the subaltern approach was that it was not only the political elite who possessed agency and a political and historical consciousness; the 'subordinate' or lower classes did as well, and they actively participated in the making of Indian history. Because the 'subordinate' classes left very few written documents, alternative means of accessing or analysing their voices and their political ideas was required. This took the form of a deconstructive reading – that is, a reading 'against the grain' – of official or colonial records in much the same way that the Annales historians had read inquisition and court records, together with a study of peasant uprisings. Subaltern historians in the 1980s and 90s were clearly influenced by Marxist ideas. They challenged the essentialism of much nationalistic history writing through foregrounding not only issues of class, but also gender and ethnicity.[19] However, in recent years members have been inspired by postmodern thinking. As such they have often questioned the Rankean-inspired historical methodology favoured by western academia, particularly the almost exclusive reliance on archival sources which, in turn, privileges the history of government and social elites. They argue that the writing of history mirrors the structure of power in society, with the politically powerless subaltern voice being excluded from official archives and thus rendered culturally speechless.[20] For example, Kancha Illaih, in an article on the Indian *Dalits* (Indians of low-caste) written for *Subaltern Studies*, wished to incorporate the *Dalit-bahujan* perspective into mainstream historical writing and in the process to 'raise Dalit-bahujan consciousness'.[21] To do this, as a political gesture, he deliberately rejected the traditional historical methodology and epistemology, arguing instead that he would write from his own direct personal experience and not qualify statements, nuance his claims or use footnotes because the discipline of history in its present form does not enable the *dalit-bahujans* to construct pasts that would help them in their struggle.

Over the past 25 years the term subaltern has broadened and has been used to describe a variety of marginalised, oppressed groups, generally in a postcolonial context. However, some theorists, such as Gayatri Chakravorty Spivak, have challenged this use and argued instead that it should only refer to those who are excluded from, and not necessarily simply oppressed by, the hegemonic imperialist discourse, or the dominant cultural narrative. Spivak, in her article 'Can the Subaltern Speak?', has also problematised the means by which the subalterns are given voice. She argues that postcolonial scholars may unconsciously reproduce in their work (neo)imperialist imperatives of cultural, economic and political exploitation and erasure, through the practice of western academics and intellectuals in effect speaking for the subaltern, or 'allowing' them a space in academia in which to speak.[22]

For the voice of the subaltern to be heard, postcolonial scholars must generally adopt the practices and protocols of western academia. Dipesh Chakrabarty notes that even, in such a politically and intellectually sympathetic space as the journal *Subaltern Studies*, there was a debate as to whether to publish Kancha Illaih's article cited above.[23] The 'western' academic thus retains the position of explanatory power. As bell hooks has said:

> No need to hear your voice when I can talk about you better than you can speak about yourself. No need to hear your voice. Only tell me about your pain. I want to know your story. And then I will tell it back to you in a new way. Tell it back to you in such a way that it has become mine, my own. Re-writing you I write myself anew. I am still author, authority. I am still colonizer the speaking subject and you are now at the center of my talk.[24]

This problematisation of the subaltern's voice is exacerbated by the favourable reception that subaltern works have received within the western academy, despite the subaltern school's opposition to the hegemony of western scholarship and historiographic practice. Indeed, many members of the subaltern school are now working in western universities or have close ties to colleagues there. This is why histories by authors such as Kancha Illaih are so important.

Feminist and LGBTQ+ history

Feminist history, like postcolonial history, is overtly political, and developed out of the new social history movement which was considerably influenced by British Marxist historiography and second-wave feminism's demands for equality in the late 1960s and 1970s. Feminist history has an overt agenda of political equality for men and women and seeks to democratise historical discourse by not only recovering women as active participants in the making of history, but also decentring the male subject and challenging patriarchal ways of thinking and institutions that are presented as natural, rather than socially constructed.[25] It is heavily influenced by postmodernist and post-structuralist ideas which prompt us to question the very categories we use to understand the past. Feminist history is now more or less an established part of mainstream academia. There are a number of well-known centres for gender or women's studies; journals, books and conferences in the field have proliferated; and most university history degrees offer courses in one or more of the overlapping fields of feminist, women's or gender history. Joan Scott, however, worries that, as academic feminism has become mainstream, it has lost its connection to the political movement that inspired it.[26]

Early feminist histories de-privileged the public sphere as the only site of meaningful and authentic historical activity and argued instead that women had been active historical subjects within the domestic or private sphere, where they created a discrete women's culture. This has been understood by some feminist historians, such as Estelle Freedman, as a generative site of feminist identity that shaped later social and political activism. To this extent women became active historical agents and histories about women were legitimised.

However, later feminist historians sought to go beyond 'finding' women in history and argued that discourses of gender could help us understand how power relationships are constructed, and how these relationships changed over time. They challenged this depoliticisation of feminist history and argued that the romanticised portrayal of female domesticity was not an effective means of challenging patriarchal structures. It perpetuated, rather than challenged, the male–female dyad inherent in traditional history. Challenges to the separate-spheres model increased particularly with demonstrations of the interrelatedness of the spheres inhabited by men and women.[27] Laurel Ulrich's study of how a midwife contributed to household sustenance and social relations in late eighteenth- and early nineteenth-century Maine, for example, demonstrated the vital role of women's labour in maintaining families and communities, and explored how this labour contributed to larger transformations in the modern gendered economy.[28]

While women's and feminist history was tolerated by some, by others it was seen as subversive, essentialist and exclusionary. Gender history offered a means of bridging the gap. Gender historians sought not only to put women back into the past, but also to recognise how gender, as a key axis of power in society, provides an important understanding of how society is organised and structured.[29] It focuses on how differences between men and women are discursively produced and therefore how different gender identities have been constructed over time and reified through social institutions and structures. For example, the socially constructed and fluid concept of 'masculinity' only makes sense in relation to its binary opposite of 'femininity', and the meaning of both changes over time. Gender history is also concerned with problematising the methodologies, periodisation and meta-narratives that historians employ. Not all feminist historians, however, welcomed the emergence of gender history into the academic field. Its deconstruction of unified subjects, its descriptions of how multiple subjectivities are discursively constituted and its rejection of meta-narratives all appeared to preclude the possibility of invoking 'women' or 'female' as stable social categories that might provide a platform for activism based around identity politics or the writing of new emancipatory narratives.[30]

Some historians are particularly interested in how gender and sexuality is constructed, and how this has shaped our understanding of the past.[31] Queer history emerged out of feminist historical critiques of sexuality, and Queer historians have struggled with some of the essentialist/constructionist debates that have dogged feminist historians.[32] Queer history seeks to make LGBTQ+ people visible in the historical record, to explore how LGBTQ+ identities are constructed, to expose the prejudice of dominant social discourses and institutions and to provide a positive history for LGBTQ+ people. Queer studies therefore has an explicit political agenda and a strong theoretical basis. Like Black history, it emerged from the establishment of university student groups, during the civil rights and social justice movement of 1960s America, which agitated for courses that were relevant to their identities and concerns.

John Howard poses the central dilemma of queer pedagogy, whether one should teach queer history or queer the teaching of history. That is, should one take historical LGBTQ+ people (and the state and society's attitudes towards them) as the subject of historical enquiry, or should one, in Howard's words 'engage audiences in the theoretical exercise of destabilising present categories, such that we all see our individual and varied collective investments in multiple histories of gender, sexuality, and difference'.[33] In other words, should it extend discourse theory's critique of normalcy and explore how ideas of deviancy were created and reproduced over time? Queer theorists argue against sexual essentialism and are therefore not so interested in searching for, or defining, the LGBTQ+ subject. Instead they focus on how LGBTQ+ subjectivities have been constituted though discourses of resistance and transgression over time. Queer theory also opposes heteronormative readings of sexuality and gender – that is, they challenge readings in which heterosexuality and the idea of gender as binary are assumed to be the natural and normative state.[34]

Lastly, there has been considerable criticism in recent years of the white ethnocentrism of much feminist history. Amos and Parmar accuse white feminist scholarship of ignoring black women or using them as 'exotic' contrasts.[35] While white women have a more visible presence in the historical record, black and brown women are still absent or marginalised. When they are present, it is through the representations of white female missionaries, educators or colonial wives. Although feminism has successfully challenged the idea that the construction and maintenance of the British Empire was an exclusively male undertaking, it has not so successfully acknowledged the racial privileges enjoyed by white women in the colonies and it has done very little to correct the invisibility of indigenous women. This has recently begun to change through the work of postcolonialist and black feminist scholars such as Antoinette Burton and her *Burdens of History: British Feminists, Indian Women and Imperial Culture* (1994).[36] Similarly, writers including Iris Berger, Sylviane Diouf and Jennifer Morgan have explored how the intersecting categories of race, gender, class, religion and region have shaped divisions of labour, movements for social reform and national liberation struggles among twentieth-century Africans and African Americans.[37]

Black history

Just as with postcolonial, non-Eurocentric, feminist and queer history, black history is explicitly political. The acceptance of black history as part of mainstream historical education in the USA and Britain only came about as a direct result of political activism in both countries. In the USA, histories before the late 1960s were basically concerned with narrating the achievements of white people, mainly white men. When white historians discussed African-Americans it was usually in the context of slavery or the period of Reconstruction, and they uniformly depicted African-Americans as less civilised and intelligent.

However, there were some radical reinterpretations of black history in the late nineteenth and early twentieth centuries by scholars such as George Washington Williams, author of *History of the Negro Race in America 1619–1880* (1882), and W.E.B. Du Bois, whose prodigious output included *The Souls of Black Folk* (1903), now considered to be one of the pre-eminent modern texts on African-American cultural consciousness, and *The Philadelphia Negro* (1899), a sociological work on the urban black population of Philadelphia. Du Bois was a historian, sociologist, teacher, pan-Africanist, envoy, editor, socialist and activist. He was the co-founder of the National Association for the Advancement of Colored People (NAACP) and worked throughout his life for African-American liberation and equality. He also supported anti-colonial and independence movements in Africa, and attended pan-African conferences. His experience teaching in the south of the USA inspired his revisionist histories of the slave trade and Reconstruction. His *Black Reconstruction in America* (1935) not only challenged the dominant view of white historians that Reconstruction had been a disaster and had given black Americans political and economic rights too quickly, but also made explicit the racist elements inherent in the arguments of such historians. In the late nineteenth century the history of Africa and African Americans was not part of the American university or school history curriculum. The scholarship and activism of Du Bois began to change this, and because of his efforts Africa was slowly accepted as a legitimate subject of historical study. Moreover, Du Bois was writing at a time when popular white American culture was suffused with racist depictions of black Americans. He challenged these views, particularly the idea that the most successful or worthy elements of African civilisation were the result of non-black Africans. In doing so he gave a sense of communal pride and identity to black Americans at a time when their rights were under great pressure.[38]

Just as second-wave feminism led to the acceptance of women's studies and women's history as a legitimate area of scholarly enquiry, the 1960s' social justice and civil rights movements in the USA instigated radical changes to American social and political organisations, including educational establishments, and led to the establishment of black studies programmes. Student agitation helped establish many black studies departments: between 1968 and 1975 over 500 programmes and departments offered black studies courses.[39] Like feminist studies and queer studies, black studies is a multidisciplinary endeavour that encompasses the social sciences, history, literature and anthropology. It attempts to redress the centuries of popular and academic representations of black people as inferior and seeks to understand how race is socially and politically constructed. It challenges canonical texts which perpetuate racist perspectives, critiques traditional politics, histories and social affairs and works to transform the existing social order to make it more inclusive and equal. Black history does not simply make black people a legitimate subject of historical enquiry, it also seeks to engage with contemporary societal issues and aims to challenge the exclusion or marginalisation of black people from mainstream political, economic and cultural life in America and the UK.

Despite the fact that black people have lived in the British Isles since Roman times, when African soldiers were part of the Roman army defending Hadrian's Wall, James Walvin has argued that, up until the 1970s, black history was completely absent from mainstream British historiography.[40] Four key factors contributed to the gradual acceptance of black history as a legitimate field of historical enquiry: the success of social history, with its emphasis on reclaiming the histories of the common people, the marginalised and the dispossessed; the rise of African studies as a result of African nationalism and independence movements; the development and proliferation of African-American studies in the USA in the 1960s and 1970s; and the activism of educationalists such as Len Garrison, who pushed for black history to be incorporated into the history curriculum and pioneered the Black Cultural Archives in Brixton.[41] However, the situation is still far from ideal and theUK Qualifications and Curriculum Authority has recently argued that '[t]oo little attention is given to the black and multi-ethnic aspects of British history. The teaching of black history is often confined to topics about slavery and post-war immigration or to Black History Month. The effect, if inadvertent, is to undervalue the overall contribution of black and minority ethnic people to Britain's past and to ignore their cultural, scientific and many other achievements'.[42] Slowly the situation is beginning to change with historians gradually telling the stories of the numerous black individuals and communities that have lived in Britain during the past 2,000 years. However, the paucity of sources poses a problem for historians. As we noted in Chapter 7, just as Indian women have no real presence in many British Indian colonial sources, so too the black presence has been consciously or unconsciously erased from British sources. For example, Bressey has demonstrated that the records and sources that we do have do not always explicitly acknowledge that an individual is black. She cites the example of two poor working-class women, Caroline Maisley and Mary Matthews, who spent some time in Colney Hatch asylum. The hospital records make no mention of their skin colour, but a photograph of the patients shows that they were black women.[43] This invisibility of black individuals in the historical record has led some commentators to argue, incorrectly, that there were few or no black people in Britain before the mid-twentieth century and thus they are not really an integral part of British life, society and culture. The work of geographers such as Bressley and others committed to making black history more widely known effectively challenges the assumption that an absence of explicit colour in the archives equates to whiteness.

Conclusion

All of these approaches to history are explicitly political and ideologically motivated – that is, they express particular perspectives and are written for specific functions. This, however, does not make them inferior histories, as they still adhere to the key protocols of the profession. Moreover, as we saw in earlier chapters, the claim that historians write objective, disinterested history for its own sake is disingenuous. While some historians may claim this is what they are doing, in reality, it is impossible to step back from our beliefs, assumptions and interpretative strategies. The above historical approaches are therefore not so different from other histories, except that the authors are open about their perspectives and their aim in writing them. Histories that celebrate Columbus or that focus on the positive aspects of British colonial domination are just as positioned and politically motivated as non-Eurocentric or postcolonial histories that focus on the suffering caused by the European colonial adventures.

History can be very conservative, that is it can be used to legitimise and justify the political, social and cultural status quo, but it can also be challenging, emancipatory and inspiring. Hayden White has argued that, because correspondence to reality is no longer an adequate or effective means of distinguishing between different historical narratives, choices are made between different histories on the basis of aesthetic preference. We would suggest that we also chose between histories on an ethical or political basis. That is, we like or agree with those accounts of the past that cohere with our own political perspective, that use interpretative models to make sense of our world and society that we think are useful and correct. Both Frank and Ferguson have written an economic history of the development of the modern world. Both have adhered to the protocols of the profession and both have used extensive, but different, sources in a professional manner. However, they have used different interpretative paradigms and have approached their subject with different assumptions as to how society works and with a different political agenda.

Chakrabarty calls for a history that makes explicit in its narrative the role it plays in narratives of identity and citizenship.[44] The histories discussed here do just that. The postmodern challenge has demonstrated the futility of trying to distinguish so-called objective histories from those that are positioned and political. Instead, when we read a history, we need to ask whose politics it represents, what is its ideological basis and what functions it serves.

Notes

1 Edward W. Said, *Orientalism* (New York: Pantheon Books, 1978) quoted in Robert J.C. Young, *Postcolonialism: A Very Short Introduction* (Oxford: Oxford University Press, 2003) 59.

2 David Landes, *The Wealth and Poverty of Nations: Why Some are so Rich and Some so Poor* (New York: W.W. Norton, 1998); E. Jones, *The European Miracle: Environments, Economies and Geopolitics in the History of Europe and Asia* 3rd ed. (Cambridge: CUP, 2003).

3 *Ibid.*, 96–98.

4 Jones, *The European Miracle* 181, 185.

5 *Ibid.*, 229.

6 John M. Hobson, *The Eastern Origins of Western Civilisation* (Cambridge: Cambridge University Press, 2004) chapter three.

7 Jack Goody, *The East in the West* (Cambridge: Cambridge University Press, 1996) chapter two.

8 Andre Gunder Frank, *ReOrient: Global Economy in the Asian Age* (Berkeley: University of California Press, 1998) 4.

9 *Ibid.*, chapter six.

10 This is despite the fact that there is substantial evidence that Benjamin Jesty inoculated his wife and two sons with cowpox, which conveys immunity from the smallpox virus, some 20 years before Jenner's similar experiments. The BBC webpage on Jenner describes Jenner as the pioneer of smallpox vaccination and the father of immunology, www.bbc.co.uk/history/historic_figures/jenner_edward.shtml accessed 20 July 2010; the Jenner museum in Gloucestershire similarly promulgates the idea that Jenner alone was responsible for the smallpox vaccine www.jennermuseum.com/index.php accessed 20 July 2010; and *The Jenner Institute for Developing Vaccines*, by taking the name of Jenner, reinforces the idea that he was responsible for curing smallpox and developing vaccination practices.

11 Robert Temple, *The Genius of China: 3,000 Years of Science, Discovery and Invention* (New York: Simon and Schuster: 1986) 136–7.

12 Mary Wortley Montagu, *Letters of the Right Honourable Lady M--y W---y M----e :written, during her travels in Europe, Asia and Africa, to persons of distinction, men of letters, &c. in different parts of Europe : which contain, among other curious relations, accounts of the policy and manners of the Turks : drawn from sources that have been inaccessible to other travelers* (London : Printed for T. Becket and P.A. De Hondt, 1763) 59–63. http://pds.lib.harvard.edu/pds/view/7320431?n=263&imagesize=1200&jp2Res=.5 accessed 20 July 2010.

13 K. Silverman, *The Life and Times of Cotton Mathar* (New York: Harper and Row, 1984) 338–9.

14 Robert J.C. Young, *Postcolonialism: An Historical Introduction* (Oxford: Blackwell Publishing, 2001) 4–5 argues for the use of this term to rather than the negative terms 'non-western' or 'third world'.

15 *Ibid.*, 10–11.

16 See Dipesh Chakrabarty, 'Postcoloniality and the Artifice of History: Who Speaks for "Indian" Pasts?', in *Representations* 37, 1992 also in Bill Ashcroft, Gareth Griffiths and Helen Tiffin (eds), *The Post-Colonial Studies Reader* 2nd ed (London: Routledge, 2006) 340–44.

17 Peter Chelkowski and Hamid Dabashi, *Staging a Revolution: The Art of Persuasion in the Islamic Republic of Iran* (London: Booth-Clibborn Editions, 2000) 88.

18 *Ibid.*, 217–8.

19 Wang, 'Cross-Cultural Developments of Modern Historiography', 205.

20 *Ibid.*, 207.

21 Kancha Ilaih, 'Productive Labour, Consciousness and History: the Dalitbahujan Alternative', in Shahid Amin and Dipesh Chakrabarty (eds), *Subaltern Studies: Writings on South Asian History and Society* (Delhi: Oxford University Press, 1996) 165–200, 168 quoted in Dipesh Chakrabarty, 'History and the Politics of Recognition', in Jenkins et al. (eds), *Manifestos* 80.

22 Gayatri Chakravorty Spivak, 'Can the Subaltern Speak?', in Cary Nelson and Lawrence Grossberg (eds), *Marxism and the Interpretation of Culture*. (Urbana, IL: University of Illinois Press, 1988) 271–313.

23 Chakrabarty, 'History and the Politics of Recognition', 80.

24 bell hooks, 'Marginality as a Site of Resistance', in R. Ferguson et al. (eds), *Out There: Marginalization and Contemporary Cultures*. (Cambridge, MA: MIT, 1990) 341–43, 343, italics in the original.

25 Joan W. Scott, 'Feminism's History', in Morgan (ed.), *Feminist History Reader* 393.

26 *Ibid.*, 389.

27 Sue Morgan, 'Introduction', in Sue Morgan (ed.), *The Feminist History Reader* (London: Routledge, 2006) 7–8.

28 Laurel Ulrich, *A Midwife's Tale* (New York: Random House, 1990), in N. Hewitt 'Gender and Feminist Studies in History', in Neil J. Smelser and Paul B. Baltes (eds), *International Encyclopedia of the Social and Behavioural Sciences, vol. 9* (Oxford: Elsevier, 2001) 5930.

29 Catherine Hall, 'Feminism and Feminist History' in Catherine Hall, *White, Male and Middle-Class: Explorations in Feminism and Feminist History* (Oxford: Polity Press, 1992) 1–40, 12 quoted in Morgan 'Introduction',10.

30 Hewitt, 'Gender and Feminist Studies in History', 5931.

31 For a classic discussion of the intersection between feminism and queer history, see Judith Butler, *Gender Trouble: Feminism and the Subversion of Identity* (New York: Routledge, 1990).

32 For more on this struggle, see Eve Kosofsky Sedgewick, *Epistemology of the Closet* (Berkeley: University of California Press, 1990).

33 John Howard, 'Where are we to Begin?', in Allida M. Black (ed.), *Modern American Queer History* (Philadelphia: Temple University Press, 2001) 8–9.

34 Morgan 'Introduction', 22.

35 See Valerie Amos and Pratibha Parmar, 'Challenging Imperial Feminism', in Morgan (ed.), *Feminist History Reader*.

36 Antoinette Burton, *Burdens of History: British Feminists, Indian Women and Imperial Culture* (Chapel Hill: The University of North Carolina Press,1994).

37 Hewitt, 'Gender and Feminist Studies in History' 5930.

38 Eric J. Sundquist (ed.), *The Oxford W.E.B Du Bois Reader* (Oxford: Oxford University Press, 1996) 'Introduction'.

39 Jacqueline Bobo, Cynthia Hudley, Claudine Michel, 'Introduction', in Bobo et al. (eds), *The Black Studies Reader* (London: Routledge, 2004) 2.

40 David Dabydeen, John Gilmore and Cecily Jones (eds), *The Oxford Companion to Black British History* (Oxford: Oxford University Press, 2007) 'Introduction' vii-ix.

41 *Ibid.*, vii.

42 *History 2004/5 Annual Report on Curriculum and Assessment* QCA/05/2169. 2005 quoted in Dabydeen et al. (eds), *Black British History* 'Introduction' vii.

43 Caroline Bressey, 'It's only Political Correctness – Race and Racism in British History', in Claire Dwyer and Carolien Bressey (eds), *New Geographies of Race and Racism* (Hampshire: Ashgate, 2008) 37–8.

44 Chakrabarty, 'Postcoloniality', 344.

Further reading

Allida M. Black (ed.), *Modern American Queer History* (Philadelphia: Temple University Press, 2001).

Jacqueline Bobo, Cynthia Hudley, Claudine Michel (eds), *The Black Studies Reader* (London: Routledge, 2004).

Andre Gunder Frank, *ReOrient: Global Economy in the Asian Age* (Berkeley: University of California Press, 1998). A global perspective on early modern economic history that challenges the linear narrative of exclusive western European economic progression, development and dominance.

John M. Hobson, *The Eastern Origins of Western Civilisation* (Cambridge: Cambridge University Press, 2004). Non-Eurocentric history of Afro-Asia that challenges the idea that Europeans had a monopoly on long-distance travelling and exploration, scientific curiosity and economic adventures.

Sue Morgan (ed.), *The Feminist History Reader* (London: Routledge, 2006). A collection of interesting articles from some leading feminist historians, with a detailed introductory essay.

Robert J.C. Young, *Postcolonialism: A Very Short Introduction* (Oxford: Oxford University Press, 2003). A very short introduction to the subject in the format of a montage.

Robert J. C. Young, *Postcolonialism: An Historical Introduction* (Oxford: Blackwell Publishing, 2001). A longer introduction to postcolonialism.

9

Popular history

History without historians

In *Theatres of Memory* (1994) Raphael Samuel wrote that history – which he regarded as a 'mass activity' – was more popular than it had ever been in Britain. We live, he argued, 'in an expanding historical culture, in which the work of inquiry and retrieval is being progressively extended into all kinds of spheres that would have been thought unworthy of attention in the past'.[1] Samuel was the first British historian to elaborate and *welcome* the many varied ways in which people incorporated references to the past into their social and private lives: visiting historic houses, buying period furniture and bric-à brac, wearing vintage trainers, reading Sir Walter Scott novels, collecting old vinyl records, keeping boxes of photographs, watching period dramas on film and television. History, he stated, was a collective form of knowledge, the work in any given instance of a thousand different hands rather than the exclusive property of the academic historian. Fifteen years after *Theatres of Memory* was published, David Harlan noticed something similar about US contemporary culture. He observed that: 'Americans are more intensely interested in history now than they've ever been'.[2] History, he pointed out, had become a staple of entertainment and leisure cultures: museums were crowded, Hollywood produced several big-budget historical dramas every year, historical documentaries like Ken Burns's works on jazz and baseball were reaching mass audiences and historical fiction had rediscovered the kind of popularity it last enjoyed in the first half of the nineteenth century.

History now pervades popular culture so thoroughly that any comprehensive attempt to investigate 'popular history' would fill multiple books. Jerome de Groot's *Consuming History: Historians and Heritage in Contemporary Popular Culture* (2016) is the best single volume to pursue this line of enquiry recently, largely in a British context, but always mindful of the transnational character of today's postmodern culture. De Groot uses the term 'historioglossia' to refer to the overflowing abundance of historical meanings that now confronts people in their daily lives, citing examples that range from digital games, *The Da Vinci Code* and *Wikipedia* to daytime television, metal detecting and 'celebrity historians'. If space had allowed, de Groot notes, he could equally have discussed other modes for feeding a sense of the past, such as vintage fashion, historical painting, what if? novels (these are counter-factual historical novels) and historical holidays.[3] De Groot argues that professional historians should recognise how the 'contemporary historical imaginary is fed by a multiplexity of consumption practices' and suggests that they should relinquish their self-appointed rights to 'mark history out, to control and boundarise it'[4]. Indeed, it is because of academic historians' collective conservatism when it comes to presenting their work that most of them have been bypassed by the popular turn towards the past. Only a very few historians have a presence within the public consciousness, mainly those who are familiar from television programmes on networks like History and Yesterday or who present the most popular history podcasts. Most of the rest remain isolated in private conversations about their research specialisms with colleagues and students. Consequently, the field has been left open for others to describe, reference or interpret the past in ways that satisfy more popular (and commercial) tastes. As novelist Yann Martel said in an interview in 2010:

> A great novel from Colombia, [Gabriel García Márquez's] *One Hundred Years of Solitude*, will be read around the world, whereas who's going to read a history of Columbia? A fraction of those people who might read *One Hundred Years of Solitude*[5].

Perhaps this puts the issue in overly stark terms (and ignores the ways in which novelists and historians mutually trade knowledge and inspiration across genre boundaries), but the main point holds true. People can (and do) engage with the past within the realms of aesthetics and sensibilities, not only within the 'hard' domains of knowledge, analysis and empirical observations that are the common currency of historians. Artists, novelists, filmmakers, poets, griots, folklorists, comic book authors, music anthologists, architects, designers and others besides have their own ways of working with the materials that the past has left behind. Moreover, they often do so in ways that resonate widely in the public sphere. So how might historians regard these other (and frequently more popular) ways of referencing the past?

Academic historians tend to think of their collective work as the 'proper' history against which all other accounts of the past are benchmarked. This means that they regard these other ways as being in some ways inferior to their own professional practices: as being 'corrupted', 'amateur' or *ersatz* history. Historians frequently complain about factual inaccuracies in popular historical accounts: perhaps, for example, the actor playing King Henry VIII in a television drama was too slim for *that* point in the reign.[6] More broadly, historians are likely to dismiss other modes of portraying or referencing past events because they see them as uncritical, intellectually undemanding and pandering to popular myths about the past. Critics such as David Lowenthal and Sean Wilentz have been particularly aggressive in their attack on popular histories for what they see as their 'mind-numbing nostalgia' and their 'sticky-sweet compounds of yearning and melancholy'. Such forms of history, they argue, provide a captivating distraction from present concerns for a popular audience, but they simultaneously castrate that audience's mind.[7] In the eyes of its harshest critics, popular history is devoid of any critical content and shorn of any qualities that might conflict with popular tastes.

In contrast, historians like David Harlan, Ann Rigney and Dipesh Chakrabarty have long argued that the future of academic history (and the historical method) should be one that sees academics welcome alternative mnemonic practices rather than dismiss them as impostors. In other words, they urge that we should stop judging other historical practices by the standards of academic history and instead acknowledge that each form of historical representation has its own methodology, its own forms, codes and conventions, and its own cultural value. Ann Rigney argues that we should widen the scope of academic history and understand historical practices in more inclusive, pluralist and multidimensional ways – thereby embracing different modes of presentation, methodologies, disciplines, institutions and topics for study.[8] She suggests that professional historians might usefully borrow some of the practices from outside their discipline in order to make their work more accessible to a public that seemingly needs narratives of the past. David Harlan thought the same. Without becoming more outward looking in terms of methodology and practice, he wrote, academic history risks becoming increasingly entombed in a 'pyramid of irrelevance', read solely by professional historians and a handful of history students.[9] This would leave academic historians excluded from the ongoing discussion of what our pasts might mean to us today. Harlan argued that academic historians had to engage with the new histories being produced in other cultural forms if they wanted to inspire people's historical imaginations in morally sustaining and politically relevant ways. Or, as Robert Rosenstone advised his fellow historians, we need to 'paint, write, film, dance, hip hop and rap the past in a way that makes the tragedies and joys of the human voyage meaningful to the contemporary world'.[10]

Digital histories

The development of digital technologies has encouraged the kind of genre-bending in historical practice that excited Rigney, Rosenstone and Harlan. It has also transformed how historical knowledge is produced, distributed and consumed, making the field more accessible than ever. Not so long ago, researchers had to visit libraries or archives in person to access most of the information that they wanted to know about the past. Now, more information about the past than any individual could hope to read and digest in their lifetime is available online. Much of this material (but not all of it) is freely available. Archives have digitised many millions of documents and other forms of data that can be downloaded anywhere, opening up possibilities for trans-national academic research projects without the costs (financial and environmental) of travel to distant archives. At the smaller scale, people tracing their family history can use online subscription services like *Familysearch, Ancestry* and *Findmypast* to consult the records of local and national state agencies. For anyone who wants to research the recent past, posts on user-generated sites like YouTube, Twitter and Facebook are valuable primary sources (see, for example, analysis of Twitter and Facebook posts from the Tahrir Square demonstrations that brought down President Mubarak in Egypt in 2011 or YouTube film of police evicting Occupy protestors from camps in New York and Oakland in 2012).[11] For those researching the more distant past, the development of digitised knowledge banks has generated tools for analysing change over long time-scales. As Guldi and Armitage explain, technologies for data mining have opened up new forms of cliometric history (that is, histories of things that can be quantitatively measured). Subjects like climate change, economics, food supply and international trade can be studied across wide chronological spans (known as the *longue durée*) with the use of digital analysis tools such as Paper Machines, MALLET, Google Ngrams and IBM's ManyEyes software. Moreover, open access resources such as the Trans-Atlantic Slave Trade Database, which contain datasets about 35,000 slave voyages between 1520 and 1866, during which more than 12 million slaves were transported, have brought archival research within easy reach of many people.[12]

Historical accounts have been made similarly accessible by the mutually reinforcing growth of the internet and mobile connectivity. The stated intention of Google founders Sergey Brin and Larry Page is 'to make the world's information as universally accessible and useful as possible, all the while respecting publishers, copyright and the role of libraries across the globe'.[13] To this end, Google Books has made some 40 million volumes discoverable (including history books). The same kind of ambition to make knowledge commonly available is behind the growth of Wikipedia, which six years after launching in January 2001 expanded to feature more than two million articles, and which soon became one of the ten most visited internet sites globally.[14] Whereas Google Books aims to bring published material within people's reach, Wikipedia seeks to transform the process of knowledge production itself by allowing anyone to write and post articles (in whole or part) on the site. These articles are open to be reviewed, amended, expanded and sometimes removed by a peer community of 'Wikipedians'. This networked community is sizeable: across more than 290 different language versions of Wikipedia there were 85 million registered users and 315,000 active users at the start of the 2020s ('active' means that they have made an edit or some other action in a given month).[15] This commitment to provide free access to knowledge that results from open collaboration sets Wikipedia apart from professional historical practice. Instead of 'gatekeeping' knowledge production by restricting it to accredited scholars, Wikipedia uses an 'accountability' model whereby a collective public decides what should be published.[16] Admittedly, the results are not always satisfactory. Illustrating Hayden White's point about how form determines content, the English version of Wikipedia reflects the preoccupations of its writers, who tend to be disproportionately male and white, and who spend a lot of their time online. The site has a reputation for favouring Western-centric content and 'geeky' articles about cult aspects of pop culture.[17] Nonetheless, it has become the principal common resource for information about the past (historical or otherwise). Jack Lynch's study of the history of encylopedias, dictionaries and atlases makes this point well: 'Everybody distrusts Wikipedia and everybody uses it'[18]. And as Murray Phillips pointed out in a detailed discussion of Wikipedia and the Australian Paralympic Movement, the site contains a vast number of articles about subjects that are otherwise ignored by academic and trade publishers, as well as traditional encyclopedias.[19]

Contrary to what might be expected, given that most of its articles can be edited by anyone and that Wikipedia itself warns that it should not be regarded as a reliable source of information, the site compares favourably with commercial encyclopedias in terms of factual accuracy.[20] Of course its content contains mistakes, including some malicious ones inserted into articles by 'vandals'. But errors are usually spotted by readers and corrected; Roy Rosenzweig refers to various cases in Wikipedia's early years where mistakes were dealt with in a matter of minutes or hours.[21] Moreover, some articles that are prone to vandalism are protected from editing or restricted to editing by certain categories of user. Despite these measures to address reliability issues, however, history students can expect to be told not to use Wikipedia and certainly not to cite it in their written work. The reasons for this are principally to do with the *type* of writing found on the site. Wikipedia's guidelines for writers state that it should not be used as a platform to present original research, that all knowledge claims should be verified by reference to 'reliable' published sources and that articles should be written from a 'neutral point of view'. These are restrictive conditions for writing about anything, including the past. It means that the site's articles tend to be weighted towards factual content and away from a strong interpretive position. Wikipedia is usually good at summarising what is already known about a given subject. But guidelines about 'neutrality', and the fact that Wikipedia's epistemic model is based around achieving a consensus of collective authorship, often combine to produce bland content. As Rosenzweig put it: 'Committees rarely write well'.[22] So, while Wikipedia is a remarkable example of the democratisation of knowledge, students are best advised to consult the academic sources that their tutors recommend, at least as long as their access to these sources is covered by an institutional licence and is therefore not prohibitively expensive.

Along with open-access platforms like Wikipedia, the rapid growth in popularity of online history games has forced us to rethink our understanding of contemporary history-making practices. According to *Forbes* magazine, the six best-selling editions of the *Call of Duty* game series have each sold between 25 and 30 million units.[23] The 2009 release of *Call of Duty: Modern Warfare II* was at the time the most successful release for any form of entertainment media form ever.[24] In 2019 the publisher Activision Blizzard reported that its *Call of Duty: Modern Warfare* game generated more than $600 million in sales during its first three days alone.[25] The *Assassin's Creed* franchise is not quite so popular, but its reach is impressive nonetheless. Ubisoft announced that sales for its series of *Assassin's Creed* games exceeded 140 million units.[26]

These levels of popularity are important because they confirm that engaging with the past via historical gaming has become a mainstream activity. It is a principal means for developing a popular historical imaginary of such times and places as ancient Rome, Renaissance Europe, feudal Japan, the American West and the Second World War. Game developers have invested considerable resources in researching periods and settings so that their products satisfy audience expectations about authenticity. But as Chapman, Foka and Westin have argued, simply citing statistics about the success of games is too defensive a way of explaining their significance. For these writers, digital games like *Call of Duty, Assassin's Creed, Total War, Civilization, Europa Universalis and Red Dead Redemption* constitute a distinctive and important historical form and mode of expression. Moreover, because developments in history theory have undermined long-held orthodoxies about what 'proper' histories should look like, there is growing interest in what historical games bring to our understanding of the various ways in which people relate to, remember and immerse themselves in a sense of the past.[27]

Unsurprisingly, some of the interest in how games function as a form of historical representation has been sharply critical. In part, the complaints levelled at gaming replicate the kind that have long been deployed by academic historians against history films. Games are likely to be dismissed as unhistorical on the grounds that they put customer satisfaction before historical accuracy, prioritise spectacle over interpretation and disregard standards of scholarly seriousness. A *New York Times* interview with Sid Meier neatly captured such criticisms, arguing that the *Civilization* game series, which Meier helped to develop, featured the level of historical detail that one would expect to find in a children's illustrated history book.[28] Other critiques of gaming's relationship to the historical past have focused on the nature of the interface between user and form. After all, it is argued, the point of a game is not to learn about its historical data but to *play it:* to beat its algorithms, to progress through its levels and to win. As Kevin Schutt pointedly remarked, whereas textbooks tell how Julius Caesar captured Gaul between 58 BCE and 51 BCE, when Schutt played the game *Rome: Total War* he was able to achieve the same feat some two hundred years ahead of schedule.[29] In short, the entertainment demands of game play and the pedagogical responsibilities of historical representation inevitably pull against each other. Moreover, the popularity of battlefield franchises within the gaming industry has led to further criticisms. Games are seen to offer stereotypically masculinised ways of engaging with the past, they over-simplify chains of cause and effect and they displace the complexities of sociopolitical and economic processes out of a virtual world in which things are invariably made to happen by acts of violent intervention.[30]

On the other hand, it is precisely the interactive and performative aspects of historical games *as play* that explain why we should think about them seriously. In one respect, the value of games lies in their capacity to counter teleological understandings of history by emphasising the contingency of sequences of events. By intervening in simulated historical settings, players can appreciate how any given present could easily have turned out differently. In another respect, historical games illustrate how the linguistic and rhetorical turns associated with poststructuralism produced a crisis of representation in historical discourse. By definition, games subvert notions of representational certainty and consolidation because they position the player as someone who actively constructs (not re-constructs) historical meaning from a place in the present.[31] As Pötzsch and Šisler argue, games like *Call of Duty: Black Ops* and *Czechoslovakia 38–89: Assassination* put players in 'problem spaces' that enable them to make choices. Admittedly, the amount of courses of action available to a player varies between games, depending on decisions taken by each game's designers and developers. But even allowing for limitations in the potential scope for re-scripting events in a game, 'every act of play will give rise to a different representation'.[32]

Screening the past

Players' ability to affect what happens on screen separates games from film representations of the past, which – allowing for local variations in censorship – remain the same on every showing. Nonetheless, when *L.A. Noire* (set in 1940s Los Angeles) became the first digital game to be screened at New York's Tribeca Film Festival in 2011, it showed that the two cultural forms also occupied mutual spaces.[33] Long before game designers raided the past for useable stories and settings, filmmakers were doing the same. The simple explanation for this is that major historical events make great visual and dramatic settings for screen narratives, and the resulting films are relatively straightforward to market to audiences who know what to expect from the story. A more cynical explanation is that film producers have long looked for ways to reassure politicians, religious groups and other guardians of public decency that feature films were not all about crime, sex and fantasy. In the industry's early decades, historical films like *Cabiria* (1914), *Battleship Potemkin* (1925), *Napoléon* (1927) and *Young Mr Lincoln* (1939) could be cited as examples to support the claim that cinema was an intellectually serious and morally responsible mass cultural form. Studio executives and producers over the years have plausibly claimed that, by making historical films, they were educating audiences and creating important sources of social memory. Still today such 'serious' films are often popular with reviewers and commonly nominated for awards. But making films about historical subjects is also a risky pursuit. All attempts to narrativise historical subjects are liable to be judged against common-sense notions of the 'real' of the past. And because filmmakers produce such a commodified media form, their work has been particularly prone to accusations that it has 'fictionalised' or 'distorted' the facts of the past for commercial reasons. Professional academic historians are often the ones who make such accusations, showing in the process that they have assigned for themselves the authority to adjudicate on a film's 'fidelity' to past events.[34] But as Marnie Hughes-Warrington has asked: 'On what grounds are historians the arbiters of historical activities, including film? And on what grounds do we place the communications of academic historians above those of other history makers?'[35]

Case Study

History on film: *The Battle of Algiers* (1966)

Historians often begin their study of a film like *The Battle of Algiers* by asking questions about its production: Who made this film? Who financed it? Why was it made? Why was it made *then?* Who was it made *for*? *The Battle of Algiers* is a feature film that dramatises the defeat of the Algerian Nationalist Army (FLN) by French colonial forces in the city of Algiers in 1956–7. It was a co-production between Casbah Films (Algerian) and Igor Film (Italian), it cost about $800,000 and it was shot on location in Algiers in the summer of 1965 – less than a decade after the events that it portrayed. It was made with the consent of the newly independent Algerian government under the then-president Ahmed Ben Bella (who was deposed in a coup as the film was being shot in June 1965). Although the film describes what was a major defeat for the FLN, it signposts Algeria's eventual victory in the war by concluding with a brief re-enactment of the popular uprising of December 1960 – which it portrays as a spontaneous and unstoppable demonstration of national will. Thus even the most serious of military setbacks, we are invited to infer from the film, cannot prevent the 'historical inevitably' of victory by the colonised over the colonisers. As writers like Frantz Fanon and Regis Debray had seemingly promised, the efforts of a small 'revolutionary vanguard' (in this case the FLN leadership in Algiers) were shown to have functioned as a starter motor (albeit with a delayed action) for mass insurgency. We might reasonably conclude here that the film was conceived as part historical record, part monument and part cultural building material for the creation of the modern Algerian nation. At a time when Algerian characters barely featured in films, it was also a vehicle for portraying Algerians to international film audiences, not as 'exotic enigmas' or 'imitation Frenchmen', but as people speaking their own language (Arabic) and with the power to act decisively.[36] Although *The Battle of Algiers* was not distributed on anything like the scale of a major US film production, it was shown in cinemas in Italy, Sweden, Denmark, USA, Belgium, West Germany, Finland and France in the late 1960s and early 1970s.[37]

Historians also rightly pay close attention to the textual properties of the film itself. But perhaps because of the dominance of narrative in history writing, they tend to focus solely on diegesis – this refers to the imaginary world that the film creates, in which characters 'live' and events 'happen' and that we as spectators are able to watch. In that regard, they would note how *The Battle of Algiers* was acclaimed from the outset for its 'realism', and for what *Time* magazine called the director's 'absence of editorial comment'.[38] Indeed, the film's Italian director, Gillo Pontecorvo, who co-wrote the screenplay with Franco Solinas, made a point of explaining that the script was produced 'after a year of studying documents and listening to eyewitness accounts of the real battle of Algiers'.[39] The screenplay also used as an important source Saadi Yacef's memoir *Souvenirs de la bataille D'Alger, Décembre 1956-Septembre 1957* (1962). Yacef had been the military leader of the FLN in the Casbah in 1956–7, he was also a co-producer of *The Battle of Algiers* (as the managing director of Casbah Films), he helped write the screenplay and he played a version of himself in the film (the character 'Djafaar'). There is not space here to look in detail at how the film organises, narrates and resolves its story. But we should point to the relatively 'even-handed' treatment in the film between the FLN and French police and paratroopers (noting, by the way, that even-handedness is itself a form of editorial comment, not its absence). Both sides are shown killing civilians indiscriminately; the French set off a bomb in the Casbah, the FLN retaliate with bomb attacks on two European cafes and an airport lounge. Both sides are allowed space within the film to articulate and defend their actions (without refutation). As spectators we are encouraged to identify with main FLN characters like Djafaar and Ali la Pointe, whose point of view is often adopted in the film. But the same also holds true for the French paratroop commander 'Lt Colonel Mathieu' (a composite representation of several senior French soldiers), who is portrayed as a sympathetic figure – humane, reasonable and honorable.[40]

Historians often focus on diegesis because they believe it will allow them to judge whether a film's portrayal of past events is 'accurate' or 'faithful' to those events themselves. On these grounds, *The Battle of Algiers* has been praised by some for its 'honest' and 'objective' depiction of events, but also criticised by others for its handling of the subject matter: for example, its failure to mention that more than one million Algerians died under French colonialism, against a far smaller number of French who died in the war in Algeria; its unwillingness to explore the psychological motivations of its characters; its failure to mention any other Algerian nationalist movements apart from the FLN; its inattention to ideological divisions within the FLN; its omission of any reference to those European Algerians who supported the FLN; and its failure to mention the importance of Egypt's support for the FLN.[41] But as Marnie Hughes-Warrington argues there are two main problems with this kind of approach to analysing historical films. Firstly, it typically resorts to using written histories as the foundation for judging questions of 'accuracy' and 'faithfulness' – on the false assumption that written histories are largely unproblematic representations of the past against which films should be held to account. Secondly, it holds that the discursive meanings and functions of films can be determined and *exhausted* from studying their diegeses alone – those things that we see and hear on screen. Yet this denies the role that spectators perform in actively constructing meanings as they watch films – indeed, we could say that there is no textual meaning without readers/viewers. And it overlooks the fact that the various ways in which spectators construct those meanings are influenced by many factors outside the film text itself. What do these include?

As viewers we watch films in different settings and for different purposes, and audience reception studies suggest that these will affect our reading of the film in question. Sometimes we watch films alone, sometimes with others. We might see a film in a cinema, at home, on a laptop, on a plane, in a university seminar room or on a mobile device, and these settings shape the ways we can interact with a film (whether we watch in silence or not, pause a film or skip parts, sing and dance along with the film, eat while we watch, fall asleep, watch DVD special features before or after the main film, throw things at the screen…). And, of course, the broader social and political context in which a film is viewed changes over time, altering the ways in which particular groups can use a film for their own purposes. In the 1960s the African-American revolutionary group the Black Panthers viewed *The Battle of Algiers* as a manual for urban guerilla warfare. In 2003

Pentagon officials screened it as the basis for discussing tactics following the military occupation of Iraq. In June 2010 the Algerian national football team watched it as a motivational tool on the eve of their World Cup match against England. Also, films come to us already laden with reviews and critical status that might direct our expectations of them. *The Battle of Algiers* has the reputation of a 'classic'. It won the Golden Lion Prize at the 1966 Venice Film Festival and was nominated for three Academy Awards. It features in academic film books and is taught in university courses. It was restored and re-released in 2003–4, including a three-disc DVD set in the US that features interviews with Gillo Pontecorvo and Saadi Yacef, a documentary narrated by Edward Said and interviews with Spike Lee, Mira Nair, Julian Schnabel, Stephen Soderbergh and Oliver Stone about its cinematic importance.[42] The film – along with accompanying interviews, commentaries and viewers posts – can also be accessed in chapters on *YouTube* and researched on sites such as the *Internet Movie Database* (where it currently has an average viewer rating of 8.1/10).[43]

Films like *The Battle of Algiers* are important mediums for constructing narratives of past events, not least because of their potential to attract a mass audience. They also have the potential to generate controversy and debate, both within and between different communities (national, political, ethnic, religious, ideological, intellectual) and as a focus for the interpretative functions of the popular media. Historians can play an important role in such debates – including pointing out those portrayals of events in a film that do not cohere with the available evidence. Nevertheless, we argue that historians are best advised to ask questions about the ways in which films generate meanings on their own terms (as films) rather than regard them as diluted forms of 'proper' history. What caused the filmmakers to make the film the way they did? What are the possible implications of making this film in that way? How have interpretations of the film (and the uses which it is seen to be able to serve) varied between times and places? What causes us (as individual historians) to read the film the way that we do?

Past presencing

The examples discussed so far are all representations or simulations of the past: products that audiences can read, play or watch. But today's consumer culture is not fully satisfied with simulation: it also craves the harder hits of 'experience' and 'authenticity' – ways of accessing the 'real thing'. What would constitute an authentic experience of the past, given that commonsense understandings of temporality hold that the past is necessarily absent from the present and therefore unavailable to us? One way of dealing with this question is to dismiss it as being based on a false premise. We could sensibly argue that we can never experience the past as such, we can only apprehend it via its mediation in a system of symbolisation (such as description, narrative, or montage). But for the sake of rehearsing some ideas that interest history theorists, we can approach the question from a different perspective. The starting point here is opposition in some quarters to the main direction of travel in history theory from the 1960s onwards. For a long time, the field was dominated by debates about how language is used to create effects of meaning in historical texts (the 'linguistic turn'). For its opponents, the problem with making linguistics and representation the main objects of attention was that questions about the 'real stuff' of the past were ignored. Their response was to focus attention back on the materiality of the past (not on written accounts of it) through the related notions of 'presence' and 'experience'. These became familiar terms in memory studies in the 1980s and 1990s, particularly where memory work was concerned with the traumatic effects of torture, violence or genocide. By the twenty-first century, experience and presence were being put to work in history theory by those who wanted to argue that the past could be accessed outside of its representational forms. Two theorists are significant here. Frank Ankersmit's work on the 'sublime historical experience' sought to move discussion of people's relationship to the past beyond epistemology. Before we do the cognitive work of knowing the past, says Ankersmit, we first have a feeling or sensation for it. In a prosaic sense, this can mean that an individual historian's work on the past evokes powerful sensations in them, to the point where they feel themselves to be a part of what they are describing. More characteristic of Ankersmit's notion of the sublime historical experience is when one looks at an old painting, a piece of furniture or a room that has been left unchanged for centuries and experiences a sensation that he describes as the highest stage of historical consciousness. In such objects, Ankersmit argues, 'the past itself can have been said to have survived the centuries and to be still present'.[44] Such encounters with the 'reality' of the past are only ever fleeting, he says, no more than a 'gift of the moment'.[45] They cannot be sought or willed, and in their intensity they can overwhelm the person who has the encounter.

Eelco Runia's theorisation of presence also starts from a desire to engage with the non-discursive 'reality' of the past.[46] Unlike Ankersmit's subject of 'sublime historical experience', who is conscious of what they are feeling, presence for Runia often manifests via the unconscious.[47] He gives the example of Dutch historians who worked on the Srebrenica Commission

(1996–2002). Their task was to investigate the actions of Dutch peacekeeping troops who failed to prevent a massacre of thousands of Bosnian Muslims in Srebrenica in 1995. Runia claims that, in compiling their report, the historians unconsciously reproduced patterns of behaviour that mirrored those of the Dutch troops they were investigating. By hiding behind an overly detailed report, refusing to make an authoritative judgement and adopting the same arguments that the soldiers used to excuse their inaction, the historians identified with or 'acted out' the actions of the troops in 1995. Runia sees this as a case of the past intruding on the historians in ways that they did not – perhaps could not – control. '[S]trangely and inexplicably,' he remarks, 'the past turned the tables and mastered these historians'[48]. Stranger still is his other often-cited claim about the 'presence' of the past at Abu Ghraib prison in Baghdad after the US-led invasion of Iraq in 2003. Runia believes that US troops' torture of prisoners at Abu Ghraib should be read as an example of the psychological 'compulsion to repeat':

> In the cells and corridors of Abu Ghraib, Saddam Hussein's torture practices were so overwhelmingly present, and the sheer possibility of using them – though horrifying – loomed so large, that sooner or later the Americans *had* to repeat them...
>
> The Abu Ghraib case suggests that the past... may have such an irresistible power that it is able to express itself in what actually happens in the real world. It opens a perspective that is almost too disturbing to accept: that the past may have a presence that is so powerful that it can use *us*, humans, as its *material*.[49]

Sceptics regard Ankersmit's and Runia's descriptions of historical experience and presence as confused wanderings into mysticism. These are understandable objections. But their work does usefully provide an intellectual supplement to a popular phenomenon, which is a desire to feel affected by the past rather than just to know about it. As Runia writes, museums and heritage sites often spend vast sums of money attempting to give visitors what they hope will be a 'deep sense of personal connection' with the past.[50] He argues that these attempts usually fail because they are too literal, too forced. But failure has not deterred people from trying to connect with the 'real' of the past. This is why attempts to conjure experience and presence continue to operate in some popular forms of history. Historical tourism trades on its promise to take people to sites where important events played out. Historical walking tours offer a similar promise of 'authenticity' by implying that traces of the past endure at given locations. In doing so, they emphasise the importance of spatiality over temporality – 'time may have passed, but this remains the exact place of a certain event'. For example, 'Buenos Aires Off the Beaten Path Tours' promises walkers a chance to become 'an eyewitness to an obscure period of our history' in Argentina.[51] It takes them to a former detention centre that was known as the 'Auschwitz of Argentina' and shows them memorial plaques of the disappeared people (Runia regards naming the victims of history as one of the most effective ways of enabling the past to intrude upon us[52]). In Belfast, walking tours of sites connected to 'the Troubles', often led by former Republican paramilitaries, have become significant features of 'political tourism' (or 'terror tourism' if viewed from a Unionist perspective). Jonathan Skinner argues that these walks are 'embodied and immersive', while for Allice Legat walking through such sites 'validates the reality of the past in the present'.[53] The idea that physically occupying a space of historical significance provides a special form of experience of the past in the present helps to explain the popularity of historical tourism. It also helps us to understand developments in the field that we turn to next – public history.

Notes

1 Raphael Samuel, *Theatres of Memory*, vol. 1, *Past and Present in Contemporary Culture* (London: Verso, 1994) 25.
2 David Harlan, '*The Burden of History Forty Years Later'*, in F. Ankersmit, E. Domanska, and H. Kellner (eds), *Refiguring Hayden White* (Stanford: Stanford California Press, 2009) 177.
3 Jerome de Groot, *Consuming History: Historians and Heritage in Contemporary Popular Culture* (Abingdon: Routledge, 2016) 311.
4 de Groot, *Consuming History* 312.
5 *The Guardian,* G2, 23 June 2010.
6 'BBC period drama *The Tudors* is 'gratuitously awful" says Dr David Starkey', *The Telegraph*, 16 October 2008.
7 Sean Wilentz, 'America Made Easy: McCulloch, Adams, and the Decline of Popular History', in *The New Republic,* 2 July 2001, quoted in David Harlan, 'Ken Burns and the Coming Crisis of Academic History', in *Rethinking History* 7/2 (2003) 183.
8 Ann Rigney, 'Being an Improper Historian', in Keith Jenkins, Sue Morgan, Alun Munslow (eds), *Manifestos for History* (London: Routledge, 2007) 153, 150.
9 Harlan, 'Ken Burns', 184.
10 Rosenstone, 'Space for the Bird to Fly,' 17.

11 See Nadia Idle and Alex Nunns (eds), *Tweets from Tahrir: Egypt's Revolution as it Unfolded, in the Words of the People who Made it* (New York: OR Books, 2011). For YouTube film of police evicting protesters in Oakland on 25 October 2011, see www.youtube.com/watch?v=wQe0twUCQwY and in New York on 15 November 2011, see www.youtube.com/watch?v=j_xg3uKS6gs both accessed 9 February 2010.

12 Jo Guldi and David Armitage, *The History Manifesto* (Cambridge: Cambridge University Press, 2014) 97; see also www.slavevoyages.org accessed 16 December 2019.

13 'Google Books History', www.google.com/googlebooks/about/history.html accessed 16 December 2019.

14 Statistics are taken from Alexa, www.alexa.com/siteinfo/wikipedia.org and Wikipedia, https://en.wikipedia.org/wiki/Wikipedia#Launch_and_early_growth both accessed 8 January 2020.

15 https://en.wikipedia.org/wiki/Wikipedia accessed 8 January 2000.

16 Marcus Messner and Marcia W. DiStaso, 'Wikipedia versus Encyclopedia Britannica: A Longitudinal Analysis to Identify the Impact of Social Media on the Standards of Knowledge', in *Mass Communication and Society,* 16/4 (2013) 482–3.

17 Dan O'Sullivan, *Wikipedia: A New Community of Practice?* (Farnham: Ashgate, 2009) 81–2.

18 Jack Lynch, *You Could Look It Up: The Reference Shelf from Ancient Babylon to Wikipedia* (New York: Bloomsbury Press, 2016) 389.

19 Murray G. Phillips, 'Wikipedia and History: A Worthwhile Partnership in the Digital Era?', in *Rethinking History,* 20/4 (2016) 523–43.

20 See, for example, Roy Rosenzweig, 'Can History be Open Source? *Wikipedia* and the Future of the Past', in *The Journal of American History,* 93/1 (2006) 117–46; and Wikipedia's own summary of judgements about its reliability at https://en.wikipedia.org/wiki/Reliability_of_Wikipedia#Assessments accessed 8 January 2020.

21 Rosenzweig, 'Can History be Open Source?', 132–3.

22 Rosenzweig, 'Can History be Open Source?', 132.

23 Niall McCarthy, 'The Best-Selling Titles in the Call of Duty Franchise', in *Forbes,* 25 October 2019. These figures were accurate for the period up to and including October 2019.

24 Robertson Allen, *America's Digital Army: Games at Work and War* (Lincoln: University of Nebraska Press, 2017) 45.

25 See *Business Insider,* 31 October 2019, https://www.businessinsider.com/call-of-duty-modern-warfare-launch-sales-records-ps4-pc-2019-10?r=US&IR=T accessed 4 December 2019.

26 Ubisoft, 'Facts and Figures', June 2019, https://ubistatic-a.akamaihd.net/0090/PROD/ubigroup/PressKit/20180611/2019_06_Press_Kit_Facts_Figures-EN.pdf accessed 4 December 2019.

27 Adam Chapman, Anna Foka and Jonathan Westin, 'Introduction: What is Historical Game Studies?', in *Rethinking History*, 21/3 (2017) 359–61.

28 Cited in William Uricchio, 'Simulation, History and Computer Games', in Joost Raessens and Jeffrey Goldstein (eds), *Handbook of Computer Game Studies* (Cambridge, MA: MIT Press, 2005) 330.

29 Kevin Schutt, 'Strategic Simulations and Our Past: The Bias of Computer Games in the Presentation of History', in *Games and Culture*, 2/3 (2007) 213.

30 Holger Pötzsch and Vít Šisler, 'Playing Cultural Memory: Framing History in *Call of Duty: Black Ops* and *Czechoslovakia 38–89: Assassination*', *Games and Culture* 14/1 (2019) 8.

31 Uricchio, 'Simulation, History and Computer Games', 333.

32 Pötzsch and Šisler, 'Playing Cultural Memory', 6–7.

33 Dawn Spring, 'Gaming History: Computer and Video Games as Historical Scholarship', in *Rethinking History*, 9/2 (2015) 212–13.

34 For a detailed study of why historians are wrong to do so, see Eleftheria Thanouli, *History and Film: A Tale of Two Disciplines* (New York: Bloomsbury Academic, 2018).

35 Hughes-Warrington, *History Goes to the Movies*, 31.

36 E. Shohat, and R. Stam, *Unthinking Eurocentrism: Multiculturalism and the Media* (London: Routledge, 1994) 252.

37 www.imdb.com/title/tt0058946/releaseinfo accessed 8 July 2010.

38 J. Mellen, *Filmguide to the Battle of Algiers* (Bloomington, London: Indiana University Press, 1973) 58.

39 *Ibid.*, 16.

40 Hugh Roberts, 'The Image of the French Army in the Cinematic Representation of the Algerian War: The Revolutionary Politics of *The Battle of Algiers*', in Martin S. Alexander, Martin Evans and J.F.V. Keiger, (eds), *The Algerian War and the French Army, 1954–62: Experiences, Images, Testimonies* (Basingstoke: Palgrave, 2002) 158.

41 Mellen, *Filmguide to the Battle of Algiers*, 60–5.

42 www.criterion.com/films/248-the-battle-of-algiers accessed 4 February 2020.

43 www.imdb.com/title/tt0058946/ accessed 4 February 2020.

44 Frank Ankersmit, *Sublime Historical Experience* (Stanford: Stanford University Press, 2005) 115.

45 Ankersmit, *Sublime*, 128.

46 See Eelco Runia, 'Presence', in *Moved by the Past: Discontinuity and Historical Mutation* (Columbia University Press, 2014) 49–83.

47 For a good comparative discussion see Anton Froeyman, 'Frank Ankersmit and Eelco Runia: the Presence and the Otherness of the Past', *Rethinking History*, 16/3 (2012) 393–415.

48 Eelco Runia, 'Spots of Time', *History and Theory*, 45/3 (2006) 308.

49 Runia, 'Spots of Time', 308.

50 Runia, 'Spots of Time', 309.

51 See https://baoffthebeatenpathtours.wordpress.com/2015/11/16/in-the-footsteps-of-dictators, accessed 9 February 2020. We are grateful to Georgia Bender for this reference.

52 Runia, 'Spots of Time', 309.

53 Jonathan Skinner, 'Walking the Falls: Dark Tourism and the Significance of Movement on the Political Tour of West Belfast', in *Tourist Studies,* 16/1 (2016) 14.

Further reading

Jerome de Groot, *Consuming History: Historians and heritage in contemporary popular culture* (Abingdon: Routledge, 2016). De Groot's revised text is the best single-volume on the many different ways in which people engage with and consume the past. Inevitably a book that discusses contemporary television, film, digital games and social media platforms dates fairly rapidly, but this book provides serious discussion of why we need to look beyond historians for our past-talk.

Ludmilla Jordanova, *History in Practice* (London: Bloomsbury Academic, 2019). This third edition contains useful chapters on history in a digital world and public history. It also ranges widely across history's relationship with other disciplines in the humanities and social sciences.

Joost Raessens and Jeffrey Goldstein (eds), *Handbook of Computer Game Studies* (Cambridge, Mass: MIT Press, 2005). This multi-disciplinary text was one of the first serious collection of pieces about gaming. It includes William Uricchio's influential essay, 'Simulation, History and Computer Games'.

Eleftheria Thanouli, *History and Film: A Tale of Two Disciplines* (New York: Bloomsbury Academic, 2018). In this theoretically sophisticated book, Thanouli seeks to bring history theory and film studies together. She argues that whereas history films are compatible with contemporary ideas about truth, meaning and knowledge, written histories are better suited to nineteenth-century epistemologies.

PART IV

HISTORY TODAY

10

Public history

What is public history?

The past has long made a claim on public attention, centuries before university historians turned it into a professional field of study. Epic tale, ecclesiastical chronicle, poetry, painting, sculpture and monument have all been used as vehicles for what we would now call public history. Histories in these forms were 'public' in the literal sense that they were produced for general audiences (not for people studying or teaching courses). More importantly, such representations of the past often served a public function. The battle site of Thermopylae in Greece, for example, displays a copy of a text that exhorted people in ancient times to remember the defeat of the Spartans by Xerxes in 480 BCE. By the nineteenth century, the idea of treating the past as a resource that could be exploited in service of social goals had taken on more modern forms. This was the era when governing regimes across Europe commissioned the building of major museums, in part to persuade people that the 'proper' way to understand the past was through the narrative template of the nation. In this way, public history was mobilised to secure popular allegiance to the relatively new idea of the nation state as a sovereign unit. In the 1970s, the term public history took on a new meaning as the name for the production and use of history that ran outside of – and in some respects parallel to – formal academic institutions. The setting up of the journal *The Public Historian* in the United States in 1978 signalled the arrival of a newly distinctive field of practice. At around the same time in the 1970s, the first academic courses to train public historians also appeared. Rather than become university historians, these graduates typically went on to work as historical interpreters, advisers and consultants in heritage organisations, museums, archives and local government. At one level, this trend was caused by an over-supply of academic historians for the number of university jobs that were available, which meant that people who wanted to make a career out of their interest in history had to look elsewhere for work. But there was also a sense of mission behind the growth of public history from the 1970s onwards. Rather than assume that there was an intrinsic value to knowing about the past for its 'own sake', public historians committed to use their practices in pursuit of named social goals. This 'applied' or 'practical' dimension of public history is still emphasised in the National Council on Public History' latest definition of the term as 'the many and diverse ways in which history is put to work in the world'.[1]

Since its emergence in North America, this contemporary iteration of public history has developed internationally. In 2012 the International Federation for Public History held its inaugural meeting in Luxembourg. A recent handbook about public history globally contained case studies from around a dozen countries.[2] This proliferation helps to explain Faye Sayer's point that public history has shifted from its position on the outskirts of orthodox academic history 'into an integrated and essential element of the subject's research and communication'.[3] This is a reasonable observation. But equally it is important to recognise that public history is more than simply a supplement to academic history's repertoire of activities. In its choice of subjects, its orientation towards different audiences, and its attitude towards questions of authority over the past, public history often employs a distinctive set of values. It attempts to do things that academic historians rarely see as being part of their collective responsibility. Take, for example, the UK's Migration Museum Project. Since 2009, this project has sought to create a museum that represents Britain's long heritage as a country of migration. Many similar museums exist elsewhere but, in 2020, the work to establish a permanent site for a British version was still ongoing.[4] The initiative for the project came from a group that included a former government minister, an immigration barrister and judge, a deputy editor of the publisher *Granta* and senior staff or associates from the Institute for Public Policy Research think-tank. The group's political ambition for the proposed museum was expressed in stark terms in a 2012 report on the project's first two years, which declared: 'Our overriding purpose is to bring about a reduction in hostility to migrants'.[5] The need to realise this goal was urgent because as the report explained: 'Attitudes to migrants in Britain are hostile and becoming more so, especially among young people'.[6] The rationale for creating a museum to shift people's views about migrants was that a cultural institution could be a 'potentially effective vehicle for influencing cultural attitudes'.[7] The original idea for the museum was that it would be mobile, consisting of nine shipping containers that could be transported to different parts of the country. However, this proposal was eventually dropped in favour of a plan to find a settled home in central London. This proved to be a major challenge, so, while the wait to find a permanent base continued, the museum staged a number of exhibitions in different spaces across the country. These included 'Germans in Britain' (which appeared in various locations between 2014 and 2017), 'Stories from Calais and Beyond' (2016–17), '100 Images of Migration' (2014–17), 'Seven Migration Moments that Changed Britain' (2017–18) and 'Room to Breathe' (2018–19).

Some of these exhibitions gave a voice to the experiences of those migrants who are defined by classificatory regimes as 'refugees'. By doing so, the museum recognised the importance of enabling refugees to talk about themselves as subjects in their own terms, rather than making aid agencies and relief organisations the principal subjects of a story in which anonymous refugees appear only as the objects of external support. The 'Room to Breathe' exhibition at Lambeth in south London, for example, featured artists-in-residence, some of whom were former refugees. It also hosted therapeutic art studios for asylum seekers and refugees. In providing a space in which refugee experiences could be articulated, a public history organisation like the Migration Museum does something that academic history largely fails to do. Peter Gatrell noted this failure more than a decade ago when he complained that historians have shown 'actual resistance rather than simple apathy' in their engagement with refugees as subjects.[8] In similar fashion, Philip Marfleet wrote in a historiographical review in 2007 that refugees are 'people whose absence from most historical writing is so marked that it constitutes a systematic exclusion'.[9]

The heritage industry

Public history is not the same as the heritage sector, but the two have much in common. Heritage work is the practice of identifying, preserving, marking and increasing people's awareness about those things that are held to be of historic and cultural significance. Such work might involve building monuments or erecting commemorative plaques to mark particular sites. It also includes preserving and conserving the material fabrics of the past, as well as old customs and habits – such as protecting historic remains, renovating old houses, curating museum exhibitions or reenacting life in a sixteenth-century kitchen. It is difficult to date the rise of the modern preoccupation with heritage. David Lowenthal argued that it dates from around 1980, at least in relation to Reagan's America, Thatcher's Britain and Pompidou's France. Alternatively, one could cite the meeting of European nations at the first historic monuments meeting in 1931 (joined by Tunisia, Mexico and Peru in 1964) and the coming into force of the World Heritage Convention in 1975 (which was extended from 20 to 80 countries in 1979).[10] This convention has resulted in a list of more than 1,100 properties (natural and cultural) across the world that are deemed to be of 'outstanding universal value' and thus worthy of international safeguards (and funding). These include sites such as Egypt's Ancient Thebes with its Necropolis, the Sydney Opera House, China's Great Wall, Brazil's Historic Town of Ouro Preto, Berlin's modernist housing estates built in 1910–33 and Britain's Stonehenge.[11] Heritage has now become a sizeable industry in its own right. In Britain, for example, the National Trust's membership climbed above one million in 1981 (in 2017 it reached more than five million). It was also estimated in 2006 that about £1 in every £1,000 in the UK economy could be directly related to the museums and galleries sector.[12]

David Lowenthal viewed the expansion of the heritage sector as problematic, complaining that by the late 1990s, '[o]ne can barely move without bumping into a heritage site'.[13] In *What Is History Now?* (2002) Felipe Fernández-Armesto set out a different line of criticism. Because there was now less history taught in schools, he argued, heritage had become many people's main point of contact with history – and for him it was a poor substitute. 'Some of this [heritage activity] is in the hands of scholarly museum curators and *fonctionnaires*. Much of it, however, is at the mercy of theme park economics, dire and dumbed down. Historians contribute relatively little guidance'.[14] Such criticisms, from the kind of commentators that Raphael Samuel called 'heritage-baiters', are as old as the heritage industry itself.[15] They rest on two main points. The first is that the heritage sector is overly nostalgic about the past. There is a joke that captures this: how many preservationists does it take to change a light bulb? Four: one to change the bulb, one to document the event and two to lament the passing of the old bulb.[16] If we apply this joke to Britain's heritage sector as it grew in the 1980s, the thing that's loss was often implicitly lamented was the country's stature as a leading international power. By offering the public an idealised version of a once 'glorious' national past, heritage acted as a supplement to the cultural-nationalist strand of the Thatcher government's ideological project. Among other objectives, this project promised to 'revive' Britain's international standing after a period of 'decline'. The problem here was not so much that heritage had become politicised. This is unavoidable. Heritage work always involves confronting political questions. What things should be preserved or commemorated? Which heritage projects should be funded? What *counts* as 'our' national heritage (who decides and, in any case, who are 'we')? The real problem was that the heritage industry had become aligned too easily with forms of popular nationalism, allowing a dominant coalition of interests to pass off their preferred version of the past as 'natural' or 'common sense', in just the same way as they did for their ideas about economics and social questions.

The second common criticism made of the heritage sector is that it represents the past as a Disneyland of the historical imagination. By this, critics mean that it turns the past into commodities and tourist kitsch – vulgar, trivialised, packaged for easy consumption and shorn of anything that might encourage serious thinking. Heritage, they argue, has become just another option for discretionary leisure spending in our overly mediated societies, reframing the past as a kind of bland shopping mall in which we can 'experience' the times of our ancestors and buy replicas of things that they used to own. Ludmilla Jordanova regards the way that museums represent the past as being typical of modern convenience culture – inauthentic, inorganic, satisfying at the point of contact but in the long run almost certainly bad for us. '[M]useums work in insidious ways,' she wrote. 'The past they present is highly refined, in the manner of manufactured foods'.[17] Underneath this criticism, of course, lies the idea that 'heritage' and 'history' are not just different concepts, but that in most important respects they are antithetical. Lowenthal invokes a conventional epistemic model of 'proper' history to make just this kind of distinction:

> Heritage is not history at all; while it borrows from and enlivens historical study, heritage is not an inquiry into the past but a celebration of it, not an effort to know what happened but a profession of faith in a past tailored to present-day purposes.[18]

Heritage sites can be as undemanding on their visitors as critics allege, aiming to provide the public with no more than a pleasant day out. But we should also recognise that there are important exceptions. For the past

20 years or so, commentators have been analysing the rise of 'dark tourism'. The term refers to the way in which former sites of genocide, torture and disaster have become visitor destinations. Places such as Auschwitz-Birkenau in Poland, Chernobyl in Ukraine, Ground Zero in New York and the Khmer Rouge's Tuol Sleng prison in Cambodia are now part of the global heritage-tourist network, offering a span of experiences that range from educational opportunities at one end to a morbid gaze at extreme suffering at the other, depending on what visitors want. Despite their best intentions, there is no way that former prisons or killing grounds can prevent people from visiting them simply to feed their darkest curiosities. Nor can they prevent people from posting disrespectful images of their visit to the site on social media. However, there are ways in which they can signal that their preservation and accessibility as public spaces is primarily linked to mourning, remembrance and reflection. Since 1999, for example, the International Coalition of Sites of Conscience has sought to use places of memory as a way of supporting efforts to promote peace and social justice.[19] These efforts include the coalition's involvement in campaigns to secure reparations for victims of human rights abuses, to support survivors of torture and to prevent the repeat of atrocities in post-conflict settings. As the organisation explains, their mission is to 'connect past to present [and] memory to action'.[20]

Transforming a place where disaster occurred into a heritage site that works on behalf of victims is a laudable aim, but any attempt to do so raises challenging issues of authority, responsibility and representation. The Remember Bhopal Museum in India, which was established in December 2014, illustrates the point. The event that the museum commemorates is a major gas leak that occurred at the US-based Union Carbide Corporation's pesticide plant in Bhopal on the night of 2–3 December 1984. Between 15,000 and 20,000 people died as a result and another half a million suffered harmful exposure to methyl isocyanate gas. After three decades of corporate and political failure to deal adequately with the disaster, survivors and activists set up their own museum in Bhopal as a way of naming and shaming those responsible and keeping their campaign for justice in public sight. It was crucial that the museum was not set up by heritage professionals or with the advice of historians. No third parties were delegated to speak on behalf of those who suffered because of the gas leak. Instead, oral testimonies from survivors dominate the museum, ensuring that they are the ones who control how the story of Bhopal is told within its walls. Moreover, by refusing all offers of government or corporate support, the collective behind the project resisted efforts to memorialise the disaster solely on the terms that the Indian state wished (an official memorial had been established to mark the disaster on its twentieth anniversary). By doing so, the survivor-led museum functions as part of a struggle for redress in the present rather than as a memorial that consigns the Bhopal disaster fully to the past and signals to the survivor community that the time has come for them to 'move on'.[21]

In similar spirit, albeit in a different context, Sharon Macdonald describes how authorities in Germany have dealt with the problem of the 'undesirable heritage' that was left by the Nazi party rally grounds at Nuremberg.[22] These grounds are the largest existing site of fascist architecture in Germany, located in a city whose name has become synonymous with Nazism. In the decades after the Second World War, authorities at city, regional and federal level had to decide what to do with the old rally grounds. There were no easy choices because any decision raised awkward questions about the relationship between the site and the current condition of German historical consciousness of the 1933–45 era. Destroying the grounds could be seen as an attempt to suppress a painful past. Allowing them to fall into ruin by deliberate neglect risked giving them an unwanted romantic allure. On the other hand, restoring the site could unintentionally revive its former glory and monumental power. The solution was to turn the old Congress Hall at the Nuremberg grounds into a Documentation Centre which, it was hoped, would require visitors to engage in 'serious cognitive work' and demonstrate 'an ability to self-distance from that which is displayed'.[23] This sense of critical purpose was reinforced by an architectural design strategy that involved inserting a large glass and steel structure into the centre of the old building. Symbolically, this insertion represented a stake through the heart of the former Congress Hall. It functioned to repurpose the building for new times and to reduce the risk of it being appropriated as a relic of the Nazi past. It was a striking visual signal that a site of 'undesirable heritage' had been preserved, but only on terms that were clearly intended to serve the democratic needs of the present.

What is shared authority?

Shared authority is a useful concept for anyone who wants to avoid drawing hard and fixed boundaries between public and academic history. The term contains semantic flexibility. It can be used with a critical edge, urging academic historians to adopt a position of 'epistemic modesty' in relation to the past. In effect, this means relinquishing a collective sense that they have a privileged descriptive or explanatory perspective on 'how things were', and recognising that they share authority with other producers of past-talk.

Alternatively, it can be applied as a simple descriptive term for collaboration between different types of contributors to past-focused projects. Using either inflection of meaning, shared authority is a phrase that reminds us that no forms of history-making are located exclusively and necessarily within singular categories of 'academic', 'public' or 'popular' histories. Instead, what matters is how any such work is conducted and turned into a particular type of representation for others to consume.

We can see how 'sharing authority' works in practice in cases like the Chinatown History Museum (later renamed as the Museum of Chinese in America), which grew out of the New York Chinatown History Project (NYCHP) which was itself set up in 1980. Developed from complementary strategies of community consultation and outreach programmes, the museum has stood as a small, but significant, counterpoint to the white Anglo-American institutional power that organisations like the New York Historical Society and the Museum of the City of New York embody. Most important of all, its presence as 'other' to the official memory repositories of New York highlights questions about what such sites of cultural authority fail to collect and exhibit, and how the absence of particular materials (and the narratives they made possible) both constitute and reproduce the racially ordered hierarchies that have played out with such iniquitous social consequences across the city. Jack (John Kuo Wei) Tchen, one of NYCHP's co-founders, explained how the kind of exclusionary practices that operated within New York's established historical culture meant that crucial social and economic networks such as Chinese laundries were almost wholly marginalised from authorised histories of the city. Consequently, it was incumbent on the city's Chinese American community to find the methods, settings and forms to represent itself historically:

> When we wanted to explore the formation of New York Chinatown in the 19th Century, we realized it was founded by the thousands of small hand laundries scattered in the New York metropolitan region. There was not documentation about this low status, racially excluded community. There were not collections. There were no academics studying this experience, except for one. There were no Chinese American historical groups. This was a subaltern history best understood by those who lived the experience and came from it.[24]

In order to work as a space for the expression of subaltern history, NYCHP created a 'dialogic museum', where its scholars and production team worked in tandem with the people whose histories it narrated. In effect, this meant a series of discussions exploring the memories and meanings of Chinatown's past between groups that included Chinese New Yorkers, Lower East Side residents, other New Yorkers, tourists, scholars and various other 'cultural producers' – the diversity of the groups involved in the dialogue was designed to reflect the complex networks of people who crossed in and out of Chinatown and interacted with its residents.[25] Although the early dialogues between these groups focused on exchanging information and recounting experiences, this was always intended to be preliminary to deeper discussions about the formation of individual and collective identities. In one of its early exhibitions on 'Memories of New York Chinatown', the museum explored the dissonance between the expressed cultural identities of Chinese New Yorkers and the tendency among the wider New York public and visiting tourists to see them as perpetual foreigners. Indeed, the museum's larger social ambition, according to Tchen, was to 'make a critical historical awareness a powerful factor in improving New York and the community for the future'.[26] In a review of the project in its early years, Tchen wrote that the museum's role in producing a more inclusive community history could help to counter the feelings of marginalisation and disempowerment experienced by Chinese Americans: feelings that resulted in no small way from the Chinese Exclusion Acts (1882–1943) and the decades of racism that these statutes legitimised. The sense of 'alienation and low self-esteem' that Tchen ascribed to the New York Chinese manifested itself as a lack of concern within the community about its own history. Documents, artefacts and other traces of the past were often discarded as rubbish in Chinatown by people who scarcely saw themselves represented in US mainstream historical culture. But by reaching out to the community with public programmes – including organising reunions, media production and curating bilingual exhibitions – the museum helped to reverse assumptions that no one was interested in recording or preserving communal memories. The more activities it staged and materials it produced, the more the museum won trust among Chinese Americans; people who were formerly reticent to collaborate became more willing to talk to its trained volunteer researchers and share their memories. This openness, in turn, helped the museum to develop an 'alternative archive' of materials, and, out of this, it has produced walking tours, radio programmes, documentaries, lectures, publications and other resources that have disseminated far beyond Chinatown.[27] In doing so, a small museum project developed into an important source of a community's collective memory.

Collective memory

Raphael Samuel, who was one of the earliest agenda setters for British public history, argued that identifying, preserving, marking and increasing people's awareness about things in the past could be socially empowering.[28] Warwick University's 'People's History of the NHS' project in the UK is a recent example of the kind of historical practice that Samuel sought to encourage. It involved gathering people's stories, memories and objects about Britain's National Health Service as it approached its 70th anniversary in 2018. By encouraging contributions from patients, staff and health service trade unions, the project aimed to inform and encourage public debate about the NHS's future. Also, by creating a grassroots record of stories and experiences, the 'People's History of the NHS' project contributed to a collective memory of a vital national institution.[29] Referring to 'collective' rather than 'personal' memory here is a way of signalling that memories are never formed in isolation; they are always formed, maintained and given meaning as part of a social group.[30] Cultures commonly have shared points of identity that are drawn from the past – often battles, victories, defeats, betrayals, atrocities or perceived injustices – and these resonate among group members in ways that can bind people together. Moreover, as Eviatar Zerubavel noted, it is possible that people are able to incorporate into their own pasts things that happened to groups that predate their membership.[31] This is why rival versions of the past adhered to by different communities often carry enormous political and affective weight: think, for example, of the Israel-Palestine question or the debates in a reunified Germany about how to mark publicly the country's recent past.[32]

The ways people relate to the past has become the focus of growing scholarly attention. By 'relate to the past' we mean all the many ways in which people selectively narrate, represent, identify and commemorate aspects of the past – including what they repress, forget or otherwise remain silent about. The study of these processes is categorised under the heading of 'memory studies', and it spans several academic disciplines – mainly anthropology, cultural studies and history, but with important contributions from psychology, sociology, literature and film studies. Instead of treating 'memory' and 'history' as being either identical or opposite terms, memory studies looks at their mutual interaction and dependence. In Dominick LaCapra's formulation, memory helps us to determine what in history deserves preservation in living traditions, and history serves to test and question memory critically.[33] Alternatively, we might say that memory is what makes history possible – because without memory humans would have no concept of the 'before now', and because all of our written sources for history are dependent upon writers' memory work at some level.[34] Moreover, the dominance (or at least popularity) of particular narratives of the past within cultures at different times helps to shape which kinds of memory are likely to find an audience within the public sphere, and which ones are likely to be marginalised and thus only articulated in private settings. As Wulf Kansteiner has argued, memory studies should aim to interrogate the interaction between several factors: 'The intellectual and cultural traditions that frame all our representations of the past, the memory makers who selectively adopt and manipulate these traditions, and the memory consumers who use, ignore, or transform such artifacts according to their own interests'.[35]

As a research field for academic historians, memory studies became established principally in the 1990s, assisted by the founding of a new journal, *History and Memory*, in 1989. The 1990s boom in memory studies also owed something to the cycle of fiftieth anniversary commemorations relating to the Second World War which were observed internationally between 1989 and 1995. These generated, according to Geoff Eley, 'an extraordinary amount of commemorative excess, saturating the spaces of public representation and the TV screens in particular'.[36] Historians (some at least) became interested in what analysis of such commemorative activities might suggest about the relationships between a series of dualisms: memory/history, past/present, public memory/private memory, academic history/popular history. Alon Confino and Peter Fritzsche describe how the 'first generation' of memory studies was principally concerned with cultural representations of memory, which they criticise for its failure to engage with questions concerning social relations, mediation and reception. Thus, they welcomed the emergence of a 'second generation' of memory studies that seeks to shift the focus away from the museum exhibit and the monument. This 'second generation' of work analyses how memory operates within social networks, it explores what people 'do' with their memories and it investigates how shared understanding of memory informs state and institutional policies and practices.[37]

Other developments in the 1990s that spurred interest in memory studies included the work of post-apartheid South Africa's Truth and Reconciliation Commission (where people related their traumatic stories of life under the old regime as part psychotherapy and part legal testimony)[38], the harnessing of mythical accounts of the past to the violent nationalist rhetoric of politicians in states in the former Yugoslavia, and significant events in Holocaust representation and remembrance, such as the release of the film *Schindler's*

List (1993) and the dedication of the United States Holocaust Memorial Museum in Washington DC in 1993.

The turn towards memory also reflected the influence of postmodernism within universities. For historians who were sceptical about conventional models of historical research and writing, the conceptual field of memory offered an alternative means of thinking critically about the past. As Katherine Hodgkin and Susannah Radstone explained in *Contested Pasts: The Politics of Memory* (2003):

> the concept of memory seems to offer a more cautious and qualified relation to the past than the absolute assertion that for some is associated with history. Working with the concept of memory – provisional, subjective, concerned with representation and the present rather than fact and the past – suggests a way out of the impasse into which historiography might have been driven by the poststructuralist assault on truth.[39]

Perhaps the most frequently cited work among historians who turned to the study of memory was *Les Lieux de mémoire* (1984–92), the multi-volume, collective study of symbolic 'memory places' in French national identity. This was supervised and edited by Pierre Nora and was later translated into English as *Realms of Memory*. Nora's collection does not focus solely on those physical places that would immediately come to mind when we think of sites of memory (although it features essays on subjects that include monuments, cathedrals, Versailles and the Eiffel Tower). It broadens its gaze to the 'remembrance of things French', the kinds of symbols and signifiers of bygone traditions that help constitute an imagined French national identity.[40] In Nora's own words, these symbols include:

> The archives and the tricolor; libraries and festivals; dictionaries and the Pantheon; museums and the Arc de Triomphe; the *Dictionnaire Larousse* and the Wall of the Fédérés (where defenders of the Paris Commune were massacred by the French Army in 1871).[41]

These realms of memory come to be regarded as such, argued Nora, because in late twentieth century France there were no longer any settings in which memory was a real part of everyday experience. Artificial memory props, he reasoned, were developed because people needed to find a means of coping with the absence of an organic memory culture that was passed down through successive generations (via collectives such as families, churches and schools). Modern society, he lamented, was fixated on the new and the future, and so it developed a sense of historical consciousness in which the present was conceptualised as breaking off from the past. Nora regretted how history (in his view) distanced people from the past. In particular, he mourned how the passage from memory to history brought about the loss of an apparent unifying sense of nationhood, which he saw as being sustained by a shared sense of continuity with tradition.[42]

The field where heritage, shared authority, memory and public history overlap and become meaningful for the largest number of people is genealogy. As Thomas Cauvin notes, family memories are 'major prisms through which people look at and understand the past', and yet academic historians tend to dismiss family history as a serious form of research.[43] They are likely to see it as insular and incidental to professional historical enquiry. This attitude holds despite – or, more likely, because of – family history's widespread appeal. Having long existed as an inter-generational memory culture based around anecdote and possession of mementos, popular interest in genealogy began to develop in more profound ways in the 1970s, spurred by the success of Alex Haley's book, *Roots: The Saga of an American Family*, and its adaptation for television. Twenty years later in his best-selling memoir, *Dreams From My Father: A Story of Race and Inheritance* (1995), Barack Obama described his project as 'a boy's search for his father, and through that search a workable meaning for his life as a black American'.[44] In the act of writing his memoir (itself a strong literary tradition within the African-American community), Obama embarked on a quest for self-knowledge via his own past experiences and those of his ancestors – both familial and cultural. The availability of online tools like *Familysearch, Ancestry* and *Findmypast* have helped millions of people to undertake their own versions of Haley's and Obama's genealogical research. Together with the proliferation of online forums, blogs and listservs, they have enabled the kind of people who enjoy popular genealogy television programmes, such as *Who Do You Think You Are?*, to become their own family historians. Moreover, user-generated sites like *Memoro: The bank of Memories* have provided a digital space where people from across the world (in this case, those who were born before 1950) can upload films in which they recount stories of their lives for later generations.[45] Collectively, these personal narratives constitute a rich archive of social experiences for researchers. But, even at the level of individual family research, genealogy can provide insights into the broader questions that interest academic historians. Mary Stewart's research into her great, great grandfather, William

McCaw, who migrated from Scotland to New Zealand in 1880, shows how genealogy can be meaningful at the 'micro' and 'macro' scales. We can read her project as a microhistory of one man's experiences, drawn from the family archive of books, letters, photos and objects that McCaw left behind. Equally, we can use it to reflect more generally on the ways that migrants in the nineteenth century inhabited many layers of belonging and maintained webs of connections and identities. McCaw used writing as a way of bridging the divides between his family in New Zealand, Scotland, Australia and America. He also saw his Presbyterian faith as something that transcended national boundaries and made him part of a global community. In finding a way to tell his story, Stewart makes no claim that her relative's experiences were typical. But she does think that her research has a relevance beyond her own family because she has successfully used 'family history to mediate the space between the personal and global perspectives in history'.[46] Moreover, as a project that was undertaken for a postgraduate degree at the University of Otago, Stewart's research illustrates how divisions between academic and public history are continuing to break down.

Notes

1 'How Do We Define Public History?', National Council on Public History, http:// https://ncph.org/what-is-public-history/about-the-field, accessed 20 August 2019.
2 Paul Ashton and Alex Trapeznik (eds), *What is Public History Globally? Working with the Past in the Present* (London: Bloomsbury Academic, 2019).
3 Faye Sayer, *Public History: A Practical Guide* (London: Bloomsbury, 2015) 1.
4 Eureka Henrich, 'Mobility, Migration and Modern Memory', in Anna Maerker, Simon Sleight and Adam Sutcliffe (eds), *History, Memory and Public Life: The Past in the Present* (Abingdon: Routledge, 2018) 101–25.
5 Migration Museum Project, 'How We Got Here: The First Two Years' (London, July 2012) 35.
6 *Ibid.*, 10.
7 *Ibid.*, 11.
8 Peter Gatrell, 'Population Displacement in the Baltic Region in the Twentieth Century: From "Refugee Studies" to Refugee History', in *Journal of Baltic Studies*, 38/1 (2007) 43–5.
9 Philip Marfleet, 'Refugees and History: Why we Must Address the Past', in *Refugee Survey Quarterly*, 26/3 (2007) 136.
10 *Ibid.*, 5.
11 whc.unesco.org/en/list accessed 8 July 2019.

12 T. Travers, *Museums and Galleries in Britain. Economic, Social and Creative Impact* (London, 2006) cited in M. Davies *Imprisoned by History: Aspects of Historicized Life* (London: Routledge, 2009) 21.

13 D. Lowenthal, *The Heritage Crusade and the Spoils of History* (Cambridge: Cambridge University Press, 1988) xiii.

14 F. Fernández-Armesto, 'Epilogue: What is History *Now*?' in D. Cannadine, (ed.), *What is History Now?* (London: Palgrave Macmillan, 2002) 158.

15 Samuel, *Theatres of Memory*, 259–73.

16 *Ibid.*

17 L. Jordanova, *History in Practice* (London: Hodder Arnold, 2006) 127.

18 Lowenthal, *Heritage Crusade* x.

19 For a full list of members see www.sitesofconscience.org/en/members/members-list/ accessed 3 September 2019.

20 www.sitesofconscience.org/en/who-we-are/about-us/ 2 September 2019.

21 Indira Chowdhury and Srijan Mandal, 'Public History in India: Towards a People's Past', in Ashton and Trapeznik (eds), *What is Public History Globally?* 79–92; Rama Lakshmi and Shalini Sharma, 'Building a Safe Space for Unsafe Memories: The Remember Bhopal Museum', in Katie Holmes and Heather Goodall (eds), *Telling Environmental Histories: Intersections of Memory, Narrative and Environment* (Basingstoke, Hampshire: Palgrave Macmillan, 2017) 133–52.

22 Sharon Macdonald, 'Undesirable Heritage: Fascist Material Culture and Historical Consciousness in Nuremberg', in *International Journal of Heritage Studies*, 12/1 (2006) 9–28.

23 *Ibid.*, 22.

24 John Kuo Wei Tchen and Liz Sevchenko, 'The "Dialogic Museum" Revisited: A Collaborative Reflection', in Bill Adair, Benjamin Filene, and Laura Koloski (eds), *Letting Go? Sharing Historical Authority in a User-Generated World* (Philadelphia: The Pew Centre for Arts and Heritage, 2011) 82–3.

25 John Kuo Wei Tchen, 'Creating a Dialogic Museum: The Chinatown History Museum Experiment', in Ivan Karp, Christine Mullen Kreamer and Steven D. Lavine (eds), *Museums and Communities: The Politics of Public Culture* (Washington: Smithsonian Institution Press, 1992) 298.

26 *Ibid*, 291.

27 Tchen, 'Creating a Dialogic Museum', 300–3.

28 Samuel, *Theatres of Memory*, 274–312.

29 See peopleshistorynhs.org

30 M. Halbwachs, *Les cadres sociaux de la mémoire* (1925) cited in G. Cubitt, *History and Memory* (Manchester: Manchester University Press, 2007) 164.

31 Eviatar Zerubavel, *Time Maps: Collective Memory and the Social Shape of the Past* (Chicago: Chicago University Press, 2003) in Dan Stone, 'Beyond the

Mnemosyne Institute: The Future of Memory after the Age of Commemoration', in Rick Crownshaw, Jane Kilby and Antony Rowland (eds), *The Future of Memory* (Oxford: Berghahn, 2010) 23.

32 See, for example, I. Pappé, (ed.), *The Israel/Palestine Question: A Reader* (London: Routledge, 2nd edn 2007).

33 D. LaCapra, 'History and Memory: In the Shadow of the Holocaust', in LaCapra *History and Memory after Auschwitz* (Ithaca: Cornell University Press, 1998) 19–20.

34 For a discussion of the idea of memory as the 'bedrock of history' see Dan Stone, 'Beyond the Mnemosyne Institute', 27–9.

35 Wulf Kansteiner, 'Finding Meaning in Memory: A Methodological Critique of Collective Memory Studies', *History and Theory*, 41/2 (2002) 180.

36 G. Eley, 'Foreword', in M. Evans, and K. Lunn (eds), *War and Memory in the Twentieth Century* (Oxford: Berg, 1997) viii.

37 Alon Confino and Peter Fritzsche (eds), *The Work of Memory: New Directions in the Study of German Society and Culture* (Chicago: University of Illinois Press, 2002) 1–21.

38 C.J. Colvin, '"Brothers and Sisters, Do Not Be Afraid of Me": Trauma, History and the Therapeutic Imagination in the new South Africa', in Katherine Hodgkin and Susannah Radstone (eds), *Contested Pasts: The Politics of Memory* (London: Routledge, 2003) 153.

39 Katherine Hodgkin and Susannah Radstone (eds), 'Introduction: Contested Pasts', in Hodgkin and Radstone (eds), *Contested Pasts*, 2.

40 L. D. Kritzman, 'Foreword: In Remembrance of Things French', in P. Nora (ed.), *Realms of Memory: Rethinking the French Past,* vol. 1, *Conflicts and Divisions*, trans. Arthur Goldhammer (New York: Columbia University Press, 1996) xiv.

41 P. Nora, 'Between Memory and History', in *Realms of Memory*, vol. 1,6.

42 *Ibid.*

43 Thomas Cauvin, *Public History: A Textbook of Practice* (Abingdon: Routledge, 2016) 96.

44 Barack Obama, *Dreams From My Father: A Story of Race and Inheritance* (New York: Random House, 1995) ix.

45 www.memoro.org/uk-en/ accessed 20 January 2020.

46 Mary Stewart, 'Expanding the Archive: The Role of Family History in Exploring Connections Within a Settler's World', in Paul Ashton and Hilda Kean (eds), *People and their Pasts* (Houndmills: Palgrave Macmillan, 2009) 256.

Further reading

Bill Adair, Benjamin Filene, and Laura Koloski (eds), *Letting Go? Sharing Historical Authority in a User-Generated World* (Philadelphia: The Pew Centre for Arts and Heritage, 2011). The distinctive feature of this anthology of essays on public history and 'shared authority' is that it is written by practitioners. Most of the essays deal with examples of museums, artists, educators and audiences in the USA.

Paul Ashton and Alex Trapeznik (eds), *What is Public History Globally? Working with the Past in the Present* (London: Bloomsbury Academic, 2019). This collection examines the state of public history in 11 countries, provides guidance abut methods and practices in the field and finishes with a set of detailed case studies of public history sites.

Thomas Cauvin, *Public History: A Textbook of Practice* (Abingdon: Routledge, 2016). This is a useful practical guide to the various ways of being a public historian. It covers debates about the ethics and responsibilities of public history. But it is light on theory and takes a traditionalist view of historians' authority over the past.

Katherine Hodgkin and Susannah Radstone (eds), *Contested Pasts: The Politics of Memory* (London: Routledge, 2003). An inter-disciplinary collection of essays inspired by Raphael Samuel's *Theatres of Memory* (1994). The book is organised using four headings: 'Transforming memory', 'Remembering Suffering: Trauma and History', 'Patterning the National Past' and 'And then Silence…'. The essays have a wide geographical range and explore different types of memorial cultural forms: including museums, television and oral testimony. There is a companion volume by the same editors, *Regimes of Memory* (London: Routledge, 2003), which focuses on different theoretical approaches to the study of memory.

Pierre Nora (ed.), *Realms of Memory: Rethinking the French Past,* 3 vols (New York: Columbia University Press, 1996–8). This English-language version (translated by Arthur Goldhammer) makes available 46 of the original 132 essays that were published in *Les Lieux de mémoire*. There is a useful foreword by Lawrence D. Kritzman, and an important general introductory essay by Pierre Nora, 'Between Memory and History', in vol. 1: *Conflicts and Divisions* (1996).

11

Liberating history

Throughout this book we have discussed the ideological positioning of histories, the popularity of history as a form of past-talk and the fact that it is very hard in the light of the postmodern challenge to continue to argue that we research and write about history 'for its own sake'. Yet history must have an important socio-political use, otherwise why would people bother with it?[1] Recently people have begun to rethink what they understand the functions of history and other forms of past-talk to be and the role that such past-focused narratives play in our culture and society. In this chapter we will look at history as a means of imagining or reinforcing the identity of individuals and societies; history as an ethical meditation on how we can make a better present and future; and history as hopefulness and as a form of political activism. But we will also look at the idea of the end of history and whether the genre of history, as opposed to other forms of past-talk, is the most useful way of engaging with, and using, narratives of the past.

Ethical meditations, identity and activism

The postmodern challenge has foregrounded the fact that history is never neutral; it is always written from a particular ethical (and political) perspective. Ethical considerations influence not only our choice of research topic, but the interpretative strategies and models we employ. David Harlan argues that, in the early part of the twentieth century, history written and consumed in America was one of the culture's main means of moral reflection, but from the 1950s this began to change. For Harlan, like Beverley Southgate, the future of history and the historical profession lies in a return to this key, earlier function. Harlan does not think that the role of professional or academic historians is simply to transmit 'professionally certified knowledge' to students, but instead that it is to help them 'develop historical imaginations that are morally sustaining and politically relevant' and to be reflective readers or viewers of all the ways their society represents the past.[2] For Harlan, history should therefore be primarily understood as a form of moral reflection; it is 'a conversation with the dead about what we should value and how we should live'.[3] Narratives of the past can provide models or exemplars of behaviour that we can choose to emulate or repudiate. They can be viewed as a means by which we can articulate values we think are important and thereby imagine a better world. Harlan argues that we should teach and write in such ways that our students develop a historical imagination that will help them say, '[t]his is how we mean to live but do not yet live; this is what we mean to value but do not yet value'.[4] Both Southgate and Harlan argue that it is the ability of Ken Burns' historical documentaries of American life and society to offer not only a sense of identity, but also hope for the future that account for their massive popularity.[5] If academic history is to become more relevant to a wider public, and if academic historians are to play a role in determining the pasts we have, then it might be useful to explore further these potential uses of history.

This is not to say that we can find absolute moral truths in the past. The past can provide examples that exemplify a range of moral values, some that we agree with and which reflect the type of people we want to be, and some that do not.[6] In this regard, the ethical dimension to history is also closely linked to the practice of identity formation. As Harlan says, 'our every attempt to define who we *have been* is [...] densely and irretrievably interwoven with our hopelessly subjective attempts to define both who we *are* and who we wish to *become*'.[7] Southgate echoes this opinion, arguing that a future role for history could perhaps be as an explicit means of constructing or reinforcing identity for both individuals and societies. Instead of constructing cultural or geographical 'others' to define ourselves against, we could instead use chronological 'others' – 'others' from the past.[8] History is thus a way of thinking about ourselves and our experiences. When we research the past, we are not so much looking to establish or determine the meaning of the past, but searching for the meaning of our present. History is a way that we can give our lives meaning, grow as individuals and work for a better, more just society.[9]

Ann Rigney similarly argues that one of the uses of history may lie in the fact that it defamiliarises the present; it allows us to look at the present from an unfamiliar view and provides a critical distance which facilitates a recalibration of our perception of the world, ethical position and self-understanding.[10] This sentiment is echoed by Robert Rosenstone, who believes that we need a 'history that surprises and startles us', which exposes us to things we have not seen, heard or felt before.[11] Alun Munslow argues along similar lines, contending that what he describes as 'history artwork' is a means of considering 'all things human' and a way of using the past to meditate upon new insights, understandings and emotions to produce an 'ethically inspired cultural catharsis'.[12]

A number of historians are therefore writing history with the explicit aim of recovering the lost histories and voices of subjugated or marginalised groups and, in doing so, empowering or raising the consciousness of present-day communities and challenging essentialist discourses. Such historians recognise history as a form of political activism. Of course, all history is political in that it provides an account and interpretation of an event from a particular perspective, but some historians, such as Joan W. Scott, explicitly argue that historians should use their narratives of the past as levers to unearth and challenge the foundational premises on which our social and political institutions rest. The point of this, she continues, would be to demonstrate that these institutions, and the concomitant assumptions and power relations inherent in them, are not natural and enduring, but are contingent, historicised and therefore open to change.[13] Southgate, like Scott, argues that we need histories that expose the contingency of our presuppositions, customs and practices because, by emphasising that things could have been different, there is therefore hope that we can make things different in the future.[14] Ramírez, quoting Mario T. García, similarly argues that oppositional histories can be used as political tools to critique oppressive institutions and to make public the stories of those often marginalised by dominant narratives, those who are erased by history.[15] Likewise, Dening does not want to understand the world, but to try to change it, to disturb 'the moral lethargy of the living to change in their present the consequences of their past'.[16] He wants to tell true stories, inclusive stories, stories that acknowledge the identity of those ignored by history, the dispossessed. He wants to help them use their words to say who they are.[17]

Historians and histories can also have very immediate political effects. For example, Chauncey describes how he participated as a professional historian in ten gay rights legal cases in which he testified as an expert witness, wrote amicus briefs and submitted affidavits on the history of sexual regulation and anti-gay discrimination, which all played a role in the final decision of the judges.[18] Similarly, three historians, David Anderson, Huw Bennett and Caroline Elkins, as a result of their research into the history of colonial British atrocities in Kenya in the 1950s, subsequently gave evidence as expert witnesses in a successful court case brought by the Kenyan Human Rights Commission against the UK government for the torture of their clients.[19]

The end of history? Vernacular forms of past-talk

In contrast with the historians discussed above, Keith Jenkins argues that the challenge of postmodernism has simply highlighted that history no longer serves any useful function. Although we could reconceptualise history as a reflexive, positioned, moral reflection on life – a means of articulating identity or a way of facilitating emancipatory thinking – Jenkins, *pace* Harlan, does not think that we need history to do this. He believes that there are more interesting ways by which we can achieve the same result. We can think about our present and future ethically, and in emancipatory and democratising ways, without the need for historical narratives of the past.[20] For example, as we noted in Chapter 1, we do not necessarily *need* to study the Nazi era in order to come to the conclusion that genocide is morally wrong. It is perfectly possible to make good ethical choices without studying history – as countless millions of people have done and continue to do.

Whereas Jenkins argues that we no longer need to 'bother' with history and can safely let it drop, Sande Cohen and Martin Davies put the case against history in stronger terms. They regard history and the historicising habit in contemporary culture as an always-oppressive force that needs to be overcome. Their arguments are elaborate and difficult to summarise, but we can note the following points. History, on their reading and echoing Hayden White, always rationalises and affirms how things are – however appalling – because it explains the present as being the product of historical 'forces' or 'processes' which have inevitably led to now. Moreover, instead of recognising the distinctiveness of our contemporary predicaments and attempting to think through solutions, historical thinking has a tranquilising and socially stabilising effect – it acts as a social anaesthetic and 'ultimately enforces public acquiesce in what is'.[21] The main problem, according to Davies, is identitary thinking – the drawing of historical parallels – because this denies that anything is new or unfamiliar (and familiarity then becomes a form of acceptability). In his words, 'a society mesmerized into seeing "everything" as the same old historical thing soon accepts phantasmic catastrophe as a normal occurrence'.[22] Instead of critiquing war, genocide, disease and famine, we historicise and therefore naturalise them as endemic features of the human condition. In effect, history works to affirm violence as historically, and thus socially and politically, normal.[23] Thus, the familiar injunction of seeing history as a guide to the present becomes an obstacle to alternative ways of thinking because it 'encourages a consciousness that is never able to arrive at criticism'.[24] It acts as a default mechanism for taking us back to what we already know, and is another way of saying that the past contains all that we can ever have. As Cohen argues, the most troubling implications of this lies in how our ways of invoking history can damage the future – by shrinking that future to our existing political and cultural 'sizes'.[25] Or, as Davies concludes:

> The world, now, suffers from severe problems of political and social justice, scandalous inequalities of opportunity and the distribution of wealth and resources, alarming and irreversible environmental damage. This is how the world has, in historical terms, turned out: this is the historicized world. Historians... are uniquely implicated in the way the historicized world is now. By their very function, their formal, social position, historians furnish the intellectual justification for its perpetuation and reproduction, for constantly symbolically re-enacting the historical changes throughout history that always perpetuate the same old thing.[26]

Here Davies argues that history functions as an 'indispensible information-management technology', whose production makes universities, as well as heritage institutions (such as museums, archives, monuments), the ideal, compliant instruments of socially dominant interests, governmental and cultural policies and neo-liberal ideology.[27] In one sense, this instrumental use of history is to be expected. As Jenkins has argued, it would be perverse for government agencies to allocate such sizeable funds to history teaching in schools and (at least until recently in the UK) universities, and to support historical research and heritage activities, unless they believed that, in doing so, they were helping to reproduce social cohesion and acquiescence in current political arrangements. Sande Cohen occupies a similar critical position, arguing that historians provide the data that give particular social formations present credibility by anchoring them to perceived traditions or inter-generationally shared values.[28]

Chantal Mouffe argues that there is nothing inherent in any articulatory practice that determines how it might be used politically.[29] That is, historical practices do not necessarily have to reinforce the status quo but could instead, as Hayden White argued, be employed in the service of emancipatory or progressive political projects.[30] But it seems to us that institutional history is, at best, outdated or, at worst, politically compromised. And, indeed, White argues in *The Practical Past* that there is little reason to hope that academic historians might be capable of performing a politically emancipatory role. However, White does not argue that all forms of past-talk are equally redundant. He argues that what he calls the 'practical past' – that is, forms of past-talk that are constituted by practices and representational forms outside the borders of academic history's professional codes and forms of past-talk employed by artists, activists, film-makers, journalists, radical archivists and campaigners – can be mobilised effectively as cultural and rhetorical resources in tactical campaigns for socio-political justice.[31]

Activists frequently employ instances of past-presencing as part of their campaigns for social and political justice. That is, they integrate the commemoration or memorialisation of past dates, people and events into present-day campaigns. In 2012, land activists, taking inspiration from the seventeenth-century Protestant radical Gerrard Winstanley, walked down the River Thames to an area of disused woodland where they set up the Runnymede eco-village. Winstanley and his *Diggers* wanted to reform the social order and create egalitarian, agrarian and rural communities. They have been seen as inspirational precursors of a variety of community-anarchist, squatting, anti-capitalist and communalist groups, including the *San Francisco Diggers*.[32] The land-activists of the Runnymede eco-village consciously situated their activities in the historical context of the *Diggers* through their writings, activities and self-description as *Diggers2012*.[33] They argue that, just like the 1649 *Diggers*, they hope to facilitate a revolution in land reform and return to people their right to live freely on the land, to grow their own food and to build their own homes. In May 2012, they issued the *Declaration from the Dispossessed*, indirectly referencing the seventeenth-century *Digger* pamphlet *A Declaration from the Poor Oppressed People of England*, arguing that everyone should have the right to dwell on and cultivate disused land.[34] Their old website also included a list of resources: including information on the history of land rights, land enclosures, the clearances and the commons, as well as many quotes from Winstanley.[35] In 2015, when their community came under threat of destruction, they contextualised historically their legal fight to retain their eco-village by reference to its location at Runnymede and the sealing of the Magna Carta.[36] On the blog and activist website *Phoenix Rising*, there are numerous entries that intertextually reference the Magna Carta and situate the struggle of the eco-village as part of an ongoing struggle by the people of England and Britain for 'democracy, land rights and other rights relating to Magna Carta', a connection facilitated by the fact that the court proceedings to evict the eco-village coincided with the 800th anniversary of the signing of the Magna Carta.[37]

Similarly, many artists have very effectively utilised past-talk (through reference to specific past events) in their work to challenge hegemonic narratives, unjust institutions, practices and unequal power relations. Emily Jacir's art often focuses on the narration of collective histories and works to dissolve 'the boundary between the present and the historical'.[38] Her *Memorial to 418 Palestinian Villages which were Destroyed, Depopulated and Occupied by Israel in 1948* (2001) is a refugee tent into which she, helped by friends and strangers who had heard of her project, stitched the names of the Palestinian villages which were ethnically cleansed, occupied or destroyed by the Israelis in 1948. The work took as its resource the edited history by Walid Khalidi, *All That Remains: the Palestinian Villages Occupied and Depopulated by Israel in 1948*, and many of the participants, themselves from diverse backgrounds, read through sections of the book as they stitched, which, in turn, gave rise to the sharing of memories, exchange of stories and conversations about the expulsion of the Palestinians from their homeland.[39] Read and discussed in this way, the book, through Jacir's tent, 'became not a record of a dead history, but a living thesis'.[40] By giving the work the title *Memorial to 418 Palestinian Villages which were Destroyed, Depopulated and Occupied by Israel in 1948*, Jacir ensures the subversion of the title into a political statement witnessing the occupation and erasure of Palestinians and their land; an unequivocal statement that would necessarily have to be included in any review of an exhibition featuring the work.

Another intervention into a political debate that employs past-talk to draw attention to how past actions can contribute to present injustices is Victoria Burgher's *Don't Let Them Drown* (2015). The work juxtaposes a print of the Brookes Atlantic slave ship plan on one side of a piece of canvas with the text "they are here because we were there" on the other. This text rewords Ambalavaner Sivanandan's aphorism on postcolonial migration, 'we are here because you were there'. In doing so, it draws attention not only to the central role that the violence, inequality and dislocation engendered by European colonialism has played in present-day migration, but also foregrounds a continuation of the attitude that the lives of some are more 'disposable' than others.[41] Her work *Plundered* (2018) similarly emphasises the fact that many migrants fleeing poverty, conflict and ecological catastrophe originate in areas of former European colonial occupation; areas where Europeans brutally oppressed the population, subverted existing property arrangements, dominated and controlled the extraction of raw resources and themselves migrated to *en masse*.[42] By juxtaposing a map of the British Empire, overlaid with a stereotypical crime-scene outline of a body, next to a photograph of a gold thermal foil blanket (the type often wrapped around freezing migrants rescued in the Mediterranean) floating in the sea, Burgher suggests a direct causality and culpability between a British imperial past and the present-day plight of migrants crossing and dying in the Mediterranean.

Working also within a context of ongoing colonial injustice Máret Ánne Sara's *Pile o' Sápmi* (2016) seeks to protest the cultural erasure and dislocation of the indigenous Sami people from their lands, which stretch across the northern areas of present-day Norway, Sweden, Finland and Russia, through restrictions imposed on reindeer herding by the Norwegian state. Norway is implementing a policy of enforced slaughter of Sami reindeer herds to reduce them by 50 per cent, under the auspices of protecting the tundra ecosystem. *Pile o' Sápmi* has taken various forms but it originally consisted of 200 reindeer heads piled up outside the Inner Finnmark District Court (Norway). Both the pile of heads and the title of the work create a number of intertextual links to past events and places, perhaps most iconically to an 1892 US photograph of a massive pile of bison skulls.[43] In the nineteenth century, the US government and army encouraged the slaughter of bison herds to the point of extinction to both facilitate the western expansion of cattle ranches and railroads in the US and to simultaneously weaken and dislocate the First Nations North American peoples by eliminating one of their key resources. The creation of a link between the state-sanctioned destruction of the buffalo and reindeer creates a parallel in the colonial appropriation of First Nations land in the nineteenth and twenty-first centuries.

The title of the work itself refers to another past-time and place, oskana ka-asastēki, which loosely translates as 'the place where the bones are piled up'. This was the name the Nêhiyawak Cree nation gave to the area where they stacked bison bones near the Wascana Creek, and which later became the settler town Regina in Canada, nicknamed Pile O'Bones. In referencing the Nêhiyawak nation and their sustainable environmental practices, specifically with regard to their relationship with the bison, Sara creates a link to the Sami's relationship with their reindeer and challenges the Norwegian state's claim that the culling of Sami reindeer herds is to protect the delicate tundra ecosystem from over-grazing. Just as the mass slaughter of the bison in North America was a means to destroy the way of life and thus dislocate the indigenous First Nations (to make way for white European settlement), so too the actions of the Norwegian state can be more coherently explained as an attempt to contain and control the indigenous pastoralist Sami in order to more effectively exploit the natural resources (including minerals, wood and water) and economic potential of their land. Further historical resonances are present in the various performances and iterations of the installation which reinforce the interpretation of the cull as *another* in a long line of Norwegian actions of oppression against the Sami, the appropriation of their land and Sami resistance. For example, the unveiling of a curtain of reindeer skulls in front of the Norwegian parliament was accompanied by speeches from a number of Sami activists including Niillas Somby, who was one of the people who went on hunger strike outside parliament in 1979 to protest the construction of the hydroelectric dam on the Alta river that would flood a Sami village and interrupt reindeer migration.[44]

Artists have also effectively drawn attention to the ways museum collections, memorials, historical monuments and heritage sites, through their performance of 'political inheriting', display, legitimise and reinforce hegemonic interests.[45] Burgher makes reference to past events to challenge and undermine the dominant, nostalgic narrative of an essentially benign British Empire. She seeks to make explicit the exploitation, violence and cost of empire. In this regard, her work has also challenged the ongoing de facto public commemoration of those involved with, and who hugely profited from, the Atlantic slave trade. The presence of statues honouring the economic acumen and civic generosity of these individuals, without effective contextualisation, not only mitigates the barbarity, violence and exploitation that underpinned their 'achievements', but it also erases the history of those subject to such violence. Burgher's *Milligan Must Fall* (2016) provides a counterpoint to the history of Robert Milligan as an eighteenth-century merchant, ship-owner and key founder of the London West India Docks. By adding a cast-sugar pound sign to the statue of Milligan at West India Quay she reminds audiences that his wealth came from his role in transporting slaves across the Atlantic and his ownership of slave plantations.[46] Her utilisation of the commodities of colonialism (in this case sugar) challenges the dominant narrative of British entrepreneurship, mercantile acuity and civic-mindedness, focusing instead on the imperial exploitation and racism at the heart of such activities. The continued presence of statues to slavers and imperialists, and the commemoration and celebration of them through the naming of public buildings and streets, whitewashes history; it perpetuates a history that reinforces and legitimises the status quo in terms of wealth distribution; and it depicts a history that ignores the contribution of the exploited in the creation of much of Britain's wealth today.

Kara Walker's sculpture *Fons Americanus* displayed in the Turbine Gallery of London's Tate Modern (2019) was inspired by, and functions as a counterpoint to, the Victoria Memorial outside Buckingham Palace.[47] The memorial, commissioned after the death of Queen Victoria, functioned not only as a commemoration of the life and reign of the Queen, but also, through her role as the head of empire, it celebrated the United Kingdom as the centre of an empire. The memorial consists of a plinth topped by a golden statue of victory beneath which are personifications of constancy and courage and two imperial eagles. On the side facing away from the palace, towards the city, is a statue of the Queen on her throne. On the other three sides there are statues representing truth, justice and motherhood: the first two, according to the designer and sculptor Thomas Brock, were the qualities that made the Queen so beloved, while the last represented her great love for her people.[48] At the base fountains flow into basins surrounded by low reliefs of mermaids and tritons: all of which represent the maritime power of the British Empire.[49]

Walker's *Fons Americanus*, in contrast to the celebration of imperial dominance of the Victoria Memorial, offers an often-forgotten narrative of the African diaspora and the experience of the Black Atlantic, while simultaneously questioning narratives of power – how the past is remembered and how history is constructed through public monuments. Instead of the traditional figural representations of military and naval might and claims to civilisational superiority that adorn many imperial-era monuments, Walker's fountain presents an allegory of the Black Atlantic, including figures that symbolise aspects of the transatlantic slave trade and 'yoke[s] together racist representation and violent expression of power, issues which tend to become romanticised and often depicted in pastoral settings'.[50] Instead of mermaids and tritons, in the fountain basin there are circling sharks and a small sinking boat which depict, figuratively and actually, the violence and de-humanising brutality experienced by enslaved people trafficked across the Atlantic by Europeans. Slavers sometimes threw dying or ill slaves overboard in order to claim the standard maritime insurance, which was generally only paid for losses resulting from 'perils of the sea' and not for 'natural deaths', 'natural wastage' or 'spoilage'.[51] On the left-hand side, in the place where the sculpture of justice is on the Victoria Memorial, Walker has placed a noose hanging from a tree – illustrating a racist justice system that African Americans often experience. The noose references a post-slavery history of violence and oppression against African Americans engendered by the racism and institutional inequality enshrined in the US legal system which ranged from racist practices of segregation enshrined in the 'Jim Crow laws' to the justice system ignoring the lynching and killing of African Americans through the nineteenth and twentieth centuries and into the present day.

The fountain also talks back to power and works to create new narratives. The figure of the captain at the front (in place of Victoria on her throne) is a composite of key black individuals, such as Marcus Garvey and François-Dominique L'Ouverture, who rebelled against European imperial dominion and exploitation. In the place of the statue representing truth, Walker has placed a kneeling man based on West Indies Governor Sir William Young, who is presented begging in a posture of remorse – perhaps having realised the truth (and horror) of European colonialism?[52] In place of winged victory, at the top of the fountain stands Venus. Not the 'Sable Venus' of Stothard's pro-slave trade engraving depicting an African Venus being taken from Angola to the West Indies on a scallop shell accompanied by cherubs and tritons, but a reclaimed Venus; a powerful priestess of Afro-Caribbean religion; 'the daughter of waters'; the mother providing sustenance to her people from her milk and blood.[53]

Walker's monument challenges the commemorative spectacle of colonial domination that is inherent in imperial-era monuments but that is often unseen or disregarded by audiences. It questions how events such as the British Empire are and, perhaps more importantly, should be, remembered. London is full of monuments and statues to merchants who profited from slavery and the exploitation of colonial labour, as well as the generals and politicians who enforced colonial dominance. There are also statues and plaques to the white supporters of the abolition of the slave trade, but there is still no monument acknowledging the incomparable suffering of those who were transported and enslaved as a result of the British slave trade. For example, the Buxton Memorial Fountain, commemorating the emancipation of slaves in the British Empire in 1834, is described on its inscription as 'intended as a memorial of those members of Parliament who with Mr Wilberforce, advocated the abolition of the British slave-trade, achieved in 1807...' not to those who suffered.[54]

To challenge this collective national amnesia concerning the slave trade, and to remind people the history of slavery in the UK is not the morally uplifting story of abolition but rather one of centuries of brutal exploitation, *Memorial 2007* was set up to erect a memorial depicting the transatlantic slave trade to break the silence surrounding it; 'to commemorate enslaved Africans and their descendants'; and remember the economic prosperity that their coerced, exploited labour provided to Britain.[55] A design for the £4m bronze and granite memorial, planning permission to site it in London's Hyde Park and the support of government departments and ministers was acquired. Despite raising funds from individuals, the project, like that of many memorials, needed financial support from the state. Such state support has recently been provided for the planned Holocaust memorial in Victoria park (£75m); to restore and repair First World War memorials across the UK (£5m); and to raise awareness of the Srebrenica genocide (£1.2m).[56] Although Boris Johnson enthusiastically endorsed the project in 2008, in late 2019 his government decided they did not have the funds to support the memorial, and the planning permission for its construction lapsed, along with it any reasonable expectation that the memorial would be built in the near future.[57]

This tendency for historical silence surrounding Britain's involvement with, and benefit from, the transatlantic slave trade and the country's subsequent colonial exploits is directly referenced in the title of Walker's work: '*[T]he Monumental Misrememberings* Of Colonial Exploits'. This prompts us not only to question how the past is re-presented and re-imagined through heritage markers in public space, but also to ask how such monuments might inscribe and reify ongoing power imbalances in public spaces.[58] In a similar way to Burgher's work, it reminds us that the legacy of colonialism and slavery, and the violence, dislocation of people, racism, exploitation and unequal distribution of resources it brought about, still have ramifications today. What does it say about present-day Britain when the public spaces of London (and other cities) are full of memorials commemorating imperialists, slavers and benefactors who made their money from the exploitation of others? Who does it exclude when these memorials become the centre of national celebrations, as the Victoria Memorial was during both the Golden and Diamond Jubilee celebrations for Queen Elizabeth II and the parade celebrating the British teams during the 2012 UK Olympics?

Colonial trophies

It is not only monuments and other memorials in the public space that commemorate the violence of imperialism, gloss over its more unsavoury aspects and neglect to interrogate the ongoing economic and socio-political inequalities that are the legacy of colonialism. Many museums (especially in former European colonial capitals) are full of artefacts looted, purchased or acquired in dubious conditions by the imperial powers and officials from countries they controlled. From the end of the nineteenth and into the twentieth century these European museums displayed such objects as colonial trophies, employing them to establish hierarchies of cultural value and to demonstrate how colonialism had not only brought the 'wonders of the world' home to the metropole, but had also, in return, generously bestowed European civilisation on to their colonised subjects. Despite the general military and political withdrawal from empire in the twentieth century by European states, many of their national museums have not effectively decolonised. Not only have the museums retained the objects but the manner in which they are displayed tends to elide or ignore the history of violence and unequal relations between colonisers and colonised which facilitated their acquisition.

London's British Museum holds many artefacts acquired within the unequal power structure of colonial occupation and military presence, including the Gweagal Shield (Gweagal Country/Australia), the Admonitions Scroll (China), the Hoa Hakananai'a *moai* statue (Rapa Nui/Easter Island) and the Benin Bronzes (Kingdom of Benin/Nigeria). They demonstrate in different ways how artefacts can be 'collected' within a broader context of imperial violence and inequality. The descendants of those from whom these objects were taken see them as integral to their culture and heritage and have unsuccessfully requested their return. The British Museum is reluctant to repatriate any artefact and its official policy 'starts from a presumption of retention'.[59] Even with objects it knows were acquired as a result of British colonial aggression, the museum only commits to re-examining the acquisition histories and caring for the objects with appropriate respect.[60] This policy of retention appears to extend to human remains because, in recent years, it has decided not to return remains to First Nations Torres Strait Islander Peoples and the New Zealand Te Papa Tongarewa, despite formal requests.[61] When loaning objects to the National Museum of Australia for their exhibition *Encounters: Revealing Stories of Aboriginal and Torres Strait Islander Objects from the British Museum* (2015–16), the British Museum only agreed after the Australian government guaranteed in law that descendants of the original owners would have no legal basis to take the objects.[62] The Australian government passed the Protection of Cultural Objects on Loan Act in order to ensure that the objects would be returned to the former colonial power and would not remain in their country of origin.[63] The Gweagal Shield, which was displayed at the *Encounters* exhibition, was taken, along with spears from the Gweagal people, by Captain Cook during a violent incident in 1770. He and some of the crew of *HMS Endeavour* landed at Kamay Bay (Botany

Bay) and fired at the Gweagal people gathered on the shore – an event that presaged British colonial occupation and a policy of aggressive dislocation of, and extreme violence towards, the First Nations peoples living there.[64] In contrast, the Hoa Hakananai'a *moai* was 'found' and taken by Commodore Richard Powell in 1868 when he arrived at Easter Island on the Royal Navy frigate *HMS Topaze*.[65] The Rapa Nui people consider it to have been taken without permission and want its return.

The Admonitions Scroll and Benin Bronzes were taken in the late nineteenth century in more aggressive colonial interventions by British forces in China and the Kingdom of Benin. The scroll was acquired in dubious circumstances in 1899 by a British officer, Captain Clarence A.K. Johnson, during a period of extensive looting following the defeat of the Chinese Imperial army by an eight-nation military alliance (including American, British, French, Japanese and Russian troops) sent to crush the anti-imperialist Yihetuan Movement (Boxer Uprising 1899–1901). Johnson subsequently sold it to the British Museum.

The Benin Bronzes is the collective name given today to several thousand plaques and sculptures of mainly bronze/brass that decorated the early modern royal palace complex of the ruler, or *Oba*, of the Kingdom of Benin in West Africa (fourteenth to the nineteenth centuries). They were looted during an act of British colonial violence and occupation. In 1897, the British Admiralty appointed Rear-Admiral Harry Lawson to lead an invasion of Benin City, which was rather disingenuously named the Benin Punitive Expedition. Benin City was destroyed during the invasion, the king exiled and the British took thousands of the bronzes back to the UK as war booty, where many were sold to museums in order to retrospectively fund the expedition.[66] Some of the bronzes are held by the British Museum and others are scattered around museums in the global north. Between 1950 and 1970, a few were sold by the British Museum to the Nigerian government.

Popular histories of the event, museum information boards on the Benin Bronzes and associated educational resources in contemporary British museums describe the expedition as retaliatory or punitive, implying that the British were only responding to an act of aggression by the people or ruler of Benin. This 'punitive' expedition was ostensibly a response to the killing of Britain's Acting Consul-General Phillips, who had requested permission to 'visit' Benin City and receive an audience with the *Oba*, but who was in fact seeking to depose the *Oba* in order to 'open up' the Kingdom of Benin and allow the British more advantageous access to its natural resources. The naming (and thus interpretation) of the incident as retribution for prior acts of violence against British officials mitigates an incident of disproportional colonial violence because it elides British intentions to extend its economic and military control from its existing protectorate and colonies in West Africa and effectively assert military, political and economic dominance over Benin.

For example, the information board next to the British Museum's display of the bronzes describes it as a punitive expedition that was in retaliation for the killing of British representatives as part of Benin's resistance to British control over southern Nigeria. Similarly, the teaching notes accompanying the British Museum's school resources mention in passing that

> [i]n 1897 British forces captured Benin City and sent the king into exile. The kingship was restored in 1914 and since then kings have continued to maintain local power in this area which is now in Edo State in modern Nigeria

But no mention is made of the violence and the looting of the treasures.[67] Information about the plaques on the British Museum's online portal simply notes that they were found/acquired in Benin City (Africa, Nigeria, Edo State, Benin City), and the accompanying curator's notes, while detailed, do not mention the manner of their capture.[68]

Two of the British Museum bronzes (which are described as depicting separately an African king and a Portuguese merchant both with manilas used as currency) are on loan to London's Victoria and Albert Museum (V&A) and displayed in the Medieval and Renaissance Rooms in a cabinet on 'merchant life', along with weights and measures, coins and other artefacts. No information is given concerning their acquisition, other than a description of them as being two brass plaques from Benin 1500–1700 (Benin City). In the British Museum and the V&A, the bronzes are contextualised as evidence of the existence of a sophisticated society in early-modern Benin which was embedded in global trade networks and produced technological, complex and beautiful artefacts that fulfilled various political and religious roles. This is accurate but, in only framing the artefacts in this way, both institutions conveniently deflect attention from the violent context in which they were brought to Britain.[69]

A more extreme example of un-decolonised museum labelling is provided by the Royal Museums Greenwich. Although they do not have a Benin Bronze, they do have an Itsekiri flag, which they report as acquired during the Benin expedition. They contextualise the expedition as having been 'launched in reprisal against an attack on a British mission in the service of Niger Coast Protectorate by forces of the Oba of Benin. [...] The famous Benin bronzes were removed as reparations by the British'.[70] By describing the bronzes as reparations, the museum frames the acquisition in legal terms as appropriate redress for a violation of law and thus implies that the colonial attack was a legitimate act.

Artists and activists are, however, drawing attention to the ways these museums continue to function as ongoing spaces of colonialism. For example, Tony Phillips's series of 12 prints entitled *A History of the Benin Bronzes* (1984) points to how the possession and display of looted artefacts creates a particularly shaped knowledge of where and to whom things belong and why – a shape of knowledge that effectively positions the objects in the museum as colonial trophies and can easily be used to ignore ongoing inequalities arising from imperialism.[71] Phillips' prints detail the bronzes' ceremonial use in the Kingdom of Benin to articulate the power of the *Oba* and ruling elite, the British attack and burning of Benin City and the subsequent inclusion, incarceration and circulation of the bronzes in the cultural institutions and practices of western colonial powers: namely the auction room, the scholarly lecture and the museum display cabinet. In so doing, Phillips draws attention to how the bronzes take on a new ceremonial role in the hands of the colonisers. In becoming objects of the western gaze, they still function as markers of power, but they now perform the superiority of the western colonising audience.

Of particular interest is the juxtaposition, or lack thereof, in the display and cataloguing of Phillips' *History of the Benin Bronzes* series and the bronzes on loan to the V&A. No connection (either with regard to digital entries or the physical artefacts) is made between the prints and the bronzes in the institution. On one level, it seems strange that a complete series of Phillips' *History of the Benin Bronzes* exists in the same museum space as two of the bronzes, yet there is no dialogue between them. It surely presents an excellent opportunity to engage with not only the violence of British colonialism, but also the ethics and issues surrounding the continued retention and display of looted cultural artefacts by former colonial powers? But this is perhaps precisely the reason there is no dialogue. Narratives positively emphasising the cultural achievements of early-modern Benin and its global trading connections are far more palatable to twenty-first century British audiences than those of violent acquisition and exploitation. Moreover, they also more effectively align with the socio-political functions that twenty-first century museums see themselves as embodying in their continued possession of these objects: that is, the creation and preservation of an interconnected global history for everyone; conservation and study of the artefacts; and the facilitation of access to the objects.

This narrative and interpretative shift from a history of colonial exploitation to the celebration of a shared world history is evident in the recent renaming of various ethnographic European museums that housed collections of artefacts acquired from former colonial dominions as 'world museums'.[72] But this framing of colonial artefacts in terms of the construction of a global history elides the fact that the continued possession and display of these objects not only functions as a material reminder of previous colonial dominance and the racist dichotomies of un/civilised that underpinned it, but also obscures an ongoing power imbalance between the global north and south, between colonial powers and the colonised. Artefacts of former colonisers are *never* in the museums of the colonised. It is the colonisers who hold the artefacts of the colonised in their gaze, subject them to scholarly investigation, utilise them in the creation of their explanatory historical narratives and determine their cultural value. When museums claim that they are caring for, interpreting and presenting aspects of global cultural heritage, we should be aware of whose intellectual authority, voices and judgement are dominant and whose are silenced or erased. Artists such as Phillips draw our attention to the way in which the refusal by the museums of the colonisers to both accept responsibility for the violent acquisition of objects and to facilitate their return, mirrors a parallel refusal by the former colonisers to adequately acknowledge historical injustices by former colonial powers, to commit to reparations and work to end ongoing inequality. In whitewashing a period of western violence and aggression against African peoples beneath a narrative of supposed education about other cultures, the current display of the Benin Bronzes not only fails to address past failures, but also ignores ongoing inequalities.

One could, perhaps provocatively, argue that if western institutions were truly committed to establishing museums of world culture to celebrate our shared humanity that were to be accessible to all, they would not only entertain the idea of returning looted artefacts but would, in the spirit of providing *actual* accessibility for everyone, also donate some treasures from European cultures to museums in the global south. Perhaps some of the Sutton Hoo collection or the Papal tiara could be given to the Nigerian National Museum to allow scholars, curators and visitors there to compare and discuss metalworking traditions and ceremonial practices in Europe and Africa.

Conclusion

The main institutional instruments of historicisation developed into their modern forms alongside the new imperialism of the nineteenth century and the shift towards the nation-state as a means of delineating geo-political space. The archive, museum, school, archaeological site and memorial all facilitated an imagination of identity *and* a rhetorics of legitimisation – they are all examples of 'political inheriting' and work to articulate and reinforce hegemonic interests.[73] The work of artists such as Walker, Phillips and Burgher challenge these institutions and offer a form of past-talk that complicates, challenges and undermines dominant narratives. These artists have deconstructed the way in which histories enacted through these institutions are intricately bound up with relations of power, ontologies and processes of legitimisation.

While there is nothing inherent to institutional or academic practices of historicisation that determines their socio-political role, in our opinion institutional history's potential to be used as a way of challenging dominant power appears weak. Historians might like to think that, by discussing previous instances of social or political change, they are encouraging belief in the possibility of analogous changes now and in the future, but there is no strong evidence that the production of histories, or indeed the more recent growth of heritage practices, has done anything to counter instances of inequality, violence and oppression. In contrast, we are more persuaded by Davies's argument that history's role in 'explaining' the present through its construction of a past that inevitably leads to a 'now' risks creating 'the illusion that the world's wrongness makes sense'.[74] Instead, we think that 'vernacular' forms of past-talk, by emphasising the heuristic benefit of plurality, contestation and intervention, have been more effectively mobilised *as cultural and rhetorical resources* in campaigns for socio-political justice, in challenging dominant narratives, institutions and practices and in unsettling common-sense assumptions that limit how we think about the social and political issues we face today. Moreover, such examples of past-talk have more effectively deconstructed the way in which institutionalised histories are intricately bound up with relations of power, ontologies and processes of legitimisation.

Greg Dening developed the idea of 'historying' – a term he used to describe a process of making histories that refuses closure, reification and the transformation of lived experience into a single authoritative narrative; a process by which pasts can be transformed into words, images or performances; a process which is polyvocal, open-ended, multifaceted and not exclusively the preserve of historians. But Dening wonders whether to be truly compassionate his 'stories' should in fact be poems. We think he may be right, and that the politics and practices of institutionalised historicisation processes do not provide an effective critique of, or practical intervention in, the unequal political and economic implications of globalisation and ongoing legacies of colonial exploitation. Maybe what is needed right now is not more history reinforcing and re-affirming the status quo, but an unhistorying.

Notes

1 Beverley Southgate, *What is History For?* (London: Routledge, 2005) 134–5.
2 David Harlan, 'Ken Burns and the Coming Crisis of Academic History', in *Rethinking History* 7 (2003) 184.
3 David Harlan, *The Degradation of American History* (Chicago: University of Chicago Press, 1997) 105.
4 Harlan, 'Ken Burns', 187 borrowed by him from Michael Walzer, *The Company of Critics: Social Criticism and Political Commitment in the Twentieth Century* (New York: Basic Books, 1988) 230.
5 Southgate, *What is History For?* 139; and Harlan 'Ken Burns', 170–1.
6 Harlan, *The Degradation of American History* 95.
7 *Ibid.*, 92.
8 Southgate, *What is History For?* 120.
9 *Ibid.*, 93.
10 Rigney, 'Being an Improper Historian', in Keith Jenkins, Sue Morgan and Alun Munslow (eds), *Manifestos for History* (London: Routledge, 2007) 153.
11 Robert A. Rosenstone, 'Space for the Bird to Fly', in Jenkins et al. (eds), *Manifestos,* 13.
12 Alun Munslow, *The Future of History* (Basingstoke: Palgrave Macmillan, 2010) 10, 185, 203.
13 Joan W. Scott, 'History-writing as Critique', Jenkins et al. (eds), *Manifestos,* 26–7
14 Beverley Southgate, 'Humani nil alienum': The Quest for "Human Nature", in Jenkins et al. (eds), *Manifestos* 71, 73; Southgate, *What is History For?* 159 and 176.
15 Horacio N. Roque Ramírez, 'A Living Archive of Desire: Teresita la Capesina and the Embodiment of Queer Latino Community History', in Antoinette Burton (ed.), *Archive Stories: Facts, Fictions and the Writing of History* (Durham: Duke University Press, 2005) 119.
16 Greg Dening, *Beach Crossings: Voyaging Across Times, Cultures, and Self* (Philadelphia: University of Pennsylvania Press, 2004) 58.
17 Dening, *Beach Crossings* 43, 18.
18 George Chauncey, 'How History Mattered: Sodomy Law and Marriage Reform in the United States', in *Public Culture: Society for Transnational Cultural Studies* 20/1 (2008); *The Public Life of History*, Special Edition ed. Bain Attwood, Dipesh Chakrabarty and Claudio Lomnitz 28.

19 David Anderson, *Histories of the Hanged: Britain's Dirty War in Kenya and the End of Empire* (London: Weidenfeld and Nicolson, 2005); Huw Bennett, 'Soldiers in the Court Room: The British Army's Part in the Kenya Emergency Under the Legal Spotlight', in *The Journal of Imperial and Commonwealth History* 39/5 (2011) 717–30; Caroline Elkins, *Britain's Gulag: The Brutal End of Empire in Kenya* (London: Jonathan Cape, 2005); Claire Norton and Mark Donnelly, *Liberating Histories* (Abingdon: Routledge, 2019) 121–25.

20 Keith Jenkins, *Why History? Ethics and Postmodernity* (Abingdon: Routledge, 1999) 2, 9, 193, 199–200.

21 Martin Davies, *Historics: Why History Dominates Contemporary Society* (Abingdon: Routledge, 2006) 8.

22 *Ibid.*, 183.

23 *Ibid.*, 7.

24 Cohen, *Historical Culture* 77.

25 Sande Cohen, *History Out of Joint* (Baltimore, MD: Johns Hopkins University Press, 2006) 17.

26 Davies, *Historics* 249.

27 Martin Davies, *Imprisoned by History. Aspects of a Historicized Life* (Abingdon: Routledge, 2010) 57, 61, 147, 194.

28 Cohen, *History Out of Joint* 118.

29 Chantal Mouffe, *Agonistics: Thinking the World Politically* (London: Verso, 2013) 13.

30 Hayden White, 'The Burden of History', in *History and Theory* 5 (1966) 111–134; White, *The Practical Past* (Evanston, IL: Northwestern University Press, 2014).

31 White, *The Practical Past* 3–24. See Norton and Donnelly, *Liberating Histories,* 14–15 for the distinction between institutionalised and vernacular forms of past-talk.

32 http://artforsocialchangetoolkit.wordpress.com/history/san-francisco-diggers accessed 5 March 2020.

33 http://diggers2012.wordpress.com/about accessed 5 March 2020.

34 http://diggers2012.wordpress.com/about/ and www.diggers.org/diggers-ENGLISH-1649/Declaration_from_the_poor_oppressed.pdf. The Diggers2012 also have a Facebook page www.facebook.com/diggers2012 accessed 5 March 2020.

35 http://diggers2012.wordpress.com/ accessed 5 March 2020; see diggers2012.wordpress.com/links/ accessed 5 March 2020 for a link to www.thelandmagazine.org.uk/articles/short-history-enclosure-britain accessed 5 March 2020.

36 http://phoenixrainbow23.blogspot.co.uk/2015/06/travesty-of-justice-as-runnymede-eco.html?utm_source=feedburner&utm_medium=email&utm_campaign=Feed:+blogspot/ZDStg+%28Phoenix+Rising%29 accessed 5 March 2020; and here for Pete Phoenix's notes citing the Magna Carta and Charter of the Forest http://phoenixrainbow23.blogspot.co.uk/2015/06/runnymede-eco-village-historic-appeal.html?utm_source=feedburner&utm_medium=email&utm_

campaign=Feed:+blogspot/ZDStg+%28Phoenix+Rising%29 accessed 5 March 2020; and here http://phoenixrainbow23.blogspot.co.uk/2015/06/runnymede-eco-village-court-defence.html?utm_source=feedburner&utm_medium=email&utm_campaign=Feed:+blogspot/ZDStg+%28Phoenix+Rising%29 accessed 5 March 2020; and here for a summary of the legal argument and references to the Forest Charter and Magna Carta www.squashcampaign.org/2015/09/runnymede-eco-village-in-epic-court-battle-sept-2015/ accessed 5 March 2020.

37 http://phoenixrainbow23.blogspot.co.uk/2015/06/runnymede-eco-village-get-stay-of.html accessed 5 March 2020.

38 Omar Kholeif, 'Europa: Performance, Narration and Reconstitution', in Emily Jacir and Omar Kholeif (eds), *Emily Jacir. Europa* (London: Prestel, 2013) 18.

39 Walid Khalidi, *All That Remains: The Palestinian Villages Occupied and Depopulated by Israel in 1948* (Washington, DC: Institute for Palestine Studies, 2nd edn 2006).

40 John Menick, 'Undiminished Returns: The Work of Emily Jacir 1998–2002', in Emily Jacir, Stella Rollig and Genoveva Rückert (eds), *Emily Jacir. Belongings: Arbeiten/Works 1998–2003* (Vienna: Folio Verlag, 2004), 25, http://johnmenick.com/writing/emily-jacir.html accessed 28 November 2017.

41 Exhibited at the *Sink Without Trace*, curated by Federica Mazzara and Maya Ramsey at P21, London (13 June–13 July), see exhibition catalogue *Sink Without Trace: Exhibition on Migrant Deaths at Sea,* 10; and also Burgher's website www.victoriaburgher.com/photography/lsvkrav99l1bike84gnfwcf9yxgvrd accessed 5 March 2020.

42 Victoria Burgher, *Plundered* (2018), www.victoriaburgher.com/photography/2018/6/19/plundered-2018 accessed 20 April 2020.

43 'Bison Skulls Await Industrial Processing at Michigan Carbon Works in Rogueville', Burton Historical Collection, Detroit Public Library (1892), http://commons.wikimedia.org/wiki/File:Bison_skull_pile.jpg accessed 5 March 2020. Sara makes explicit this link textually, and in the juxtaposition of her work and the photo of bison skulls on the website for the work www.pileosapmi.com/pile-o-sapmi-tittelverket-av-maret-anne-sara/ accessed 5 March 2020.

44 http://en.wikipedia.org/wiki/Alta_controversy accessed 5 March 2020.

45 Benedict Anderson, *Imagined Communities: Reflections on the Origin and Spread of Nationalism* (London: Verso, 2nd edn 1991) 178.

46 Victoria Burgher, *Milligan Must Fall* (2016), www.victoriaburgher.com/photography/2016/10/7/milligan-must-fall-2016-cast-sugar-22x10x2cm accessed 5 March 2020. The title of Burgher's work references the Rhodes Must Fall campaign that started in 2015 at the University of Cape Town and which sought to 'decolonise education' by effecting the removal of a statue commemorating British imperialist and businessman Cecil Rhodes at the university. The protest inspired similar movements to decolonise public spaces through the removal, or

contextualisation, of statues and the renaming of institutions that commemorate those who profited from imperialism. The statue of Milligan was re-erected in its original location at West India Quay 1997 by the London Docklands Development Corporation after having been previously sited at a number of locations and kept in storage for a while. It lacks any contextualisation or reference to Milligan's involvement with the slave trade.

47 Kara Walker, *Fons Americanus* (2019), www.tate.org.uk/art/artists/kara-walker-2674/kara-walkers-fons-americanus; http://en.wikipedia.org/wiki/Victoria_Memorial,_London both accessed 5 March 2020.

48 http://en.wikipedia.org/wiki/Victoria_Memorial,_London accessed 12 March 2020.

49 www.royalparks.org.uk/parks/st-jamess-park/things-to-see-and-do/monuments-fountains-and-statues/the-queen-victoria-memorial accessed 5 March 2020.

50 www.tate.org.uk/art/artists/kara-walker-2674/kara-walkers-fons-americanus#figures accessed 5 March 2020.

51 Robin Pearson and David Richardson, 'Insuring the Transatlantic Slave Trade', in *The Journal of Economic History* 2/79 (2019) 417–499 2020, www.cambridge.org/core/journals/journal-of-economic-history/article/insuring-the-transatlantic-slave-trade/F1E2354A667CF7A4DB989838F37B2DC2/core-reader accessed 10 March.

52 www.tate.org.uk/art/artists/kara-walker-2674/kara-walkers-fons-americanus#figures accessed 10 March 2020.

53 www.tate.org.uk/art/artists/kara-walker-2674/kara-walkers-fons-americanus accessed 10 March 2020.

54 Extract from the inscription on the fountain, see http://en.wikipedia.org/wiki/Buxton_Memorial_Fountain accessed 10 March 2020.

55 www.memorial2007.org.uk/about accessed 10 March 2020.

56 www.gov.uk/government/news/millions-of-pounds-to-support-restoration-and-repair-of-first-world-war-memorials; http://en.wikipedia.org/wiki/UK_Holocaust_Memorial; www.gov.uk/government/news/pm-pledges-12-million-to-remember-victims-of-srebrenica accessed 10 March 2020.

57 www.theguardian.com/world/2019/dec/10/slave-trade-memorial-charity-uk-government-refusal-of-funding-boris-johnson accessed 10 March 2020.

58 Kara Walker, *Fons Americanus* (2019) – full title is written on the wall of the Turbine Room, www.tate.org.uk/art/artists/kara-walker-2674/kara-walkers-fons-americanus accessed 18 March 2020.

59 Extract from the Minutes of a Meeting of the Board of Trustees of the British Museum, 17 April 2008, 7.4 www.britishmuseum.org/our-work/departments/human-remains/policy-and-governance/request-repatriation-human-remains-torres-strait-islands accessed 11 March 2020.

60 www.britishmuseum.org/about-us/british-museum-story/collecting-histories accessed 11 March 2020.

61 www.britishmuseum.org/our-work/departments/human-remains/policy-and-governance/request-repatriation-human-remains-new-zealand accessed 11 March 2020.

62 *Encounters: Revealing Stories of Aboriginal and Torres Strait Islander Objects from the British Museum*, National Museum Australia, 27 November 2015 to 28 March 2016, www.nma.gov.au/exhibitions/encounters accessed 20 April 2020.

63 Paul Daley, 'Encounters Exhibition: A Stunning but Troubling Collection of Colonial Plunder', *The Guardian* (27 November 2015) accessed 20 April 2020. www.theguardian.com/artanddesign/2015/nov/27/encounters-exhibition-a-stunning-but-troubling-collection-of-colonial-plunder.

64 www.theguardian.com/australia-news/2016/sep/25/the-gweagal-shield-and-the-fight-to-change-the-british-museums-attitude-to-seized-artefacts accessed 11 March 2020.

65 http://research.britishmuseum.org/research/collection_online/collection_object_details.aspx?objectId=512302&partId=1 accessed 11 March 2020.

66 Thomas Uwadiale Obinyan, 'The Annexation of Benin', *Journal of Black Studies* 19/1 (1988) 29–40.

67 www.britishmuseum.org/learn/schools/ages-7–11/africa/visit-resource-benin accessed 12 November 2019.

68 http://research.britishmuseum.org/research/collection_online/collection_object_details.aspx?objectId=8849&partId=1 accessed 12 November 2019.

69 The summary information accompanying the digital record of Tony Phillip's prints held in the V&A, and discussed below, does describe the British attack on Benin city as an 'unsavoury aspect of British history' and a punitive raid motivated by a desire on the part of the British to end the monopoly on the trade of palm oil and other commodities held by the *Oba* of Benin. See for example http://collections.vam.ac.uk/item/O45656/v-odudua-dancers-print-phillips-tony/ accessed 15 November 2019.

70 http://collections.rmg.co.uk/collections/objects/557.html accessed 11 March 2020.

71 Tony Phillips, *History of the Benin Bronzes* (1984) http://collections.vam.ac.uk/name/phillips-tony/A4285/ accessed 11 March 2020.

72 www.volkenkunde.nl/en/about-volkenkunde/mission accessed 11 March 2020. The National Museum of Ethnology, together with the Museum of the Tropics and the Africa Museum in the Netherlands, have all been renamed under the broader title of the National Museum of World Cultures; similarly, the Swedish Museum of Ethnography has been brought together with three other institutions under the umbrella title of the Museums of World Culture. The Museum of Ethnology in Vienna is now the Weltmuseum.

73 Anderson, *Imagined Communities* 178.

74 Martin L. Davies, 'Disobedience Reconsidered: History, Theory, and the Morality of Scholarship', *Rethinking History: The Journal of Theory and* Practice 17/2 (2013) 195.

Further reading

Martin Davies, *Historics: Why History Dominates Contemporary Society*, (Abingdon: Routledge, 2006).

David Harlan, *The Degradation of American History* (Chicago: University of Chicago Press, 1997).

Alun Munslow, *The Future of History* (Basingstoke: Palgrave Macmillan, 2010).

Claire Norton and Mark Donnelly, *Liberating Histories* (Abingdon: Routledge, 2019).

Hayden White, *The Practical Past* (Evanston, IL: Northwestern University Press, 2014).

Bibliography

Acton, John Emerich Edward Dalberg 'Letter to Contributors to the Cambridge History', 12 March 1898, appendix in *Lectures on Modern History*, (London: Macmillan, 1906).

Adair, Bill, Benjamin Filene, and Laura Koloski (eds) *Letting Go? Sharing Historical Authority in a User-Generated World* (Philadelphia: The Pew Centre for Arts and Heritage, 2011).

Allen, Robertson *America's Digital Army: Games at Work and War* (Lincoln: University of Nebraska Press, 2017).

Allison, Graham *Essence of Decision: Explaining the Cuban Missile Crisis* (New York: Longman, 2nd edn 1999).

Amos, Valerie and Pratibha Parmar 'Challenging Imperial Feminism', in Sue Morgan (ed.) *The Feminist History Reader* (London: Routledge, 2006) 284–294.

Anderson, Benedict *Imagined Communities: Reflections on the Origin and Spread of Nationalism* (London: Verso, 2nd edn 1991).

Anderson, David *Histories of the Hanged: Britain's Dirty War in Kenya and the End of* Empire (London: Weidenfeld and Nicolson, 2005).

Andrews, C.M. *The Colonial Background of the American Revolution: Four Essays in American Colonial History* (New Haven: Yale University Press, 1924).

Ankersmit, F.R. *Sublime Historical Experience* (Stanford: Stanford University Press, 2005).

———'Historiography and Postmodernism', in Keith Jenkins (ed.) *The Postmodern History Reader* (London: Routledge, originally published in 1997 reprint 1998) 277–97.

Ankersmit, F. and H. Kellner (eds) *A New Philosophy of History* (London: Reaktion Books, 1995).

Antoniou, Vasilia Lilian and Yasemin Nuhoglu Soysal, 'Nation and the Other in Greek and Turkish History Textbooks', in Hanna Schissler and Yasemin Nuhoglu Soysal (eds) *The Nation, Europe, and the World: Textbooks and Curricula in Transition* (New York: Berghahn Books, 2005) 105–21.

Appleby, Joyce, Lynn Hunt and Margaret Jacob *Telling the Truth About History* (London: W.W. Norton and Company, 1994).

Arendt, Hannah 'The Concept of History, Ancient and Modern', in Arendt *Between Past and Future: Eight Exercises in Political Thought* (Harmondsworth: Penguin, 1977, first published 1954) 41–90.

Armstrong, Catherine *Using Non-textual Sources: A Historian's Guide* (London: Bloomsbury Academic, 2016).

Art for Social Change Toolkit. 'Diggers Welcome'. Accessed 21 November 2016. http://artforsocialchangetoolkit.wordpress.com/history/san-francisco-diggers

Arthurs, Joshua W. '(Re)presenting Roman History in Italy, 1911–1955', in Claire Norton (ed.) *Nationalism, Historiography and the (Re)construction of the Past* (Washington: New Academia Publishing, 2007) 29–43.

Arnold, John H. *History: A Very Short Introduction* (Oxford: OUP, 2000).

Ashton, Paul and Alex Trapeznik (eds) *What is Public History Globally? Working with the Past in the Present* (London: Bloomsbury Academic, 2019).

Attwood, Bain 'In the Age of Testimony: The Stolen Generations Narrative, "Distance", and Public History', in *Public Culture: Society for Transnational Cultural Studies* 20/1 (2008) *The Public Life of History* special edition ed. Bain Attwood, Dipesh Chakrabarty and Claudio Lomnitz, 75–95.

Ballantyne, Tony 'Mr Peal's Archive: Mobility and Exchange in Histories of Empire', in Antoinette Burton (ed.) *Archive Stories: Facts, Fictions, and the Writing of History* (Durham: Duke University Press, 2005) 87–110.

Barber, Sarah and Corinna M. Peniston-Bird *History Beyond the Text: A Student's Guide to Approaching Alternative Sources* (London: Routledge, 2009).

Beattie, John *Other Cultures: Aims, Methods, and Achievements in Social Anthropology* (London: Cohen & West, 1964).

Becker, C. *The History of Political Parties in the Province of New York, 1760–1776* (Madison: University of Wisconsin, 1909).

Bede, *The Ecclesiastical History of the English People* trans. J. McClure and R. Collins (Oxford: Oxford University Press, 1994).

Bennett, Huw 'Soldiers in the Court Room: The British Army's Part in the Kenya Emergency Under the Legal Spotlight', in *The Journal of Imperial and Commonwealth History* 39/5 (2011) 717–30.

Bentley, Michael *Modern Historiography: An Introduction* (London: Routledge, 1999).

Berger, Stefan, Heiko Feldner and Kevin Passmore (eds), *Writing History: Theory and Practice* (London: Arnold, 2003).

Bisha, Robin 'Reconstructing the Voice of a Noble Woman of the Time of Peter the Great: Daria Mikhailovna Menshikova. An Exercise in (Pseudo)autobiographical

Writing', in Alun Munslow and Robert A. Rosenstone (eds) *Experiments in Rethinking History* (London: Routledge, 2004) 183–194.

Blaut, J.M. *Eight Eurocentric Historians* (London: The Guildford Press, 2000).

———*The Colonizer's Model of the World: Geographical Diffusionism and Eurocentric History* (London: The Guildford Press, 1993).

Bloch, Marc *The Royal Touch: Sacred Monarchy and Scrofula in England and France* trans. J.E. Anderson (London: Routledge and Kegan Paul, 1973).

Blundevill, Thomas *The True Order and Methode of Wryting and Reading Hystories* (London: William Seres, 1574).

Bobo, Jacqueline, Cynthia Hudley, Claudine Michel 'Introduction', in Bobo et al. (eds) *The Black Studies Reader* (London: Routledge, 2004) 1–10.

Booth, Robert 'UK Government Refuses to Fund Slavery Memorial Endorsed by Johnson in 2008', *The Guardian* 10 December 2019. Accessed 20 April 2020. www.theguardian.com/world/2019/dec/10/slave-trade-memorial-charity-uk-government-refusal-of-funding-boris-johnson

Bourke, Joanna 'Foreword', in Keith Jenkins, Sue Morgan and Alun Munslow (eds) *Manifestos for History* (London: Routledge, 2007) xi-xii.

Braun, Robert 'The Holocaust and Problems of Representation', in Keith Jenkins (ed.) *The Postmodern History Reader* (London: Routledge, originally published in 1997 reprint 1998) 418–425.

Braudel Fernand *The Mediterranean and the Mediterranean World in the Age of Philip II* (University of California Press, reprint edition 1996).

Bressey, Caroline 'It's Only Political Correctness – Race and Racism in British History', in Claire Dwyer and Carolien Bressey (eds) *New Geographies of Race and Racism* (Hampshire: Ashgate, 2008) 29–39.

British Museum 'Request for Repatriation of Human Remains to New Zealand'. Accessed 20 April 2020. www.britishmuseum.org/our-work/departments/human-remains/policy-and-governance/request-repatriation-human-remains-new-zealand

———'Collecting Histories'. Accessed 20 April 2020. www.britishmuseum.org/about-us/british-museum-story/collecting-histories

Brown, Callum G. *Postmodernism for Historians* (Harlow: Pearson Longman, 2005).

Bunzl, Martin *Real History: Reflections on Historical Practice* (London: Routledge, 1997).

Burgher, Victoria *Plundered* (2018). Accessed 20 April 2020. www.victoriaburgher.com/photography/2018/6/19/plundered-2018

———*Milligan Must Fall* (2016). Accessed 20 April 2020. www.victoriaburgher.com/photography/2016/10/7/milligan-must-fall-2016-cast-sugar-22x10x2cm

———*Don't Let Them Drown* (2015). Accessed 20 April 2020. www.victoriaburgher.com/photography/lsvkrav99l1bike84gnfwcf9yxgvrd

Burke, Peter *What Is Cultural History?* (Cambridge: Polity Press, 2nd edn 2008).

———*History and Social Theory* (Cambridge: Polity Press, 2nd edn, 2005).

Burton, Antoinette (ed.) *Archive Stories: Facts, Fictions, and the Writing of History* (Durham and London: Duke University Press, 2005).

———*Burdens of History: British Feminists, Indian Women and Imperial Culture* (Chapel Hill: The University of North Carolina Press, 1994).

Butler, Judith *Gender Trouble: Feminism and the Subversion of Identity* (New York: Routledge, 1990).

Cauvin, Thomas *Public History: A Textbook of Practice* (Abingdon: Routledge, 2016).

Chakrabarty, Dipesh 'Postcoloniality and the Artifice of History: Who Speaks for "Indian" Pasts?', in *Representations* 37, (1992) also in Bill Ashcroft, Gareth Griffiths and Helen Tiffin (eds) *The Post-Colonial Studies Reader* (London: Routledge, 2nd edn 2006) 340–44.

——— 'History and the Politics of Recognition,' in Keith Jenkins, Sue Morgan, Alun Munslow (eds) *Manifestos for History* (London: Routledge, 2007) 77–87.

Chapman, Adam, Anna Foka and Jonathan Westin 'Introduction: What is Historical Game Studies?', in *Rethinking History* 21/3 (2017) 358–71.

Chauncey, George 'How History Mattered: Sodomy Law and Marriage Reform in the United States', in *Public Culture: Society for Transnational Cultural Studies* 20/1 (2008) *The Public Life of History* special edition eds Bain Attwood, Dipesh Chakrabarty and Claudio Lomnitz 27–38.

Chaunu, Pierre et al. (eds) *La Mort à Paris* (Paris: 1978).

Chelkowski, Peter and Hamid Dabashi *Staging a Revolution: The Art of Persuasion in the Islamic Republic of Iran* (London: Booth-Clibborn Editions, 2000).

Chowdhury, Indira and Srijan Mandal, 'Public History in India: Towards a People's Past', in Paul Ashton and Alex Trapeznik (eds) *What is Public History Globally? Working with the Past in the Present* (London: Bloomsbury Academic, 2019) 79–92.

Cohen, Sande *History Out of Joint*, (Baltimore, MD: Johns Hopkins University Press, 2006).

———*Historical Culture: On the Recoding of an Academic Discipline* (Berkeley, Los Angeles: University of California Press, 1988).

Collingwood, R.G. *The Idea of History: With Lectures 1926–28*, 1946 (ed) Jan Van Der Dussen (Oxford: Oxford University Press, revised edn 1993).

———Collingwood, R.G. 'Lectures on the Philosophy of History (1926)', in *The Idea of History*.

Collini, S. and B. Williams, 'Collingwood, Robin George (1889–1943)', in *Oxford Dictionary of National Biography* (Oxford University Press, September 2004; online edn October 2008) www.oxforddnb.com/view/article/32503

Colvin, C.J. '"Brothers and Sisters, Do Not Be Afraid of Me": Trauma, History and the Therapeutic Imagination in the New South Africa', in K. Hodgkin and S. Radstone (eds) *Contested Pasts: The Politics of Memory* (London: Routledge, 2003).

Comnena, Anna *The Alexiad of Anna Comnena* trans. E.R.A. Sewter (Harmondsworth: 1969 reprinted 1985).

Confino, Alon and Peter Fritzsche (eds) *The Work of Memory: New Directions in the Study of German Society and Culture* (Chicago: University of Illinois Press, 2002).

Cubitt, Geoffrey *History and Memory* (Manchester: Manchester University Press, 2007).

Curthoys, Ann 'The History of Killing and the Killing of History', in Antoinette Burton (ed.) *Archive Stories: Facts, Fictions, and the Writing of History* (Durham: Duke University Press, 2005) 351–373.

Curthoys, Ann and John Docker *Is History Fiction?* (Sydney: University of South Wales Press, 2nd edn 2010).

Dabydeen, David, John Gilmore and Cecily Jones (eds) *The Oxford Companion to Black British History* (Oxford: Oxford University Press, 2007).

Daddow, O. 'Debating History Today', in *Rethinking History* 8/1 (2004) 143–7.

Daley, Paul 'The Gweagal Shield and the Fight to Change the British Museum's attitude to seized artefacts', *The Guardian*, 25 September 2016. Accessed 20 April 2020. www.theguardian.com/australia-news/2016/sep/25/the-gweagal-shield-and-the-fight-to-change-the-british-museums-attitude-to-seized-artefacts

———'Encounters Exhibition: A Stunning but Troubling Collection of Colonial Plunder', *The Guardian*, 27 November 2015. Accessed 20 April 2020. www.theguardian.com/artanddesign/2015/nov/27/encounters-exhibition-a-stunning-but-troubling-collection-of-colonial-plunder

David, Paul A. et al. *Reckoning with Slavery: A Critical Study in the Quantitative History of American Negro Slavery* (New York: 1976).

Davies, Martin L. *Historics: Why History Dominates Contemporary Society* (London: Routledge, 2006).

———*Imprisoned by History. Aspects of a Historicized Life* (Abingdon: Routledge, 2010).

de Certeau, Michel *The Writing of History* trans. Tom Conley (New York: Columbia University Press, 1988).

de Groot, Jerome *The Historical Novel* (London: Routledge, 2010).

———*Consuming History: Historians and Heritage in Contemporary Popular Culture* (London: Routledge, 2009).

Deeds Ermarth, Elizabeth *History in the Discursive Condition: Reconsidering the Tools of Thought* (Abingdon: Routledge, 2011).

Dening, Greg 'Performing Cross-culturally', in Keith Jenkins, Sue Morgan and Alun Munslow (eds) *Manifestos for History* (London: Routledge, 2007) 98–107.

———*Beach Crossings: Voyaging Across Times, Cultures, and Self* (Philadelphia: University of Pennsylvania Press, 2004).

———*Mr Bligh's Bad Language: Passion, Power and Theatre on the Bounty* (Cambridge: Cambridge University Press, Canto edn 1994, first published by CUP 1992).

Diamond, Jared *Guns, Germs and Steel: The Fates of Human Societies* (New York: Norton, 1997).

Diggers2012. Accessed 21 November 2016. http://diggers2012.wordpress.com/about

Diggers2012 Facebook page. Accessed 29 February 2016. www.facebook.com/diggers2012

Dobson, M and B. Ziemann (eds) *Reading Primary Sources: The Interpretation of Texts from Nineteenth- and Twentieth-Century History* (London: Routledge, 2009).

Droysen, J.G. *Historik Rekonstruktion der ersten vollständigen Fassung der Vorlesungen (1857). Grundriss der Historik in der ersten handschriftlichen (1857/1858) und in der letzten gedruckten Fassung (1882)* ed. Peter Ley, (Stuttgart-Bad Cannstatt: Fromann-Holzboog, 1977).

Eaglestone, Robert *The Holocaust and the Postmodern* (Oxford: Oxford University Press, 2004).

Eaton, Dave *World History Through Case Studies: Historical Skills in Practice* (New York: Bloomsbury Academic, 2019).

Eley, G. 'Foreword', in M. Evans, and K. Lunn (eds) *War and Memory in the Twentieth Century* (Oxford: Berg, 1997).

Elkins, Caroline *Britain's Gulag: The Brutal End of Empire in Kenya* (London: Jonathan Cape, 2005).

Elton, Geoffrey *The Practice of History* (Oxford: Blackwell, 2nd edn, 1992).

Encounters: Revealing Stories of Aboriginal and Torres Strait Islander Objects from the British Museum. National Museum Australia, 27 November 2015 to 28 March 2016. Accessed 20 April 2020. www.nma.gov.au/exhibitions/encounters

Engels, Friedrich and Karl *Marx The Communist Manifesto* at Project Gutenberg www.gutenberg.org/catalog/world/readfile?fk_files=165453&pageno=2

Evans, Richard J. 'Cite Ourselves!', in *London Review of Books* vol. 31 no. 23 (3 December 2009) 12–14.

———*In Defence of History* (London: Granta, 2018 edn).

Faroqhi, Suraiya *Approaching Ottoman History: An Introduction to the Sources* (Cambridge: Cambridge University Press, 1999).

Fayard, Jean-François *Des enfants sans histoire* (Paris, 1984).

Febvre, Lucien *Philippe II et la Franche-Comté, etude d'histoire politique, religieuse et morale* (Paris: 1911).

Ferguson, Niall *Empire: How Britain Made the Modern World* (London: Penguin, 2004, first published by Allen Lane in 2003).

———(ed.) *Virtual History: Alternatives and Counterfactuals* (London: Picador, 1997).

Fernández-Armesto, F. 'Epilogue: What is History *Now*?', in D. Cannadine (ed.) *What is History Now?* (London: Palgrave Macmillan, 2002).

Flynn, M.K. and Tony King 'Renovating the Public Past: Nation-building, Symbolic Reparation and the Politics of Heritage in Post-apartheid South Africa', in Claire Norton (ed.) *Nationalism, Historiography and the (Re)construction of the Past* (Washington: New Academia Publishing, 2007) 45–60.

Foucault, Michel *The Archaeology of Knowledge* trans. A.M. Sheridan Smith (London: Routledge, 2002).

———'Nietzsche, Genealogy, History', in *Language, Counter-Memory, Practice,* trans. Donald F. Bouchard and Sherry Simon, ed. with an introduction by Donald F. Bouchard (Ithaca, New York: Cornell University Press, 1977) 139–64.

———'An Exchange with Michel Foucault', in *New York Review of Books* 31 March 1983.

Frank, Andre Gunder *ReOrient: Global Economy in the Asian Age* (University of California Press, 1998).

Friedländer, Saul (ed.) *Probing the Limits of Representation: Nazism and the Final Solution* (Cambridge, MA: Harvard University Press, 1992).

Froeyman, Anton 'Frank Ankersmit and Eelco Runia: The Presence and the Otherness of the Past', in *Rethinking History,* 16/3 (2012) 393–415.

Gatrell, Peter 'Population Displacement in the Baltic Region in the Twentieth Century: From "Refugee Studies" to Refugee History', in *Journal of Baltic Studies,* 38/1 (2007) 43–60.

Geyl, P. *Napoleon, For and Against* trans. O Renier (London: Cape, 1949).

Ghosh, Durba 'National Narratives and the Politics of Miscegenation', in Antoinette Burton (ed.) *Archive Stories: Facts, Fictions, and the Writing of History* (Durham: Duke University Press, 2005) 27–44.

Gibbon, Edward *The Decline and Fall of the Roman Empire* (London: Strahan and Cadell, 1776–89).

Ginzberg, Carlo *The Cheese and the Worms: The Cosmos of a Sixteenth Century Miller* trans. John and Anne Tedeschi (Baltimore, MD: Johns Hopkins University Press, 1992).

Goffman Daniel *The Ottoman Empire and Early Modern Europe* (Cambridge: Cambridge University Press, 2002).

Goldstone, Jack A. *Revolution and Rebellion in the Early Modern World* (Berkeley: University of California Press, 1991).

Goodman, James *Stories of Scottsboro* (New York: Vintage Books, 1995).

Gottlob, Michael (ed.) *Historical Thinking in South Asia: A Handbook of Sources from Colonial Times to the Present* (Oxford: Oxford University Press, 2003).

Green, Anna and Kathleen Troup (eds) *The Houses of History: A Critical Reader in Twentieth-Century History and Theory* (Manchester: Manchester University Press, 1999).

Guldi, Jo and David Armitage, *The History Manifesto* (Cambridge: Cambridge University Press, 2014).

Gumbrecht, Hans Ulrich *In 1926: Living at the Edge of Time* (Cambridge, MA: Harvard University Press, 1997).

Halbwachs, M. *On Collective Memory,* trans. and ed. Lewis A. Coser from *Les cadres sociaux de la mémoire* and *La topographie légendaire des évangiles en terre sainte* (Chicago: Chicago University Press, 1992).

Hall, Catherine 'Feminism and Feminist History', in Catherine Hall *White, Male and Middle-Class: Explorations in Feminism and Feminist History* (Oxford: Polity Press, 1992) 1–40.

Hardy, G.R. 'Objectivity and Interpretation in the "Shih chi"' (PhD thesis, Yale University, 1988).

Harlan, David, '*The Burden of History Forty Years Later*', in F. Ankersmit, E. Domanska, and H. Kellner, (eds) *Refiguring Hayden White*, (Stanford: Stanford California Press, 2009).

———'Ken Burns and the Coming Crisis of Academic History', in *Rethinking History* 7 (2003), 169–192.

———*The Degradation of American History* (Chicago: University of Chicago Press, 1997).

Hempel, Carl 'The Function of General Laws in History', in *Journal of Philosophy*, 39/1 (1942) 35–48.

Henrich, Eureka 'Mobility, Migration and Modern Memory', in Anna Maerker, Simon Sleight and Adam Sutcliffe (eds) *History, Memory and Public Life: The Past in the Present* (Abingdon: Routledge, 2018) 101–25.

Herrnstein Smith, Barbara *Belief and Resistance: Dynamics of Contemporary Intellectual Controversy* (Cambridge, MA: Harvard University Press, 1997).

Hewitt, N. 'Gender and Feminist Studies in History', in Neil J. Smelser and Paul B. Baltes (eds) *International Encyclopedia of the Social and Behavioural Sciences, vol. 9* (Oxford: Elsevier, 2001).

Hobsbawm, Eric *Interesting Times: A Twentieth-Century Life* (London: Abacus, 2002).

———*Age of Extremes: The Short Twentieth Century, 1914–1991*(London: Abacus, 1995).

———*On History* (London: Abacus, 1998).

Hobson, John M. *The Eastern Origins of Western Civilisation* (Cambridge: Cambridge University Press, 2004).

Hodes, Martha 'Knowledge and indifference in the New York City race riot of 1900: an argument in search of a story', *Rethinking History*, 15/1 (2011) 61–89.

Hodgkin, Katherine and Susannah Radstone 'Introduction: Contested Pasts', in Katherine Hodgkin, and Susannah Radstone (eds) *Contested Pasts: The Politics of Memory* (London: Routledge, 2003).

Hoffman Berman, Constance (ed.) *Medieval Religion: New Approaches* (Abingdon: Routledge, 2005).

Hollinshead, Byron and Theodore K. Rabb, (eds) *I Wish I'd Been There: Twenty Historians Revisit Key Moments in History* (London: Macmillan, 2008).

hooks, bell 'Marginality as a Site of Resistance,' in R. Ferguson et al. (eds) *Out There: Marginalization and Contemporary Cultures* (Cambridge, MA: MIT, 1990) 341–43.

Hookway, Christopher, 'Pragmatism', in *The Stanford Encyclopedia of Philosophy (Spring 2010 Edition)*, Edward N. Zalta (ed.), URL = http://plato.stanford.edu/archives/spr2010/entries/pragmatism/

Horne, John and Alan Kramer *German Atrocities, 1914: A History of Denial* (New Haven and London: Yale University Press, 2001).

Howard, John 'Where are we to Begin?', in Allida M. Black (ed.) *Modern American Queer History* (Philadelphia: Temple University Press, 2001) 3–10.

Hughes-Warrington, Marnie *History Goes to the Movies: Studying History on Film* (London: Routledge, 2007).

———*Fifty Key Thinkers on History* (London: Routledge, 2000).

Hume, David *The History of England*, e-version based on the 1778 edition at the Online Library of Liberty http://oll.libertyfund.org/ToC/0011.php

Ibn al-Athir *The Chronicle of Ibn al-Athir for the Crusading Period from al-Kamil fi'l-ta'rikh*. Parts One and Two translated and with an introduction by D.S. Richards (Aldershot: Ashgate, 2006 and 2007).

Ibn Khaldun *The Muqaddimah: An Introduction to History* trans. and introduced by Franz Rosenthal with a new introduction by Bruce B. Lawrence (Princeton: Princeton University Press, 2005).

Idle, Nadia and Alex Nunns (eds) *Tweets from Tahrir: Egypt's Revolution as it Unfolded, in the Words of the People who Made it* (New York: OR Books, 2011).

Iggers, Georg, Q. Edward Wang and Supriya Mukherjee *A Global History of Modern Historiography* (London: Longman, 2008).

Iggers, G. Georg *Historiography in the Twentieth Century: From Scientific Objectivity to the Postmodern Challenge* (Middletown CT: Wesleyan University Press, 2005).

Ilaih, Kancha 'Productive Labour, Consciousness and History: the Dalitbahujan Alternative', in Shahid Amin and Dipesh Chakrabarty (eds) *Subaltern Studies: Writings on South Asian History and Society* (Delhi: Oxford University Press, 1996) 165–200.

Jacir, Emily *Memorial to 418 Palestinian Villages Which Were Destroyed, Depopulated, and Occupied by Israel in 1948* (2001).

Jarausch, K.H. and P.A. Coclanis, 'Quantification in History', in Neil J. Smelser and Paul B. Baltes (eds) *International Encyclopedia of the Social and Behavioral Sciences*, (Oxford: Elsevier, 2001) 12634–38.

Jenkins, Keith *At the Limits of History: Essays on Theory and Practice* (London: Routledge, 2009).

———*Re-figuring History: New Thoughts on an Old Discipline* (London: Routledge, 2003).

———*Rethinking History* with a new preface and conversation with the author by Alun Munslow 2nd edition (London: Routledge Classics, 2003).

———*Why History? Ethics and Postmodernity* (London: Routledge, 1999).

———*The Postmodern History Reader* (London: Routledge, 1997).

———*On* 'What is History?' *From Carr and Elton to Rorty and White* (London: Routledge, 1995).

Jenkins, Keith and Alun Munslow *The Nature of History Reader* (London: Routledge, 2004).

Jones, Eric *The European Miracle: Environments, Economies and Geopolitics in the History of Europe and Asia* (Cambridge: Cambridge University Press, 1981).

Jordanova, L. *History in Practice* (London: Hodder Arnold, 2006).

Judt, Tony *Reappraisals: Reflections on the Forgotten Twentieth Century* (London: Vintage, 2009).

Kansteiner, Wulf 'Finding Meaning in Memory: A Methodological Critique of Collective Memory Studies', in *History and Theory*, 41/2 (2002) 179–97.

Kaye, Harvey J. *The British Marxist Historians* (New York: Polity Press, 1984).

Khalidi Walid *All That Remains: The Palestinian Villages Occupied and Depopulated by Israel in 1948* (Beirut: Institute for Palestine Studies, 1992).

Kholeif, Omar 'Europa: Performance, Narration and Reconstitution', in *Emily Jacir. Europa* ed. Emily Jacir and Omar Kholeif (London: Prestel, 2013).

Kirsch, Gesa E. and Liz Rohan (eds) *Beyond the Archives: Research as a Lived Process* (Carbondale: Southern Illinois University Press, 2008).

Kosofsky Sedgewick, Eve *Epistemology of the Closet* (Berkeley: University of California Press, 1990).

Kosambi, D.D. *Introduction to the Study of Indian History* (Bombay: Popular Book Depot, 1956).

Kritzman, L.D. 'Foreword: In Remembrance of Things French', in P. Nora (ed.) *Realms of Memory: Rethinking the French Past,* vol. 1, *Conflicts and Divisions*, trans. Arthur Goldhammer (New York: Columbia University Press, 1996).

Labrousse, Ernest *Esquisse des mouvements du prix et des revenues* (Paris: 1933).

LaCapra, D. *History and Its Limits: Human: Animal, Violence* (Ithaca: Cornell University Press, 2009).

———'History and Memory: In the Shadow of the Holocaust', in Dominick LaCapra *History and Memory after Auschwitz* (Ithaca: Cornell University Press, 1998) 8–42.

Laiou, Angeliki 'Introduction: Why Anna Komnene?', in Thalia Gouma-Peterson (ed.) *Anna Komnene and Her Times* (New York: Garland Publishing Inc., 2000) 1–14.

Lakshmi, Rama and Shalini Sharma, 'Building a Safe Space for Unsafe Memories: The Remember Bhopal Museum', in Katie Holmes and Heather Goodall (eds) *Telling Environmental Histories: Intersections of Memory, Narrative and Environment* (Basingstoke, Hampshire: Palgrave Macmillan, 2017) 133–52.

Landes, David *The Wealth and Poverty of Nations: Why Some are so Rich and Some are so Poor* (New York: Norton, 1998).

Lemon, M.C. *Philosophy of History: A Guide for Students* (London: Routledge, 2003).

———*The Discipline of History and the History of Thought* (London: Routledge, 1995).

Le Roy Ladurie, Emmanuel, *Montaillou: Cathars and Catholics in a French Village*, 1294–1324 trans. Barbara Bray (London: Penguin, 2002).

Lindqvist, Sven *A History of Bombing* (London: Granta Books, 2002).

Loewen, James W. *Lies My Teacher Told Me: Everything Your American History Textbook Got Wrong* (New York: Simon and Schuster, 1995).

Lowenthal, D. *The Heritage Crusade and the Spoils of History* (Cambridge: Cambridge University Press, 1988).

Lynch, Jack *You Could Look It Up: The Reference Shelf From Ancient Babylon to Wikipedia* (New York: Bloomsbury Press, 2016).

Macaulay, G.C. trans. *The History of Herodotus: The Third Book of the Histories, Called Thaleia*, http://ebooks.adelaide.edu.au/h/herodotus/h4m/index.html

Macdonald, Sharon 'Undesirable Heritage: Fascist Material Culture and Historical Consciousness in Nuremberg', in *International Journal of Heritage Studies,* 12/1 (2006) 9–28.

Macrides, Ruth 'The Historian in the History', in Costas N. Constantinides, et al. (eds) ΦΙΛΕΛΛΗΝ *Studies in Honour of Robert Browning* (Venice: Istituto Ellenico di Studi Bizantini e Postbizantini di Venezia per tutti i paesi del mondo, 1996) 205–224.

Mann, Michael *The Sources of Social Power: vol. 1 A History of Power from the Beginning to A.D.1760* (Cambridge: Cambridge University Press, 1986).

Marfleet, Philip 'Refugees and History: Why we Must Address the Past', in *Refugee Survey Quarterly*, 26/3 (2007) 136–48.

Marwick, Arthur *The Nature of History* (Basingstoke: Macmillan, 3rd edn1989).

———*The New Nature of History: Knowledge, Evidence, Language* (Basingstoke: Palgrave, 2001).

———'"A Fetishism of Documents"? The Salience of Source-based History', in *Developments in Modern Historiography* ed. H. Kozicki (London: Macmillan, 1993).

Marx, Karl *Selected Writings* ed. D McLellan (Oxford: Oxford University Press, 1977).

Masalha, Nur *The Palestine Nakba: Decolonising History and Reclaiming Memory* (London: Zed Books, 2011).

——— '*Present Absentees* and Indigenous Resistance', in Ilan Pappé (ed.) *The Israel/ Palestine Question: A Reader* (London: Routledge, 2nd edn 2007).

Mazlish, B. 'The Question of *The Question of Hu*', in *History and Theory,* 31/2 (1992) 143–52.

Mazzara, Federica and Maya Ramsey (eds) *Sink Without Trace: Exhibition on Migrant Deaths at Sea* exhibition catalogue (2019).

McCullagh, C. Behan *The Logic of History: Putting Postmodernism in Perspective,* (London: Routledge, 2004).

———*The Truth of History* (London: Routledge, 1998).

———*Justifying Historical Descriptions* (Cambridge: Cambridge University Press, 1984).

Mellen, J. *Filmguide to the Battle of Algiers* (Bloomington, London: Indiana University Press, 1973).

Memorial 2007. Remembering Enslaved Africans and their Descendants 1807–2007. Accessed 20 April 2020. www.memorial2007.org.uk/about

Menick, John 'Undiminished Returns: The Work of Emily Jacir 1998–2002', in *Emily Jacir. Belongings: Arbeiten/Works 1998–2003*, ed. Emily Jacir, Stella Rollig and Genoveva Rückert (Vienna: Folio Verlag, 2004).

Messner, Marcus and Marcia W. DiStaso, 'Wikipedia versus Encyclopedia Britannica: A Longitudinal Analysis to Identify the Impact of Social Media on the Standards of Knowledge', *Mass Communication and Society,* 16/4 (2013) 465–86.

Migration Museum (UK), 'How We Got Here: The First Two Years' (London, July 2012).

'Millions of Pounds to Support Restoration and Repair of First World War Memorials'. Accessed 20 April 2020. www.gov.uk/government/news/millions-of-pounds-to-support-restoration-and-repair-of-first-world-war-memorials

Montagu, Mary Wortley *Letters of the Right Honourable Lady M--y W---y M----e :written, during her travels in Europe, Asia and Africa, to persons of distinction, men of letters, &c. in different parts of Europe : which contain, among other curious relations, accounts of the policy and manners of the Turks : drawn from sources that have been inaccessible to other travellers.* (London : Printed for T. Becket and P.A. De Hondt …, 1763).

Morgan, Gwenda. *The Debate on the American Revolution* (Manchester: Manchester University Press, 2007).

Morgan, Sue 'Introduction', in Sue Morgan (ed.) *The Feminist History Reader* (London: Routledge, 2006) 1–48.

Morris-Suzuki, Tessa 'The Frontiers of Japanese Identity', in Stein Tonneson and Hans Antlöv (eds) *Asian Forms of the Nation* (Richmond: Curzon Press, 1996) 41–66.

Moses, A. Dirk 'Coming to Terms with Genocidal Pasts in Comparative Perspective: Germany and Australia', in *Aboriginal History,* 21 (2001) 91–115.

Mouffe, Chantal *Agonistics: Thinking the World Politically* (London: Verso, 2013).

Müller, Philipp 'Understanding History: Hermeneutics and Source-criticism in Historical Scholarship', in Dobson and Ziemann (eds) *Reading Primary Sources: The Interpretation of Texts from Nineteenth- and Twentieth-Century History* (London: Routledge, 2009) 21–36.

Munslow, Alun *The Future of History* (Basingstoke: Palgrave Macmillan, 2010).

———*Narrative and History* (Basingstoke: Palgrave Macmillan, 2007).

———*Deconstructing History* (London: Routledge, 2nd edn 2006).

———*Routledge Companion to Historical Studies* (London: Routledge, 2nd edn 2006).

———*The New History* (Harlow: Pearson, Longman, 2003).

Munslow, Alun and Robert A. Rosenstone (eds) *Experiments in Rethinking History* (London: Routledge, 2004).

Mustafa Naima, *Tarih-i Naima* also known as *Ravat al-husayn fi khulāsat-i akhbar al-khāfikayn* (Istanbul: Matbaa-i âmire, 1281–3 [1864–6]).

National Council on Public History, 'How Do We Define Public History?' http://ncph.org/what-is-public-history/about-the-field

Ng, On-cho and Q. Edward Wang *Mirroring the Past: The Writing and Use of History in Imperial China* (Honolulu University of Hawai'i Press, 2005).

Nietzsche, Friedrich 'On the Uses and Disadvantages of History for Life', (1874), reprinted in Daniel Breazeale (ed.) trans. R.J. Hollingdale, *Friedrich Nietzsche: Untimely Meditations* (Cambridge: Cambridge University Press, 1997).

Nora, P. 'Between Memory and History', in P. Nora (ed.) *Realms of Memory: Rethinking the French Past,* vol. 1, *Conflicts and Divisions*, trans. Arthur Goldhammer (New York: Columbia University Press, 1996).

Norton, Claire "Narrating the 'Yoke of Oppression": Twentieth Century Hungarian Scholarship of the Ottoman-Hungarian Borderlands', in Claire Norton (ed.) *Nationalism, Historiography and the (Re)construction of the Past* (Washington: New Academia Publishing, 2007) 187–200.

——— '"The Lords of Lewdness": Imagining the "Other", in Ottoman *Fethnames*', in Robert Born and Andreas Puth (eds) *Osmanischer Orient und Ostmitteleuropa. Perzeptionen und Interaktionaen in den Grenzzonen zwischen dem 16. Und 18. Jahrundert* (Stuttgart: Franz Steiner Verlag, 2014) 281–299.

Claire Norton and Mark Donnelly *Liberating Histories* (Abingdon: Routledge, 2019).

Novick, Peter *That Noble Dream: The 'Objectivity Question' and the American Historical Profession* (Cambridge: Cambridge University Press, 1988).

Obama, Barack *Dreams From My Father: A Story of Race and Inheritance* (New York: Random House, 1995).

Obinyan, Thomas Uwadiale 'The Annexation of Benin', in *Journal of Black Studies,* 19/1 (1988) 29–40.

O'Sullivan, Dan *Wikipedia: A New Community of Practice?* (Farnham: Ashgate, 2009).

Özkirimli, Umit *Theories of Nationalism: A Critical Introduction* (Basingstoke: Palgrave, 2000).

Pappé, I. (ed.) *The Israel/Palestine Question: A Reader* (London: Routledge, 2nd edn 2007).

Partner, Nancy 'Historicity in an Age of Reality-Fictions', in F. Ankersmit and H. Kellner (eds) *A New Philosophy of History* (London: Reaktion Books, 1995) 21–39.

Pearson, Robin and David Richardson 'Insuring the Transatlantic Slave Trade', in *The Journal of Economic History,* 2/79 (2019) 417–499.

Phillips, Tony *History of the Benin Bronzes* (1984).

Phillips, Murray G. 'Wikipedia and History: A Worthwhile Partnership in the Digital Era?', in *Rethinking History,* 20/4 (2016) 523–43.

Pinto, Sarah 'Emotional Histories and Historical Emotions: Looking at the Past in Historical Novels', in *Rethinking History,* 14/2 (2010) 180–207.

Piterberg Gabriel *An Ottoman Tragedy: History and Historiography at Play* (Berkeley: University of California Press, 2003).

'PM pledges £1.2 million to Remember Victims of Srebrenica' Accessed 20 April 2020. www.gov.uk/government/news/pm-pledges-12-million-to-remember-victims-of-srebrenica

Pötzsch, Holger and Vít Šisler, 'Playing Cultural Memory: Framing History in *Call of Duty: Black Ops* and *Czechoslovakia 38–89: Assassination*', in *Games and Culture,* 14/1 (2019) 3–25.

Prakash, Gyan 'Subaltern Studies as Postcolonial Criticism', in Catherine Hall (ed.), *Cultures of Empire: Colonizers in Britain and the Empire in Nineteenth and Twentieth Centuries. A Reader* (New York: Routledge, 2000) 120–136.

Price, Richard *First-Time: The Historical Vision of an African American People* (Chicago: University of Chicago Press, 2nd edn 2002).

———*Alabi's World* (Baltimore, MD: Johns Hopkins University Press, 1990).

Raessens, Joost and Jeffrey Goldstein (eds) *Handbook of Computer Game Studies* (Cambridge, MA: MIT Press, 2005).

Ramírez, Horacio N. Roque 'A Living Archive of Desire: Teresita la Capesina and the Embodiment of Queer Latino Community History', in Antoinette Burton (ed.) *Archive Stories: Facts, Fictions and the Writing of History* (Durham: Duke University Press, 2005) 111–135.

Renan, E 'What is a Nation?', in Homi Bhabbu (ed.) *Nation and Narration* (London: Routledge, 1990) 8–22.

Richards, D.S. 'Ibn al-Athir and the Later Parts of the *Kamil*: a Study of Aims and Methods', in D.O. Morgan (ed.) *Medieval Historical Writing in the Christian and Islamic Worlds* (London: School of Oriental and African Studies, 1982) 76–108.

Ricoeur, Paul *Time and Narrative*, trans. Kathleen McLaughlin and David Pellauer (vols 1 and 2), trans. Kathleen Blamey and David Pellauer (vol. 3), (Chicago: University of Chicago Press, 1984–8).

Rigney, Ann 'Being an Improper Historian,' in Keith Jenkins, Sue Morgan, Alun Munslow (eds) *Manifestos for History* (London: Routledge, 2007) 149–59.

Roberts, Hugh 'The Image of the French Army in the Cinematic Representation of the Algerian War: The Revolutionary Politics of *The Battle of Algiers*', in Martin S. Alexander, Martin Evans and J.F.V. Keiger (eds) *The Algerian War and the French Army, 1954–62: Experiences, Images, Testimonies* (Basingstoke: Palgrave, 2002) 152–63.

Rorty, Richard 'Solidarity or Objectivity?', in K. Brad Wray (ed.) *Knowledge and Inquiry: Readings in Epistemology* (Peterborough Ont., Ormskirk: Broadview Press, 2002) 422–37.

———*Truth and Progress: Philosophical Papers* (Cambridge: Cambridge University Press, 1998).

Rosenstone, Robert A. *Mirror in the Shrine: American Encounters with Meiji Japan* (Cambridge, MA: Harvard University Press, 1988).

———'Space for the Bird to Fly', in Keith Jenkins, Sue Morgan, Alun Munslow (eds) *Manifestos for History* (London: Routledge, 2007) 11–18.

Rosenthal, F. 'Ibn al-Athir', in *Encyclopaedia of Islam* P.J. Bearman et al. (eds) (Leiden: Brill, 2004) CD-ROM ed. Windows version.

Rosenzweig, Roy 'Can History be Open Source? *Wikipedia* and the Future of the Past', in *The Journal of American History*, 93/1 (2006) 117–46.

Roth, Paul *The Philosophical Structure of Historical Explanation* (Evanston, Illinois: Northwestern University Press, 2019).

——— 'Whistling History: Ankersmit's neo-Tractarian Theory of Historical Representation', *Rethinking History*, 17/4 (2013) 548–69.

——— 'The Pasts', *History and Theory*, 51/3 (2012) 313–39.

Rublack, Ulinka (ed.) *A Concise Companion to History* (Oxford: Oxford University Press, 2011).

Runia, Eelco *Moved by the Past: Discontinuity and Historical Mutation* (Columbia University Press, 2014).

——— 'Spots of Time', in *History and Theory*, 45 (2006) 305–16.

Sahadeo, Jeff '"Without the Past There is No Future": Archives, History, and Authority in Uzbekistan', in Antoinette Burton (ed.) *Archive Stories: Facts, Fictions, and the Writing of History* (Durham: Duke University Press, 2005) 45–67.

Said, Edward W. *Orientalism* (New York: Pantheon Books, 1978).

Samuel, Raphael *Theatres of Memory*, vol. 1, *Past and Present in Contemporary Culture* (London: Verso, 1994).

Sara, Máret Ánne *Pile o' Sápmi* (2016). Accessed 20 April 2020. www.pileosapmi.com/pile-o-sapmi-tittelverket-av-maret-anne-sara/

Sayer, Faye *Public History: A Practical Guide* (London: Bloomsbury, 2015).

Schama, Simon *Dead Certainties (Unwarranted Speculations)* (London: Granta Books, 1998).

Schutt, Kevin 'Strategic Simulations and Our Past: The Bias of Computer Games in the Presentation of History', in *Games and Culture*, 2/3 (2007) 213–35.

Scott, Joan W. 'History-writing as Critique', in Keith Jenkins, Sue Morgan and Alun Munslow *Manifestos for History* (London: Routledge, 2007).

———Joan W. Scott, 'Feminism's History', in Sue Morgan (ed.) *The Feminist History Reader* (London: Routledge, 2006) 387–98.

Segal, Marshall H., Donald T. Campbell, and Melville J. Herskovits, *The Influence of Culture on Visual Perception* (Indianapolis: In: Bobbs-Merrill, 1966).

Sewell, William H. *Logics of History: Social Theory and Social Transformation* (Chicago: University of Chicago Press, 2005).

Shapiro, Ann-Louise 'Fixing History: Narratives of World War I in France', in *History and Theory: Studies in the Philosophy of History* Theme Issue 36 'Producing the Past: Making Histories Inside and Outside the Academy', 111–30.

Shohat, E. and R. Stam, *Unthinking Eurocentrism: Multiculturalism and the Media* (London: Routledge, 1994).

Silverman, K. *The Life and Times of Cotton Mathar* (New York: Harper and Row, 1984).

Simon, Bryant 'Narrating a Southern Tragedy: Historical Facts and Historical Fictions', in Alun Munslow and Robert A. Rosenstone (eds) *Experiments in Rethinking History* (London: Routledge, 2004) 156–82.

Sink Without Trace: Exhibition on Migrant Deaths at Sea exhibition at P21, London (2019). Accessed 20 April 2020 p21.gallery/exhibitions/past-exhibitions/2019-exhibitions/exhibition-sink-without-trace/ and www.sinkwithouttrace.com

Skinner, Jonathan 'Walking the Falls: Dark Tourism and the Significance of Movement on the Political Tour of West Belfast', in *Tourist Studies*, 16/1 (2016) 1–17.

Smiles, Samuel *Self-Help; with Illustrations of Conduct and Perseverance* (London: John Murray, 1890).

Smith, Charles D. 'Historiography of World War 1', in Israel Gershoni, Amy Singer, and Y. Hakan Erdem (eds) *Middle East Historiographies; Narrating the Twentieth Century* (Seattle: University of Washington Press, 2006) 39–69.

Southgate, Beverley *History Meets Fiction* (Harlow: Longman, 2009).

——— '"Humani nil alienum": The Quest for "Human Nature"', in Keith Jenkins, Sue Morgan and Alun Munslow (eds) *Manifestos for History* (London: Routledge, 2007) 67–76.

——— *What is History For?* (London: Routledge, 2005).

——— *History: What and Why? Ancient, Modern and Postmodern Perspectives* (London: Routledge, 2nd edn 2001).

Spence, Jonathan D. *The Question of Hu* (London: Faber and Faber, 1989).

Spiegel, Gabrielle M. (ed.) *Practicing History: New Directions in Historical Writing after the Linguistic Turn* (London: Routledge, 2005).

Spivak, Gayatri Chakravorty 'Can the Subaltern Speak?', in Cary Nelson and Lawrence Grossberg (eds) *Marxism and the Interpretation of Culture* (Urbana, IL: University of Illinois Press, 1988) 271–313.

Spohr Readman, Kristina 'Memoranda', in Miriam Dobson and Benjamin Ziemann (eds) *Reading Primary Sources: The Interpretation of Texts from Nineteenth- and Twentieth-Century History* (London: Routledge, 2009) 123–140.

Spring, Dawn 'Gaming History: Computer and Video Games as Historical Scholarship', in *Rethinking History*, 9/2 (2015) 207–21.

Stewart, Mary 'Expanding the Archive: The Role of Family History in Exploring Connections Within a Settler's World', in Paul Ashton and Hilda Kean (eds) *People and their Pasts* (Houndmills: Palgrave Macmillan, 2009) 240–59.

Stone, Dan 'Beyond the Mnemosyne Institute: The Future of Memory after the Age of Commemoration', in Rick Crownshaw, Jane Kilby and Antony Rowland (eds) *The Future of Memory* (Oxford: Berghahn, 2010) 15–34.

———*Constructing the Holocaust: A Study in Historiography* (London: Vallentine Mitchell, 2003).

Stone, Lawrence 'Madness', in *New York Review of Books* 16 December 1982.

Sundquist, Eric J. (ed.) *The Oxford W.E.B Du Bois Reader* (Oxford: Oxford University Press, 1996).

Swann Nancy Lee *Pan Chao: Foremost Woman Scholar of China First Century A.D.* (New York: Russell and Russell, 1968, originally published in 1932).

Swoyer, Chris 'Relativism', in *The Stanford Encyclopedia of Philosophy* (Winter 2010 Edition), Edward N. Zalta (ed.), forthcoming URL = hhtp://plato.stanford.edu/archives/win2010/entries/relativism/

Sydnor, Synthia 'A History of Synchronized Swimming', in *Journal of Sport History,* 25/2 (1998) 252–67.

Symonds, D.A. 'Living in the Scottish Record Office', in E. Fox-Genovese and E. Lasch-Quinn (eds) *Reconstructing History* (New York: Routledge, 1999) 164–75.

Tchen, John Kuo Wei 'Creating a Dialogic Museum: The Chinatown History Museum Experiment', in Ivan Karp, Christine Mullen Kreamer and Steven D. Lavine (eds) *Museums and Communities: The Politics of Public Culture* (Washington: Smithsonian Institution Press, 1992) 285–326.

Tchen, John Kuo Wei and Liz Sevchenko, 'The "Dialogic Museum" Revisited: A Collaborative Reflection', in Bill Adair, Benjamin Filene, and Laura Koloski (eds) *Letting Go? Sharing Historical Authority in a User-Generated World* (Philadelphia: The Pew Centre for Arts and Heritage, 2011) 80–97.

Temple, Robert *The Genius of China: 3,000 Years of Science, Discovery and Invention* (New York: Simon and Schuster: 1986).

Thanouli, Eleftheria *History and Film: A Tale of Two Disciplines* (New York: Bloomsbury Academic, 2018).

Thatcher, Margaret *Downing Street Years* (London: Harper Collins, 1993).

Thomas, Lewis V. *A Study of Naima* ed. Norman Itzkowitz (New York: New York University Press, 1972).

Thompson, E.P. *The Making of the English Working Class* (London: Victor Gollancz, 1963).

Thucydides, *History of the Peleponnesian War*, four vols, trans. C.F. Smith, Loeb Classical Library (London: Heinemann, 1969)

Tosh John (ed.) *Historians on History* (Harlow: Pearson Education, 2nd edn 2009).

Tosh, John *The Pursuit of History: Aims, Methods and New Directions in the Study of History* (Abingdon: Routledge, 6th edn 2015).

Travers, T. *Museums and Galleries in Britain. Economic, social and creative impact*, (London, 2006), in M. Davies *Imprisoned by History: Aspects of Historicized Life* (London: Routledge, 2009).

Ulrich, Laurel *A Midwife's Tale* (New York: Random House, 1990).

Uricchio, William 'Simulation, History and Computer Games', in Joost Raessens and Jeffrey Goldstein (eds), *Handbook of Computer Game Studies* (Cambridge, Mass: MIT Press, 2005) 327–38.

von Bothmer, Bernard *Framing the Sixties: The Use and Abuse of a Decade from Ronald Reagan to George W. Bush* (Amherst: University of Massachusetts Press, 2010).

Vovelle, Michel *Piété baroque et déchristianisation* (Paris, 1973).

Walker, Jonathan *Pistols! Treason! Murder! The Rise and Fall of a Master Spy* (Baltimore, MD: Johns Hopkins University Press, 2007).

Walker, Kara *Fons Americanus* (2019). Hyundai Commission Tate Modern, 2 Ocotber 2019 to 5 April 2020, accessed 20 April 2020. www.tate.org.uk/whats-on/tate-modern/exhibition/hyundai-commission-kara-walker

Walzer, Michael *The Company of Critics: Social Criticism and Political Commitment in the Twentieth Century* (New York: Basic Books, 1988).

Wang, Q Edward 'Cross-Cultural Developments of Modern Historiography: Examples from East Asia, the Middle East, and India', in Q Edward Wang and Franz L. Fillafer (eds) *The Many Faces of Clio: Cross-cultural Approaches to Historiography, Essays in Honor of Georg G. Iggers* (New York: Berghahn Books, 2007) 187–209.

Watson, B. *Ssu-ma Ch'ien, Grand Historian of China* (New York: Columbia University Press, 1958).

Weber, Max *The Protestant Ethic and the Spirit of Capitalism* (New York: Scribners 1958).

Whorf, Benjamin Lee *Language. Thought and Reality* (Cambridge, Mass: M.I.T. Press, 1956).

White, Hayden *The Practical Past* (Evanston, IL: Northwestern University Press, 2014).

——— 'The Burden of History', in Hayden White *Tropics of Discourse: Essays in Cultural Criticism* (Baltimore, MD: Johns Hopkins University Press, 1978) 27–50.

——— 'Historicism, History, and the Imagination', in *Tropics of Discourse* 101–20.

——— 'Interpretation in History', in *Tropics of Discourse* 51–80.

——— *Metahistory: The Historical Imagination in Nineteenth-Century Europe* (Baltimore, MD: Johns Hopkins University Press, 1973).

Wilentz, Sean 'America Made Easy: McCulloch, Adams, and the Decline of Popular History', in *The New Republic,* 2 July 2001.

Windschuttle, K. 'A Critique of the Postmodern Turn in Western Historiography', in Q Edward Wang and Georg G Iggers (eds), *Turning Points in Historiography: A Cross-Cultural Perspective* (Rochester, NY: University of Rochester Press, 2002) 271–86.

Winks, R.W. (ed) *The Oxford History of the British Empire, Volume 5: Historiography* (Oxford: Oxford University Press, 2001).

Wittgenstein, Ludwig *Philosophical Investigations* (New Jersey: Prentice Hall, 1973).

Woolf, Daniel 'Of Nations, Nationalism and National Identity: Reflections on the Historiographic Organization of the Past', in Q Edward Wang and Franz L. Fillafer (eds) *The Many Faces of Clio: Cross-cultural Approaches to Historiography, Essays in Honor of Georg G. Iggers* (New York: Berghahn Books, 2007) 71–103.

Young, Robert J.C. *Postcolonialism: A Very Short Introduction* (Oxford: Oxford University Press, 2003).

———*Postcolonialism An Historical Introduction* (Oxford: Blackwell Publishing, 2001).

Zerubavel, Eviatar *Time Maps: Collective Memory and the Social Shape of the Past* (Chicago: Chicago University Press, 2003).

Zinsser, Judith P. 'A Prologue for La Dame d'Esprit. The Biography of the Marquise Du Châtelet', in Alun Munslow and Robert A. Rosenstone (eds) *Experiments in Rethinking History* (London: Routledge, 2004) 195–208.

Index